BRITISH NAV
WORL

British Naval Aviation in World War II

The US Navy and Anglo-American Relations

Gilbert S. Guinn and G. H. Bennett

Revised paperback edition published in 2012 by I.B.Tauris & Co Ltd
6 Salem Road, London W2 4BU
175 Fifth Avenue, New York NY 10010
www.ibtauris.com

Distributed in the United States and Canada
Exclusively by Palgrave Macmillan
175 Fifth Avenue, New York NY 10010

Copyright © 2012, 2007 Gilbert S. Guinn and G. H. Bennett
First published in hardback by Tauris Academic Studies, an imprint of
I.B.Tauris & Co Ltd, 2007

The right of Gilbert S. Guinn and G. H. Bennett to be identified as the authors
of this work has been asserted by the authors in accordance with the Copyright,
Designs and Patent Act 1988.

All rights reserved. Except for brief quotations in a review, this book, or any
part thereof, may not be reproduced, stored in or introduced into a retrieval
system, or transmitted, in any form or by any means, electronic, mechanical,
photocopying, recording, or otherwise, without the prior written permission of
the publisher.

ISBN: 978 1 78076 034 6

A full CIP record for this book is available from the British Library
A full CIP record for this book is available from the Library of Congress

Library of Congress catalog card: available

Printed and bound by CPI Group (UK) Ltd, Croydon, CR0 4YY
Camera-ready copy edited and supplied by the author

CONTENTS

Acknowledgements	vi
Preface	vii
1. Aircraft and aircrew required urgently	1
2. British aircrew training in the USA	14
3. Aircrew induction in the United Kingdom	31
4. Living and training in the USA	49
5. Primary and intermediate flight training	69
6. Washouts and other aircrew	88
7. Advanced, conversion and operational training	104
8. War service and post-war life	134
9. Conclusions	148
Notes	167
Sources	177
Glossary of Abbreviations	197
Index	203

ACKNOWLEDGEMENTS

As authors we are indebted to the many other people who have made contributions to the writing of this book. In particular, we would like to thank the British Academy, who generously funded some of the research, and also the British Association of American Studies, whose travel grant for another purpose incidentally yielded additional material for this project. We would like to thank our colleagues at Lander and Plymouth Universities for their support while the book was being written. Others to whom we owe a debt of thanks are the staffs of the Roosevelt Library, Washington Navy Yard and the National Archives of both the United States and Great Britain.

A special thank you is merited by Susan Guinn, who has been supportive and helpful throughout, and Roy Bennett, who provided considerable editorial and secretarial help.

Lastly, and most importantly, we must thank the large number of people whom we have interviewed and with whom we have corresponded over the years. Their names are found in the list of sources, as they have provided the essential first-hand material for our research. Many of them are no longer with us, and it is to their memory that we dedicate this book.

Gilbert S. Guinn
G. H. Bennett

PREFACE

The usual gravitas born of personality, family history and high office were gone. The big man simply sobbed with the emotion of the moment. For Winston Churchill, dining in room 21 of the North British Hotel in Glasgow on 17 January 1941, it had been a long day in a long war. As First Lord of the Admiralty in 1939 he had overseen the early phases of the war at sea. In May 1940 he had become Prime Minister as Germany launched her assault against the Low Countries. The following month, as Germany completed her conquest of Western Europe, he had prepared his country for the possibility of invasion. From that moment on, beleaguered Britain's future depended on the sea. In the late summer of 1940 that had meant maintaining the Royal Navy's ability to intervene in the English Channel, which any German invasion fleet would have to cross. In the winter of 1940-1 and beyond, it would involve maintaining Britain's sea lines of communication to North America and the rest of the world. On the merchant ships plying their trade across the Atlantic depended Britain's ability to feed her people and maintain her economy.

Those sea communications were imperilled by the German Kriegsmarine and Luftwaffe. They were charged with the task of starving the British into submission while Hitler prepared to unleash the German Army against the Soviet Union. The principal weapons in this war on commerce would be the submarine, the surface raider and the land-based bomber. Britain was lucky that Germany did not have any operational aircraft carrier at the start of the Second World War, and misfortune was to dog her attempts to develop one.

The resources of the Royal Navy were over-stretched in trying to protect the North Atlantic convoy routes, and air power could not yet contribute much to their defence. The result, in the second half of 1940, had been the loss of over 2,400,000 gross tons of merchant shipping and a steady throttling of the British war economy.

Although this threat was severe, by January 1941 Churchill was aware of an even more pressing danger to the British war economy and to her ability to import the materials required to sustain the war effort. Britain was running out of money. In September 1939 the Roosevelt administration had departed from the policy of strict neutrality, which had been forced on it by an isolationist Congress reacting to the danger to peace posed by Germany, Italy and Japan in the 1930s. Instead, a policy of 'cash and carry' had been adopted for any belligerent nation making purchases in the United States. The British could have access to US markets, but they would have to pay for their purchases in cash and transport them to Britain in non-American vessels. That policy provided the basis for a rapid expansion of trans-Atlantic trade which, while essential to the British, also gave a boost to the American economy, still struggling to escape from the great depression. American industry could provide aircraft and other war material, which the British war economy was unable to produce in sufficient quantity and range. The only problem was that by early 1941 Britain was running out of the money and liquid assets to fund purchases on a 'cash and carry' basis. Britain faced effective bankruptcy and the collapse of her war effort. Churchill knew it and, less than a year into his premiership, the outlook seemed bleak. His and Britain's hopes now depended on the President of the United States.

There was no secret as to the American president's sympathies in the on-going conflict, but his desire to aid Great Britain was curbed by American public opinion, which opposed entry into the war. Nevertheless, after the fall of France in June 1940, he had given increasing support to Britain, against the advice of Joseph Kennedy, the American Ambassador in London, who considered that British power was broken. After the Royal Air Force's victory in the Battle of Britain, regarded by many as the first key step in denying Germany control of the English Channel, and following his re-election as president in November 1940, Roosevelt signalled his increasing support for the British. The most startling example came through the 'destroyers for bases' deal, by which the United States exchanged 50 surplus destroyers of World War I vintage for long leases on British bases in the Caribbean and Newfoundland. It could be defended as a good deal for the American nation, in line with the Monroe Doctrine, the construction of the Panama Canal and Theodore Roosevelt's earlier policies in the Caribbean, but few could have been under any illusions that the United States was not being drawn further into the war.

PREFACE

In January 1941 Roosevelt sent Harry Hopkins across the Atlantic to Britain. One of the president's closest associates and chief 'fixer' of the New Deal, Harry Hopkins was a dynamo of a man who had been undaunted by the task of putting America back to work. Now the president had a new job for him. He was to meet Churchill and form his own assessment of the British prime minister, the state of British power and her ability to prosecute the war to a successful conclusion. On the evening of 17 January 1941, in the North British Hotel, Hopkins was Churchill's dinner guest. They had spent the day at the British fleet anchorage at Scapa Flow in the Orkneys. It was a symbolic as well as a practical visit. Churchill and Roosevelt knew that the outcome of the war hinged on the North Atlantic supply lines. Both leaders were obsessed by the sea – in romantic and geopolitical terms – and by the navies which dominated it. If the flow of trade to Britain were cut, Britain would lose the war and America would find herself alone. On the outcome of the German campaign against British commerce would hinge the future of humanity.

Hopkins was evidently impressed by what he saw at Scapa Flow. Turning to Churchill, he voiced the question in everyone's mind: 'I suppose you want to know what I am going to say to President Roosevelt on my return. Well, I'm going to quote you one verse from that Book of Books . . . "Thy people shall be my people and thy God my God" . . . Even to the end.'[1] That declaration of American support for the British cause was as significant as it was theatrical. Churchill could see a turning point in Britain's military fortunes.

From this point on, the flow of war material across the Atlantic would increase dramatically. Aided by the passage of the Lend-Lease Act in March 1941, under which the American taxpayer would bankroll the British war effort for the duration of the war, and by America's own entry into the conflict in December 1941, the war at sea would form a pivot on which the outcome of the World War would hinge. Lend-Lease and the productivity of American industry had the potential to tip the balance against the Axis. The German, Italian and Japanese Navies had the job of preventing that from happening by disrupting the flow of trade and reinforcements to the battlefronts in Europe, the Mediterranean and the Far East. American industry would be expected to turn out the escort vessels, patrol aircraft, aircraft carriers and replacement merchant ships to combat the Axis threat.

The importance of American industry to the outcome of World War II has been well recognised by historians since 1945. What they have usually overlooked, in relation to Lend-Lease, is the fact that the United States provided more than just the industrial and financial muscle vital to Allied victory. The 'great arsenal of democracy' was also involved in the supply of highly trained personnel who could operate the more complex products of American industry. In other words, during World War II America provided both the weapons and the trained military personnel that would defeat the Axis. Nowhere was this more apparent than in the development of British naval aviation, so vital to the countering of the Axis submarine and surface threat. In 1939 Britain did not have the naval aircraft or the aircrew to provide effective support to Royal Navy surface vessels in all their escort and combat operations. As well as producing vitally needed aircraft, the United States would turn out thousands of pilots and other aircrew – sons of Lend-Lease – who would learn, in the skies above the United States of America, to fight the enemy menace at sea.

The provision of military training while simultaneously engaged in large-scale military operations has always presented difficulties for nations at war. The people best able to conduct the training – experienced and mature individuals – were needed, more often than not, at the front line. The front would also have to be given priority in terms of the weapons also needed for training, and there would always be tensions over the allocation of the best recruits between particular branches of the military. With the advent of total war in the 20th century, further difficulties were added to the process of training. An individual undergoing training far behind the lines was no longer safe from aerial bombardment, long-range artillery fire, the effects of blockade, poison gas attack or biological warfare. By the advent of the Second World War, the issue of training in the midst of war had become more difficult, rather than less. Greatly expanded armies, navies and air forces could not be created overnight.

To make ready for war, Germany had begun major military preparations as early as 1935. Aircraft pilots, in particular, took a long time to train, as became only too evident in the summer of 1940, when the Royal Air Force contested control of the skies over the English Channel and Southern England with the German Luftwaffe.

In 1941, as Britain strove to take the offensive in the air and at sea, the need for pilots increased exponentially. To meet that need, much pilot training would be transferred overseas to the Empire and, from mid-1941, to a non-belligerent, if far from strictly neutral, United States. The expansion of British air training would be so successful that the Royal Air Force faced a surplus of pilots by 1944, and the Fleet Air Arm was in a position to stage group attacks from several aircraft carriers.

This book examines part of the expansion of British pilot training during the war. The Towers scheme, which operated in the United States from 1941 to 1945, saw the training of pilots and other aircrew for the Royal Navy's Fleet Air Arm and Royal Air Force Coastal Command. The book seeks to contribute to military history, in that it examines a critical, but often overlooked, area of the Anglo-American war effort. In addition, it sheds light on aspects of the social history of the two countries. Trainee British pilots arriving in the United States found American society remarkably different from their own and far removed from what they had been led to expect by Hollywood and the newspapers. On both sides adjustments had to be made on matters ranging from social manners to attitudes concerning racial segregation. The book also makes a contribution to diplomatic history, in that the setting up and continued operation of the training scheme formed an important feature of Anglo-American relations and of American engagement in the Second World War. A further claim for the book might be that, by examining the training of aircrew, it seeks to contribute to the history of a specialised branch of education.

Pilot training is a complicated and difficult process. The methods employed by the United States Navy, in putting foreign nationals through an intensive course while the training establishment was being robbed of many of its best instructors and of potential replacement aircraft, represented the state of the art in the 1940s. Basic ground simulators were in operation well before the days of the computer, and the latest in psychological thinking was employed to teach students such things as aircraft recognition. Methods of teaching and assessment were devised which sought to negate or minimise the weaknesses of a training establishment suffering from rapid expansion and a consequent diminution in the quality of training that it was able to offer.

Perhaps the final claim that the authors would wish to make is that the book represents an exercise in Anglo-American co-operation. The Towers scheme was a remarkable element in wartime co-operation between the two countries. Writing about it has been an exercise in peacetime co-operation. In the 1980s and 1990s scores of Towers trainees set down their stories on paper for a project which became an investigation into human memory as much as into the recent past. Memories are always fallible, but what was surprising was the degree to which the narratives provided by the former Towers cadets overlapped or were directly comparable. Key moments in the life of an aviation cadet, from first day on board a trans-Atlantic passenger ship to going solo for the first time, impressed themselves on the minds of each and every one of them. A few former cadets, like Frank Robinson and William Warner, were able and willing to lend their wartime correspondence. Despite a degree of sanitisation in the letters, as the writers tried not to worry their readers thousands of miles away, the wartime letters of aircrew provided another check on the post-war memories of former cadets. Many of them had passed away before the two authors (Professor Gilbert Guinn of Lander University in South Carolina, and Dr G.H. Bennett of Plymouth University in England) could begin the task of collating their experiences into this volume. No book could ever do justice to the life stories and sacrifices of the many men who found themselves training to fly and fight in the United States under the Towers scheme. For every personal narrative that illuminates the rather drab and dry official record of a training scheme that closed more than sixty years ago, the authors have had to omit another dozen which confirmed or mirrored the extract chosen for publication. The authors hope that other researchers can make use of the book's source material, including extensive correspondence with veterans in the United Kingdom and New Zealand. The papers are now preserved in the Guinn Aviation History Archive at the University of South Carolina at Columbia. Where specific references for quotations are not provided, they relate to material preserved in this archive, which is as yet uncatalogued. They are identified simply by the name of the respondent.

1

AIRCRAFT AND AIRCREW REQUIRED URGENTLY

The Royal Air Force came into being on 1st April 1918, when the Royal Flying Corps and the Royal Naval Air Service were combined into one organisation. The creation of this third branch of Britain's armed forces was a recognition that aircraft had played an increasingly important ancillary role in military and naval operations during the 1914-18 war. It also recognised that aviation had the potential to develop into a powerful weapon, which might eventually make its own unique contributions to warfare beyond the traditional spheres of the army and navy. In the 1920s and 1930s modest numbers of RAF aircrew were trained in the United Kingdom and in Iraq and Egypt, while fledgling air forces began to appear in parts of the British Empire such as Canada, Australia, New Zealand, India, Southern Rhodesia and South Africa.

The development of the Royal Air Force did not receive generous financial support, however. In the inter-war years British governments, which had to cope with the costs of wartime debts, post-war reconstruction, unemployment, industrial unrest and world economic crises, were reluctant to vote vast sums of money for the new force. They might well worry about the threat of Bolshevik revolution, or even the growth of French air power, but they preferred to put their faith in the illusion of collective security provided by the covenant of the League of Nations and world disarmament conferences. If those well-meaning efforts were unavailing, they would always have the Royal Navy to protect the home islands and the empire. The politicians were inclined to value the Royal Air Force mainly for the cost-effective way in which it could act as a 'flying policeman' to overawe dissident tribesmen in places like Iraq and the northwest frontier of India, and for the publicity value of air pageants and long-distance flights.

The Royal Navy remained the nation's chief bulwark against foreign aggression, and in the 1920s and early 1930s no British government could see a serious threat to Britain's ability to dominate the sea lanes. Only the American fleet could rival that of Great Britain, and war with the USA was unthinkable. Anglo-American naval rivalry was carefully managed through an on-going dialogue between the two countries. That process began at the Washington Naval Conference in 1921-2, when Britain and the USA agreed strict limits on the development of capital ships to preserve parity between themselves and guarantee Anglo-American hegemony over the sea lanes. Only the Japanese saw that aircraft carriers, on which no limits were set, might be developed into an effective means of challenging Anglo-American naval hegemony while remaining inside the strict treaty limits of the Washington Conference. Beyond mavericks such as General Billy Mitchell, few experts in the USA or Britain foresaw how the threat from the air might one day topple Anglo-American naval superiority. Similarly, the menace of the submarine, which had proved so dangerous in World War I, was discounted in British and American government circles, because of the development of anti-submarine detection equipment. The potential of the submarine and the mine was not lost, however, on the smaller naval powers such as Germany and Italy.

In 1932, the year after Japan had seized Manchuria from China and one year before Adolf Hitler rose to power in Germany, the total estimates approved by parliament for expenditure on the British armed forces amounted to just over £104 million, of which the Royal Air Force was allocated little more than £17 million – less than 16½ per cent.[1] For a military service which needed to keep pace with rapidly changing technology, that sum could hardly be regarded as adequate funding.

In the early 1930s, for both economic reasons and sincerely held political beliefs, the national all-party government of Ramsay Macdonald was deeply committed to a policy of trying to bring about international disarmament. At least in its public pronouncements, the government could see little point in spending vast sums on the Royal Air Force. As one very senior minister explained, 'the man in the street [has] to realise that there is no power on earth that can protect him from being bombed'.[2] Winston Churchill, at that period out of office, was one of the few who would not accept that council of despair. He responded with a newspaper article advising the government 'to place our Air Force in such a condition of power and efficiency that it will not be worth anyone's while to come here and kill our women and children in the hope that they may blackmail us into surrender.'[3]

From that time on, Churchill set about the task of gathering information from various sources about the state of Britain's air defences in comparison with the strength of other nations' air forces. He mounted a determined campaign, in conversations, letters, articles and speeches, to compel the government to overcome its reluctance to spend money on defence, especially on the air force. Towards the end of 1933 he was drawing attention to 'the great dominant fact that Germany . . . has already begun to rearm'.[4] Germany was already developing its military aviation and the German navy was engaged in the debates which would lead to the development of Plan Z in the mid-1930s. Under Plan Z, by 1944 Germany would have a force of eight super-battleships of over 42,000 tons, supported by two battle-cruisers, three pocket battleships, a large fleet of submarines and two aircraft carriers. They would permit her to wage a commerce war against Great Britain.[5] Forced to spread her naval forces across the ocean by a war on commerce, the Royal Navy's elderly battleships would be tracked down by hunter-killer super-battleships of the *Bismarck/Tirpitz* class and their even larger successors. Early in 1934 Churchill was urging that there ought not to be any delay 'in establishing the principle of having an Air Force at least as strong as that of any Power that can get at us'.[6] A month later he indicated where the real threat lay by admitting, 'I dread the day when the means of threatening the heart of the British Empire should pass into the hands of the present rulers of Germany'.[7] The Luftwaffe and Plan Z would be the means of threatening the heart of the empire, and the Royal Air Force and Fleet Air Arm were ill-prepared to meet it. It is rather strange that, while politicians regarded the bomber as the inevitable scourge of civilian populations in wartime, the belief persisted that the heavily armoured ships of the Royal Navy had little to fear from aerial attack.

Behind the scenes, the government's own professional advisers had been drawing attention to the manifest inadequacies in Britain's armed forces. In February 1934 a report by the Defence Requirements Committee forecast that, within a few years, Germany would become 'a serious menace to Britain'.[8] Probably influenced more by that closely argued report than by Churchill's alarmist denunciations, Stanley Baldwin assured the House of Commons that the government would 'see to it that in air strength and air power this country shall no longer be in a position inferior to any country within striking distance of our shores'.[9]

True to that promise, national governments led by Baldwin from 1935 and Neville Chamberlain from 1937 reluctantly set about rearming Britain, a process in which high priority was to be given to the Royal Air Force, and a new naval building programme was also initiated. While Churchill continued to thunder that the government's policies were both dilatory and inadequate, Hitler pursued his territorial ambitions in Europe. Foreign correspondents and photo-journalists provided people all over the world with compelling accounts and illustrations of the destruction and carnage brought about by the ruthless application of Japanese air power in China, Italian air power in Abyssinia, and German/Italian air power in the Spanish Civil War. Governments, politicians and voters could see from publications and cinema newsreels why the case for strengthening the Royal Air Force could no longer be ignored. The increasing expenditure on the Royal Air Force, both in absolute terms and in relation to the other armed forces, may be judged from the net annual estimates (plus various supplementary estimates) voted by parliament in the last peacetime years before 1939:

1934	Just under £18 million (about 15½ per cent of total voted for armed forces);
1935	Just over £27½ million (almost 21 per cent);
1936	Almost £50 million (almost 27 per cent);
1937	Over £137½ million (over 46 per cent);
1938	Almost £200 million (almost 50 per cent).[10]

Those considerable sums of money – whether spent on recruiting more men, building new airfields, funding scientific research, gathering intelligence, buying barrage balloons, developing new aircraft and weapons, or paying for the production of faster fighter aircraft and multi-engine bombers – would ultimately depend for their effectiveness on the quality of the aircrew, who would have to fly and fight the aircraft whenever and wherever they came into contact with an enemy. Could sufficient men of the right physical, mental and psychological calibre be found? Could enough instructors and training establishments be provided? How could recruits be trained to a level where they would be capable of flying faster and faster aircraft, navigating longer and longer distances, shooting at faster-moving targets, bombing accurately from greater heights, nursing more sophisticated engines, and maintaining radio contact over longer distances? And could an adequate flow of such trained men be organised in wartime to replace the heavy casualties which might be anticipated, not only from aircraft lost in action with the enemy, but also from the accidents which were inevitable, given the unforgiving element in which airmen plied their trade?

As early as May 1936 the Air Ministry set up a separate Training Command to be responsible for training both aircrew and ground crew, but it had no easy task.[11] Forward planning was in a constant state of flux, as the projected rate of expansion had to be adjusted ever upwards to match intelligence estimates of the growth of the German air force. Meanwhile, new types of aircraft took so long to bring into production that some of them were virtually obsolescent within a year of two of entering squadron service.

For most of the inter-war years the aviation element of the Fleet Air Arm had been under RAF control – an unhappy arrangement which resulted in endless bickering between the Air Ministry and the Admiralty about the needs of 'sailors who fly'. In 1937 responsibility for the Fleet Air Arm was restored to the Admiralty, but the actual implementation of that decision was not completed for a further two years. The change created a new set of administrative, political and practical divisions in the management of British military aviation, and it left too little time for building a powerful air arm to support the fleet, as Geoffrey Till has pointed out:

> One of the most obvious weaknesses of the Fleet Air Arm at the outbreak of war was its small size. In September 1939 there were 147 torpedo/spotter/reconnaissance aircraft, 41 amphibians of various kinds and 30 fighters serving the fleet – a tiny fraction of the number deployed by the US and Japanese navies of the time. Such small numbers greatly restricted the quality and performance of aviation at sea.[12]

Flying training schools in the United Kingdom, increased from four to nine in 1936, provided excellent initial training, but for only a limited number of carefully selected trainees annually. It was difficult to see how they could cope with training aircrew in far greater numbers. Even if they could, learning to fly a wood and fabric biplane was a very far cry from being equipped in every respect to fly more sophisticated aircraft operationally in the stressful conditions of actual combat. Much of the training still remained to be done after newly-qualified aircrew had been posted to their squadrons. Air Chief Marshal Sir Edgar Ludlow-Hewitt, Commander-in-Chief of Bomber Command from September 1937, pulled no punches in drawing the attention of the Air Ministry to the shortcomings he found. He argued that training needed 'to be carried out in all conditions of weather [as part of] a more realistic Aircraft Crew policy, with the object of providing efficient crews, adequate to the tasks required of them in War, without which the Air Force will never become an efficient War organisation'.[13] His damning verdict was that 'a fair-weather air force is relatively useless and is certainly not worth the vast expenditure now being poured out on the air arm of this country. And yet today our Bombing Force is, judged from a war standard, practically useless'.[14]

How far his plea for realism was ignored is illustrated by the fact that, in the two-year period 1937-8, Bomber Command aircraft flew just over 300,000 hours, of which fewer than 24,000 were flown by night.[15] Only six weeks before the outbreak of war Ludlow-Hewitt was reporting, 'I fear that the standard of efficiency of air gunners and their ability to resist hostile attack remains extremely low.'[16] As late as August 1939 an exercise showed that 'over 40 per cent of a force of [Ludlow-Hewitt's] bombers were unable to find a target in a friendly city in broad daylight'.[17] It must also be remembered that, by 1939, a significant number of qualified pilots were probably too old, too unfit or too senior in rank for combat flying duties. The ability of the British bomber force to launch retaliatory attacks against German cities in the event of Luftwaffe terror raids, and to impede the development of the Kriegsmarine, was highly questionable.

On the outbreak of war in September 1939, 17 squadrons from Bomber Command had to be removed from the immediate order of battle to take on the role of advanced training units. That serious reduction in immediate offensive capability was justified as the only way to ensure the building up of an adequate force to carry on the war in the longer term.[18] For those who did engage in operations, even in the period of so-called 'phoney war', there were ominous signs that high casualty rates could be expected, especially in daylight operations.

On 4 September, for example, 15 Blenheim bombers were sent to attack German ships in Wilhelmshaven; five returned without locating the target, and of the 10 which did attack, five were lost. On 29 September, out of 12 Hampden bombers sent to attack shipping near Heligoland, five were shot down. In another attack by 12 Wellington bombers on shipping in Schillig Roads on 14 December, five aircraft were shot down and another crashed on landing back at base. Four days later, 24 Wellingtons were sent to attack the Wilhelmshaven area; 12 were shot down and three others had to make forced landings on their return.[19]

The loss of aircraft was serious, but so was the loss of regular RAF aircrew, crushed in the mangled remains of their aircraft, burned to death, drowned in the North Sea, so grievously injured that they would never fly again, or caged in German prisoner-of-war camps for the foreseeable future. If losses on that scale were to be the price for what were, in effect, merely 'tip and run' raids across the North Sea, how many more men and machines would be lost on raids deep into the German heartland, which many senior RAF officers were hoping to launch as soon as the four-engine bombers came into service? Would they then be able to prove that independent strategic use of air power could win a decisive victory without the frightful slaughter which First World War battles like Ypres, Verdun, Gallipoli and the Somme had burned into the collective memory of their generation?

To the wastage of Bomber Command aircrew must be added the operational losses incurred in other RAF commands and the men killed in flying accidents. There were also the losses suffered by the Fleet Air Arm, including those drowned when the aircraft carrier HMS *Courageous* was sunk by *U-29* on 17 September 1939. Even worse casualties among aircrew were incurred in the following year. First came the unavailing campaign in Norway, where the Luftwaffe provided an object lesson in the exercise of air superiority. Then followed the sinking of another aircraft carrier, HMS *Glorious*, with heavy loss of life, including RAF pilots who, without any training in deck landings, had bravely landed their fighters on board rather than abandon them in Norway.

Before the Norwegian campaign had ended, the German blitzkrieg had fallen on Holland, Belgium and France. There, in the short space of six weeks, the RAF lost over 900 aircraft, either in aerial combat or on the ground. In killed, wounded or missing, the RAF suffered 915 aircrew casualties, of whom 534 were pilots.[20] Three weeks after forming his coalition government, Winston Churchill wrote on 3 June 1940 to Sir Archibald Sinclair, the Secretary of State for Air:

> The Cabinet were distressed to hear from you that you were now running short of pilots for fighters, and that they had now become the limiting factor. This is the first time that this particular admission of failure has been made by the Air Ministry. We know that immense masses of aircraft are devoted to the making of pilots, far beyond the proportion adopted by the Germans. We heard some months ago of many thousands of pilots for whom the Air Ministry declared they had no machines . . . How then is this new shortage to

be explained? Lord Beaverbrook has made a surprising improvement in the supply and repair of aircraft . . . I greatly hope that you will be able to do as much on the personnel side, for it will indeed be lamentable if we have machines standing idle for want of pilots to fly them.[21]

Then, from August to October 1940 followed an even more intense period of air operations, now known as the Battle of Britain. The RAF had to fight off a determined aerial assault on the home islands and, at the same time, make every effort to disrupt by bombing the enemy's preparations for launching an invasion by sea. Different authorities show marked variations in their calculation of how many British airmen lost their lives in this period, but the scale of loss may be judged from the 1,494 aircrew from various RAF commands whose names are commemorated on the Roll of Honour in the Battle of Britain Memorial Chapel in Westminster Abbey.[22]

At the height of the battle, the shortage of pilots was so acute that reinforcements drawn from Bomber Command, Coastal Command and the Fleet Air Arm, some flying instructors, and inexperienced youngsters fresh from the training schools all had to be rushed in to fill the gaps. The RAF was also lucky in being able to call on competent flyers from various parts of the empire, foreign airmen from Poland, Czechoslovakia and other German-occupied countries, and a few volunteers from the neutral United States.

During 1939 and 1940, in addition to the output of its flying schools and the 'windfall' of foreign airmen, the Royal Air Force was fortunate in being able to call on a reserve of aircrew who, alongside their civilian employment, had trained in their spare time for flying duties in the Royal Air Force Volunteer Reserve. The RAFVR had been conceived in 1936 as a flying equivalent of the part-time Territorial Army. Although recruiting for the aircrew training programme had only begun in April 1937, by the outbreak of war the RAFVR had trained 6,646 pilots, 1,623 observers and 1,948 wireless operator/air gunners.[23] That was a considerable – even invaluable – contribution, but it was difficult to see how aircrew, in the far greater numbers then required, could be trained in an overcrowded island, notorious for its changeable weather, and beset by many conflicting wartime demands on manpower, land and other resources.

Those problems were further complicated once large areas of sky over southern England had been turned into a dangerous combat zone following the fall of France. In his post-war memoirs, Hugh Popham describes how, after volunteering for the Fleet Air Arm in 1940, his training as a pilot at Luton was rudely interrupted. Scheduled to practise spinning in a Miles Magister, he had been told to go ahead, climb into the aircraft and wait for the instructor to join him:

> I humped my parachute on to my shoulder and started off across the tarmac. Two or three mechanics were standing in a group looking south. 'Must be one of ours,' I heard one of them say. 'Silly beggars – trying to put the wind up us' . . . They were over the southern boundary now, sweeping straight in across the aerodrome. 'Showy lot of . . .' and, at that moment, the first bombs went off. [24]

Popham was able to reach one of the air raid shelters, but not before he had been wounded in the foot. It was to be some time before he was released from hospital and could resume his training. Learning to fly was difficult enough without the intervention of the Luftwaffe. How would aircrew training continue if many more RAF airfields suffered the fate of Brize Norton, where a Luftwaffe raid destroyed no fewer than 46 trainer aircraft on 16 August 1940?[25]

At the same time as the training of British aircrew was becoming increasingly fraught, in 1940 the German submarine arm was proving that it had the capacity to wage an effective war on British commerce, even if the balanced surface fleet envisioned in Plan Z was not yet ready to face the British fleet in decisive surface engagements. With a rising toll of merchant ships sunk in the English Channel and the Atlantic, and with German shipyards planning to turn out large numbers of new submarines, Britain's security was under serious challenge. The Luftwaffe might not be able to gain control of the skies above the Channel, and the Kriegsmarine might not have enough surface units to cover a German invasion force bound for Kent, but Admiral Dönitz's submarines could perhaps provide the means to bring Britain to her knees. In any case, by late 1940 it appeared that Britain was not in a position to contest German domination of the Continent, and the submarine campaign would keep it that way, even if the British were not starved into submission. Hitler would be free to turn his attention to his long-cherished plan to invade Russia.

Everything seemed to hang on British sea power, and yet Britain was desperately short of the means to combat the German threat. The many destroyers lost off Norway and in the evacuation of British, French and Belgian forces from Dunkirk were no longer available to provide sufficiently powerful escorts for convoys, while the remaining destroyers had to be held available to guard against a possible invasion. Naval aviation could not make good the shortage of flotilla craft. Britain had too few aircraft carriers, and neither the land-based aircraft nor the flying boats of Coastal Command had the long-range capability for operations far out over the western approaches to the British Isles. In 1940 Britain did not possess an effective air-launched depth charge, while the bombs of the RAF and Fleet Air Arm were mostly too small to cause serious damage to major German warships.

Royal Air Force and Fleet Air Arm aircrew had always been volunteers, and they remained so. From the outbreak of war, volunteers had come forward from all parts of the United Kingdom, from far flung corners of the Empire/Commonwealth, and from expatriate British families in such places as South America and China. Most of them had a common British ancestry, a strong desire to defend their heritage, or an intense hatred of enemies who threatened their homeland. No doubt, many of them were also attracted by a sense of adventure and the glamour which attached to flying duties. Before they could be trained as pilots, observers (navigators), air bombers, wireless operator/air gunners or, as the Royal Navy preferred, TAGs (telegraphist/air gunners), all volunteers underwent qualifying examinations. The aptitude examination was not considered particularly rigorous, but tales of the aircrew medical examination raised the alarming spectre of needles being injected directly into chests to ward off chronic ailments – a distinctly off-putting procedure. Years later, many of the entrants could recall cursory personal interviews by boards of officers at such regional depots as Uxbridge, Cardington, Padgate, Edinburgh and other locations. Under wartime pressure, these RAF Aircrew Examining Boards, which would normally have rejected dozens of men to find one truly outstanding candidate, now put aside any personal or regular service prejudices about such matters as accent, family background, limitations of formal education or restricted experience. Men were selected on the basis of aptitude, as far as that could be determined. If it was to find crews for thousands of aircraft, the service could no longer afford to reserve flying opportunities for a few, carefully chosen from the more privileged sections of society.

In recognising that fact, the RAF had to overcome some firmly held convictions about 'keeping one's station in life'. Because of attitudes deeply embedded in a paternalistic and elitist society, many young men from the British working classes were hesitant about aspiring to what they saw as high positions. Even if they had no doubts about their native intelligence and abilities, the class system and authoritarian parents seemed to discourage them from aspiring to become pilots or observers. Hundreds of otherwise intelligent and able young men volunteered to be air gunners, wireless (radio) operators or photographers when they were perfectly well qualified to train as pilots.

As the recruiting drive gathered momentum, both the Air Ministry and the Admiralty offered flying training to men with the necessary aptitude who were already serving in other branches of the services and, if necessary, suitable candidates were provided with preparatory courses to get them up to the standard needed to cope with an aircrew training course.

Basic induction courses, personnel depots, many technical courses, rest and recreation facilities, medical and disciplinary centres, and initial training wings were established in towns and cities with convenient transport links, most often in the hotels and guest houses of coastal resorts, holiday camps, and in former student accommodation in boarding schools or university towns. If permanent buildings were not available, tents and other types of temporary structures such as Nissen huts were used. In fact, the amount of land and the number of buildings requisitioned for personnel, ground training, and technical purposes almost equalled the area used for airfields and aircraft-related activities.

Direct entry aircrew candidates were separated from ground crew personnel and sent to scattered aircrew receiving wings at such places as Blackpool and Morecambe on the Lancashire coast, Babbacombe, Torquay, and Paignton on the coast of Devon, and Stratford-on-Avon. Emerging from their short induction courses with the rank of Aircraftman Second Class (AC2), they were posted temporarily to RAF training or operational stations to perform domestic or ground defence duties until room could be found for them in initial training wings (ITWs). In these ITWs aircrew candidates underwent a period of rigorous academic and physical training, normally lasting about eight weeks but, in practice, it might vary between six weeks at a regular ITW to nine months in a university ITW. Each ITW was made up of two or more squadrons, and each squadron contained three or four 50-man flights.

The Royal Air Force syllabus included more than 500 instructional hours, with intensive work in mathematics, navigation, Morse code with buzzer and Aldis lamp, meteorology, aircraft recognition, customs of the service, drill and physical training – a varied programme designed to prepare young men for the rigours of flying training. Graduates of ITWs were usually promoted to the rank of Leading Aircraftman (LAC), but only if they successfully mastered Morse code and signals.

Since all the different aircrew categories required a great deal of individual training, the Royal Air Force, like every other air force in the world, was never equipped, organised, staffed or administered in such a way that it could provide immediate training for all the eager volunteers. The bitter winter of 1940-1 also curtailed flying training. Unwilling to risk losing suitable volunteers, both the Royal Air Force and the Fleet Air Arm adopted the concept of 'deferred service' to hold young men until such time as a revised and expanded training system could absorb them.

Even before the outbreak of war, discussions had begun about giving an imperial dimension to the training of aircrew by utilising the open spaces in Britain's overseas dominions and colonies. There, free from any immediate threat from the enemy, suitable recruits would be able to concentrate on mastering the complex skills needed by pilots, navigators, air gunners and other categories of flying personnel. Into the training pipeline would be channelled volunteers, not only from the United Kingdom, but also from all parts of the empire, true to Britain's long-established practice of supplementing her own limited manpower by calling on the men of the dominions and colonies. The self-governing dominions saw this as a fine opportunity to develop their own air forces. Out of those discussions, on 17 December 1939 emerged the Empire Air Training Scheme (later renamed the British Commonwealth Air Training Plan). In May 1940 the resulting increase in aircrew training led to the division of RAF Training Command into a Technical Training Command and a Flying Training Command.[26]

The Empire Air Training Scheme could not be expected to produce an immediate flow of trained aircrew but, between 1940 and the end of the war in 1945, the number of aircrew trained under the scheme was impressive: 137,739 in Canada, 88,022 in the United Kingdom, 27,387 in Australia, 24,814 in South Africa, 10,033 in Southern Rhodesia, 5,609 in New Zealand, and smaller numbers in India, the West Indies and the Middle East.[27] From its inception, it was believed that the main centres for training would be located in Canada. That dominion was nearest to the United Kingdom geographically, and the regular two-way flow of merchant shipping across the Atlantic would make it easy to ship recruits westward and trained flyers eastward on completion of their courses.

The great disadvantage of Canada lay, however, in the certainty of very harsh winter weather conditions. There were, of course, parts of North America where far milder conditions could be guaranteed – and where there was no shortage of facilities and instructors – but those areas lay within the neutral United States.

Under the leadership of President Franklin Roosevelt, the USA had been gradually adopting policies which favoured Britain in her struggle against Germany. The sale of arms and other supplies came first, then the 'destroyers for bases' deal and the advancement of America's Atlantic sea frontier eastward as far as Iceland, thus denying large areas of the North Atlantic to the German U-boats. Eventually, on 11 March 1941, the United States Congress approved the Lend-Lease aid programme (ironically designated HR1776, the year in which the former American colonies had declared their independence from Britain). Lend-Lease reduced Britain's financial burden, paved the way for massive material assistance, and opened the door for the training of British aircrew in the United States.

In writing about the Empire Air Training Scheme's achievements, British historians have usually chosen to include also the contribution made by the training of over 17,000 British aircrew in the United States from 1941 onwards.[28] Convenient though this may be, it hardly seems appropriate to assume, so long after the Declaration of Independence, that the USA can be treated as just one of the many far-flung corners of the British Empire. Even if that reinstatement is accorded only an honorary, purely nominal, temporary and guest status, the role of the USA in training Britain's airmen deserves a closer consideration in its own right. It was to make a significant contribution to Allied victory.

2

BRITISH AIRCREW TRAINING IN THE USA

During the 1930s, as increasing awareness of the destructive potential of air power became linked to decreasing faith in the long-term effectiveness of collective security, air attachés of all countries were active in gathering as much information as they could about aviation developments in the countries to which they were accredited. The extensive civil aviation network, the industrial infrastructure, the eagerness to embrace innovation, the climate, and the common language, all served to make the United States of America a country of particular interest to the Royal Air Force. In each of the years 1936 to 1938, the British Air Ministry sent experienced air officers to the United States to examine military and civil aircraft, observe techniques, and report on important new developments. In time these delegations also placed orders for aircraft, instruments and engines.

British manufacturers voiced their protests. They did not like the idea of profitable orders being placed overseas, but Lord Swinton (Secretary of State for Air 1935-7) insisted on exploring what American inventiveness had to offer. In later life, as he looked back on his career, he recalled one aspect of this liaison which played an important role in training British airmen:

> I ought to say a word about the Link Trainer. This ingenious American invention does for the pilot what the mechanical horse does for the rider in a riding school, but does it with infinitely more variety and efficiency. Sitting in a cabin in a room, for the cost of a few pennyworth of electricity, the pilot pupil can sit at the controls and drive his plane on a long journey under artificial conditions

which reproduce the conditions he would encounter on a voyage of a thousand miles. Air Commodore A.W.J. Tedder, who was Director of Training, was greatly struck by this machine, and was all for making full use of it. I shared his enthusiasm. Curiously enough, although this American invention was being used by the American Civil Airlines, the American Air Force had not used it to any extent. We immediately placed an order for fifty of these trainers. They were rapidly installed, and proved the greatest success, not only in initial but also in advanced training. We followed this up by further orders and by arranging for the manufacture of Link Trainers in Canada. Later on, new varieties of this device were introduced which would enable a complete bomber crew to be trained and practised in a dummy fuselage.[1]

In April 1938 the Air Ministry set up the British Purchasing Commission to expedite the placing of orders in the United States. Air Commodore A.T. Harris was a member of the commission, one of the main aims of which was to buy instruments and aircraft suitable for training and reconnaissance purposes. Harris, the future Air Officer Commanding-in-Chief of Bomber Command in 1942-5, was among those sent to look at the Lockheed Super Electra airliner, which they considered might, with certain modifications, make a suitable reconnaissance aircraft. He was amazed at Lockheed's ability to produce a mock-up of the modified aircraft for his inspection within 24 hours.[2] In July 1938 the RAF placed an initial order for 200 of the modified version, which in British service was called the Hudson, and by 1943 over 2,000 Hudsons had joined the RAF order of battle. They did yeoman service in Coastal Command during the war, and they were also used as navigation trainers and for communications duties.[3]

Another order was placed for 200 advanced single-engine aircraft based on the North American AT-6, which came to be known as the Harvard in British service. The total cost of the Hudson and Harvard contracts was £5,400,400.[4] After the outbreak of war in 1939, Britain's orders for aircraft and all manner of other supplies from the United States were greatly increased, even though the US 'cash and carry' policy required everything to be paid for in dollars before shipment. Britain entered the war with 4.5 billion dollars in foreign currency, gold and disposable assets, but the demands of war and the policy of 'cash and carry' meant that this pool of money was expended at an alarming rate. After the fall of France in June 1940 the British took over a number of French contracts in the United

States for the supply of aircraft and other war materials essential to a country facing the threat of invasion. These purchases only accelerated the rate at which funds for financing orders in the United States continued to diminish. By late 1940, with the British also providing American arms manufacturers with capital to build new plants to meet Britain's war requirements, it was clear that the situation would soon reach crisis point. Britain would shortly run out of the cash needed to make purchases in the USA. With President Roosevelt running for a third term of office in November 1940 – in contravention of the two-term convention set by George Washington – a decisive moment arrived. Would American public opinion, which wanted to keep the nation out of the war, support Roosevelt? Would he be able to find a way of solving the financial crisis facing Britain's war purchases in the United States?

At the polls, in November 1940 the American public once again put their faith in Roosevelt. He decided that it was in America's best interest to help the British. The possibility of a humiliating armistice between the British and the Germans might involve the handing over of the Royal Navy to the Nazis. That would in turn prejudice the security of the United States. The loss of British war orders in the USA would also harm an American economy still coming out of the great depression. These considerations, allied to personal sympathy for a fellow democracy with which the United States shared a common heritage, meant that Roosevelt felt, after his re-election, that the United States could not afford to let Britain's war effort falter through lack of funds.

He was spurred on by a frank admission by Lord Lothian, the British ambassador in Washington, who declared publicly, 'Britain's broke'. In early 1941 the Roosevelt administration came forward with a plan by which 'cash and carry' would be set aside. In its place, the United States would lend or lease to Britain the materials needed to fight the war. The Lend-Lease Bill was signed by the president on 12 March 1941.[5] Under it the British would be able to order hundreds of aircraft, along with other materials of war, to take the fight to Nazi Germany. Hundreds of aircraft would require thousands of aircrew to operate them, and the Lend-Lease Bill could be used to provide schemes to train the airmen.

As the Battle of the Atlantic continued to grow in ferocity and extent, Britain's need for trained aircrew and aircraft was insatiable. The only effective means of taking the offensive to Nazi Germany lay with RAF Bomber Command. In 1941 it lacked both the aircrew and types of aircraft needed to make a significant impact on the enemy's war effort. A further limitation was imposed on 6 June, when Churchill issued a directive giving Coastal Command priority, for a time, in aircrew and aircraft. Seventeen squadrons were diverted to Coastal Command. Some 204 of the finest long-range aircraft were lost to the bomber offensive.[6] Thanks to the productivity of Anglo-American industry, aircraft could be built relatively quickly: trained aircrew took infinitely longer to produce. The Lend-Lease Bill recognised the urgent need for both the aircraft and the aircrew to fly them.

The first US-based training scheme saw the arrival of ten Royal Air Force students at the Pan-American Airways Navigation School at Coral Gables and Dinner Key, Florida, on 24 March 1941. Here they were trained in the complexities of navigation by some of the best in the business – men who were used to precise navigation over featureless oceans. Help in getting this scheme started came from Group Captain George C. Pirie MC, DFC, British air attaché in Washington until June 1941. The Pan-American Airways facility was also used by students from the United States Army Air Corps (re-named the US Army Air Force after 20 June 1941). When the USAAF established their own navigation schools in Louisiana, Texas and California, the Royal Air Force was persuaded to take up the spare capacity with Pan-Am by increasing its draft to 150 students in July 1941.

Originally lasting 12 weeks, the course was extended to 15 weeks, and much work was done to make it relevant to the needs of the RAF. British maps and charts were used, and simulated combat conditions were created to make the training as realistic as possible. In nine cohorts, some 1200 British navigators passed through the Pan-American Airways scheme between 24 March 1941 and 17 October 1942. Since the RAF navigation course was based in a private, church-linked university, it did not qualify for Lend-Lease funds, so the British Treasury had to pay all the costs.

In May 1941, Group Captain D.V. Carnegie, a former flying boat captain in World War I and frequent visitor to the United States, was appointed Director of UK Training in the USA. In that capacity, he was responsible, in due course for establishing the six British Flying Training Schools (BFTSs) for what became known as the All Through Training Scheme (ATTS). Under the oversight of RAF officers, these schools, located in Florida, Texas, Oklahoma, Arizona and California, were operated by civilian contractors who employed civilian instructors, maintenance and domestic staff. The schools were established relatively quickly with the aim of producing 2,000 pilots a year. The RAF students were trained under the provisions of the Royal Air Force training syllabus. Between June 1941 and September 1945, the British Flying Training

Schools enrolled almost 8,000 trainee pilots, of whom some 6,600 qualified.[7]

A third contribution to the expansion of British aircrew training facilities in the United States came about thanks to the United States Army Air Corps. In April 1941, Major-General Henry H. Arnold, United States Army Deputy Chief of Staff and Chief of the Air Corps, visited the British Air Ministry and offered to use one-third of the Army Air Corps pilot training capacity to train RAF pilots alongside American aviation cadets. He also offered to increase the British intake under the Pan-American Airways scheme to 150 on each course. The latter proposal was accepted only with some reluctance because of the dollar drain, but the Army Air Corps pilot-training offer was accepted gladly. It did not get off to the smoothest of starts, however. Churchill wrote to President Roosevelt on 10 May:

> I expect you are now acquainted with the splendid offer which General Arnold made to us of one-third of the rapidly expanding capacity for pilot training in the United States to be filled with pupils from here. We have made active preparations, and the first 550 of our young men are now ready to leave, as training was to have begun early next month. A second batch of 550 will follow on their heels. I now understand there are legal difficulties. I hope, Mr President, that these are not serious, as it would be very disappointing to us and would offset our arrangements if there were now to be delay. General Arnold's offer was unexpected and a very welcome addition to our training facilities. Such ready-made capacity of aircraft, airfields and instructors all in balance we could not obtain to the same extent and in the same time by any other means. It will greatly accelerate our effort in the air.[8]

Ten days later, Roosevelt was able to reassure the prime minister: 'All plans discussed with you by Arnold for training pilots have been approved here. There are no legal difficulties in the way and training will begin promptly.'[9] Under these training arrangements, which became known as the Arnold scheme, the United States Army Air Force trained 4,370 pilots out of a total enrolment of 7,885 British students.

In fierce rivalry with the US Army Air Corps, the United States Navy responded in May 1941, on the suggestion of Air Commodore Pirie, with its own plan for training British aircrew.[10] The US Navy had been expanding its aircrew training establishments since 1938, when Germany,

Italy and Japan launched expansion programs which convinced Roosevelt that the United States had to prepare for war. By May 1941 the number of US Navy aviators had increased to 4,600, from a mere 1,700 in 1938. With some training capacity to spare, Admiral Towers (Chief of the US Navy's Bureau of Aeronautics) advised the British that the US Navy was willing to train pilots, navigators, and wireless operator/air gunners for both the Royal Air Force and the Fleet Air Arm.[11] The initial offer was quite limited in scope. The Air Ministry was informed on 18 June 1941:

> Admiral Towers USN informs me that President has agreed in principle that US Navy Air Service could train some RAF and FAA pilots and air crews for flying boats and FAA types. Initially US Navy would have to limit the number of pilots under training to 100. They would be prepared to start some time in July. Americans requested release of lend-lease aircraft 6 flying boats and 12 carrier-borne fighters (Martlet).[12]

Admiral Towers felt that his offer of aircrew training was not only in keeping with his own and President Roosevelt's desire to help the British wage war against Germany, but was also a fitting response by the US Navy to the US Army commitment. The Army's aircrew training proposal had won General Arnold considerable praise and improved his personal standing in the eyes of the president. The US Navy's offer to train British airmen was quickly accepted and became known as the Towers scheme.

The original Towers scheme called for a first cohort of 102 men (62 RAF and 40 Fleet Air Arm) to enter training in July 1941. A second cohort (90 RAF and 10 Fleet Air Arm) would begin training the following month. Thereafter, every month a fresh cohort of 70 RAF and 30 Fleet Air Arm aviation cadets would report for training. From RAF and RN depots, the aircrew trainees would be assembled and cross the Atlantic by ship to Halifax (Nova Scotia), and then travel to the Royal Canadian Air Force Manning Depot at Toronto for processing before being posted to flight training in the United States.

The initial cohort had their first experience of flying training at the United States Naval Air Station, Pensacola, Florida. Their entry into training was the subject of a blaze of publicity in both the United States and Great Britain. The *War Illustrated* devoted a five-photo spread to their training under the title 'In America They're Training for the RAF'.[13] Subsequent drafts were posted to the United States Naval Reserve Air Station at Grosse Ile, Michigan, where they were subjected to an, ominously named, elimination course (later re-named an elementary flying training course). At every stage, the performance of the cadets was checked and, if they were found to be deficient on two occasions, they would 'wash out' of training unless they managed to talk their superiors into granting extra time and a further attempt at a particular stage. Those early students who successfully completed elementary flying were transferred to Pensacola, where they underwent intermediate flying training.

At this point RAF and Fleet Air Arm pilots parted company. RAF flying boat pilots completed intermediate flying and continued both advanced and operational training at Pensacola. After completing this section of training, many of the flying boat pilots were posted to a general reconnaissance course on Prince Edward Island, Canada, after which some of them were assigned to ferry new flying boats from Elizabeth City, North Carolina, via Bermuda, to the United Kingdom; others were assigned to Ferry Command or returned to Britain aboard ships.

On completion of the intermediate flying course at Pensacola, Fleet Air Arm pilots were promoted before being assigned to carrier flying training at Opa Locka, near Miami, Florida. At first, after completing advanced flying training at Miami, Fleet Air Arm pilots would be sent to squadrons in Virginia in order to undergo conversion training to more powerful tactical aircraft. As the war progressed (and especially after the Japanese attack on Pearl Harbour on 7 December 1941 brought about direct American involvement in the conflict), the United States Navy embarked on a programme of training 30,000 of its own pilots annually. That action brought a number of changes in aircrew training in order to cope with the increased numbers. All elementary flying training was shifted to US Naval Reserve Air Stations, while intermediate and advanced training were concentrated at Pensacola, Florida. A US Naval Operational Training Command was established.

British students under the Towers scheme received their elementary flying training at Grosse Ile, Michigan, until March 1944, when it was transferred to St Louis, Missouri. Finally, in November 1944 it was moved again to the US Naval Air Station at Bunker Hill, Indiana.[14] Intermediate and advanced flying training remained at Pensacola until November 1944, when both intermediate and advanced flying training for British Fleet Air Arm pilot trainees were transferred to Corpus Christi, Texas. In order to accommodate the growing number of British aircrew under instruction, operational training units for British squadrons were shifted from air stations in Virginia to Rhode Island, Massachusetts and Maine.

The introduction of operational training courses for fighter pilots and others was beset, however, by such difficulties as shortage of aircraft and maintenance staff. As a result, pre-squadron entry training was limited to a one-month pre-operational course, sometimes without the use of tactical aircraft. Initially, a Martlet fighter operational training unit was established at Opa Locka, near Miami, Florida.[15] In July 1943 a two-month operational training course was established for torpedo aircraft at Fort Lauderdale, and in January 1944 a Corsair fighter operational training unit was established at Jacksonville, Florida. In the meantime, the number of Royal Navy and Royal Air Force pilots in training under the Towers scheme had continued to grow. In the middle of 1942 the Admiralty asked the United States Navy to accept up to 50 trainee pilots each month, and to set up courses for dive-bomber and torpedo bomber pilots. By September 1943 the Admiralty was asking to increase the drafts from 50 to 66 men each month.[16]

On completion of their courses with operational training units, some FAA pilots and navigators were posted to Rhode Island, Massachusetts or Maine for assignment to squadrons being worked up for active service. Others flew back across the Atlantic as members of crew in new aircraft being delivered by RAF Ferry Command, and still other aircrew returned aboard troopships or small (Woolworth) escort carriers. Back in the United Kingdom, they usually underwent further training before being posted to service aboard carriers or to other combat units, depending upon the particular branch of the service to which they had been assigned.

Since they were then experiencing a surplus of qualified flying boat pilots for service with Coastal Command, the Royal Air Force arranged to stop sending men for training under the Towers scheme, with effect from November 1944. As a result, from September 1944 the Fleet Air Arm draft was increased once more to 80 pupils each month.[17] Every two weeks, 40 new Royal Navy aviation cadets would enter Towers flying training. The war in Europe might then be coming to a bloody climax, but the Royal Navy faced the possibility – even the likelihood – that Britain's mainly naval contribution to war in the Pacific might well have to continue into 1946 or 1947. The Towers scheme was hugely important to the Fleet Air Arm. By November 1944 it was providing 44 per cent of the pilots required by the Royal Navy.[18] In particular, the Fleet Air Arm had come to rely on the scheme to turn out the pilots needed to fly the American aircraft on which it increasingly depended.

The range and complexity of the training schemes for British aircrew in the United States called for an increase in administrative and support staff.

In 1941 it had been considered sufficient just to nominate one of the RAF trainees and one from the Royal Navy as senior men in each of the various contingents sent for training, but this led to difficulties which may have contributed to a worryingly high failure rate among the early drafts on the Towers scheme. By the time primary training was relocated from Pensacola to Grosse Ile, Michigan, Royal Navy and Royal Air Force pilots with combat experience were being posted to American training stations to act as senior officers to provide British students with leadership, advice and, if necessary, a 'shoulder to cry on'. By the end of 1944, when primary training relocated to Bunker Hill, Indiana, British staff included a senior naval officer in addition to four navigation officers. Navigation officers were also assigned to serve with senior British naval officers at Corpus Christi (intermediate and advanced training), Jacksonville (operational fighter training), Fort Lauderdale (torpedo bomber operational training) and Vero Beach (dive-bomber training). The senior British officers were responsible not only for training and discipline, but for every aspect of the lives of British aviation cadets.

In October 1943, the Royal Navy's Director of Air Warfare and Training expressed the view that training for flying American types of aircraft should be concentrated as far as possible in the USA. In his view the ideal arrangement would be to base all training for British aircraft types in the United Kingdom and all training for US aircraft in the US.[19] Britain had been purchasing large numbers of American aircraft since 1938, and by early 1941 had obtained an American pledge to share its aircraft production 50/50 with Britain, an agreement modified by the Arnold-Portal Accord of June 1942. Lend-Lease made it possible for American aircraft manufacturers, who were justly proud of their production achievements, to build thousands of training aircraft. In addition, they also built for Britain thousands of reconnaissance, transport and combat aircraft, such as Hudsons, Catalinas, Liberators, Corsairs, Avengers, Mitchells, Bostons, Tomahawks, Mustangs and Dakotas. The British aircraft manufacturers could concentrate on their own aircraft types, such as Lancasters, Halifaxes, Spitfires, Hurricanes, and Typhoons.

The four US training programs for British aircrew were just a small part of the responsibilities of the RAF Delegation (RAFDEL) and the British Admiralty Delegation (BAD) in Washington DC. Staffed with specialists in various fields, including aircrew training, the two delegations exercised a general oversight over the training programmes and assisted the British Air Commission in the procurement of aircraft and all kinds of matériel in the United States. Both RAFDEL and BAD were surrogate, semi-independent, overseas sub-ministries directed by senior RAF and Royal Navy officers and civil servants who were responsible to the London offices of the Treasury, Air Ministry, and Admiralty.

In the middle of the war the Royal Navy, fearing that its specialised aviation needs might not be adequately represented, pressed for the appointment of an Assistant Naval Attaché (Air) to the British Embassy in Washington. The intention was simple. The Admiralty telegraphed the British Air Delegation at Washington in March 1943:

> We want to convince US Navy that we appreciate that no naval development is of more importance than naval air warfare. Moreover, we have in mind that RAF have an Air Attaché who is a Group Captain and we ought not to be too far behind in the diplomatic racket if we are to keep our end up.[20]

After some wrangling, a Lieutenant-Commander was duly appointed as Assistant Naval Attaché (Air).

To minister to the growing numbers and needs of Royal Navy personnel, two shore establishments known as HMS *Saker* and HMS *Asbury* were set up in the United States.[21] HMS *Saker*, with offices in the Barbizon Plaza Hotel at 25 Broadway, New York, and adjacent to Central Park, managed the accounting and personnel needs of all branches of the Royal Navy (not just Fleet Air Arm) in the United States. HMS *Saker* also controlled several other facilities, including part of the US Navy's receiving barracks at the Brooklyn Navy Yard, New York, a former Civilian Conservation Corps camp at Peekskill (some 40 miles north of New York City), and part of the Fargo Barracks in Boston. In addition to these facilities, HMS *Saker* effectively took over the Barbizon Plaza Hotel to provide accommodation for RN officers passing through New York.[22] The resident Senior British Naval Officer (SBNO) in New York acted as commanding officer of HMS *Saker*.

HMS *Asbury*, housed in two hotels in Asbury Park, New Jersey, carried out similar functions in accounting and receiving seamen. It could accommodate up to four thousand men, and was used particularly for providing crews for ships built in the United States for the Royal Navy. HMS *Asbury* was closed in February 1944, leaving HMS *Saker* as the shore base for all Royal Navy personnel in the United States until the end of the war. Fleet Air Arm personnel would typically be appointed to HMS Saker, even though their aircrew training took place many hundreds of miles from New York.

Both Fleet Air Arm and Royal Air Force cadets spent three months in primary training, three to four months on the intermediate and advanced stages and a further two months on operational training. At each stage the cadets were taught a flight syllabus designed by the United States Navy. That syllabus was up-dated throughout the war, and many changes were introduced at the behest of the British Air Ministry. With regard to the ground syllabus, which was taught alongside the flight syllabus, the United States Navy was even more accommodating. By the end of the war, one British naval officer was happy to report that the ground school syllabus had 'been altered to suit our requirements on many occasions, particularly in navigation and armament, and at the time of writing the navigation and armament syllabi being used were drawn up by R[oyal] N[avy] officers and accepted by the USN for the instruction of RN students, the navigation now actually being taught by a staff of RN Observer officers.'[23]

The details set out below show the extent to which the ground school syllabus changed from time to time to meet the requirements of the Royal Navy and the United States Navy. The frequency of those changes shows that the officers in charge of training were certainly not guilty of inertia or complacency. Within the constraints imposed by the limited resources at their disposal, they tried to take into account the latest theories, the knowledge and skills found to be important under active service conditions, and the need to remedy perceived weaknesses revealed in student assessments or combat reports.

GROUND TRAINING SYLLABUS "C"
Effective 1 September 1942

Communication	66 periods
Navigation	97 periods
Ship and Aircraft Recognition	33 periods
Power Plants	24 periods
Theory of Flight	30 periods
Aerology	24 periods
Aircraft Indoctrination	12 periods
Gunnery	11 periods
Military Drill	33 periods

Duration: 11 weeks for six days each.

GROUND TRAINING SYLLABUS "D"
Effective 8 December 1942

Navigation	96 periods
Aerology	24 periods
Ship and Aircraft Recognition	32 periods
Power Plants	24 periods
Theory of Flight	32 periods
Physical Training	64 periods
Communications	*

*Communications taught while students wait on the flight line.

Duration: 8 weeks for six days each.

REVISED GROUND TRAINING SYLLABUS "D"
Effective 4 March 1943

Navigation	90 periods
Aerology	21 periods
Ship and Aircraft Recognition	33 periods
Power Plants	24 periods
Theory of Flight	33 periods
Physical Training	88 periods
Communications	39 periods

Duration: 11 weeks for six days each.

REVISED GROUND TRAINING SYLLABUS "D"
Effective 19 May 1943

Aerology	21 periods
Code Practice	11 periods
Voice Procedure	12 periods
Gunnery	22 periods
Navigation	90 periods
Power Plants	25 periods
Recognition	33 periods
Theory of Flight	24 periods
Health and Fitness	4 periods
Physical Training	88 periods

Duration: 11 weeks for six days each.

GROUND TRAINING SYLLABUS "E"
Effective 2 October 1943

Navigation	99 periods
Aerology	33 periods
Recognition	33 periods
Communications	44 periods
Gunnery	33 periods
Physical Training	88 periods

Duration: 11 weeks for six days each, later extended to 13 weeks.

GROUND TRAINING SYLLABUS "F"

Navigation	90 periods
Aerology	45 periods
Recognition	45 periods
Gunnery	33 periods
Principals of Flying	12 periods
Essentials of Naval Service	30 periods
Drill	30 periods
Physical Training	120 periods

Duration: 15 weeks for six days each.

Such frequent changes to the syllabus brought their own difficulties. The changes were often a response to the diagnosis of some specific problem. For example, the increased emphasis on physical training resulted from the fact that British aviation cadets generally had a lower standard of physical fitness than their American counterparts, and they were accepted into the service with lower standards in critical areas such as eyesight. Some British aviation cadets were simply not able to handle the physical aspects of gruelling training in an unfamiliar climate, but during the training most of them gained weight and got into better physical condition than ever before.

Within the subjects delivered by a constantly up-dated syllabus, there were further changes in the light of wartime experience. For example, in the early stages of the war British students were taught aircraft recognition according to the WEFT system (wings, engine, fuselage, tail) by which they would analyse four features of an aircraft. In practice, however, it was found that aircraft recognition had to be instantaneous if it was to be effective. In combat there was not sufficient time to analyse the profile of an aircraft according to the WEFT system. Dr Samuel Renshaw of the

Ohio State University Research Foundation put forward in 1942 a new technique that the Navy adopted across its training. It called for students to learn the profile of an aircraft in total from any particular angle. In terms of teaching 'the system featured the use of slides, flashed onto a screen at rates varying from an initial 1/10 of a second working up for a while to 1/75 of a second'.[24]

New teaching and learning methods were introduced to deliver the syllabus, and British aviation cadets experienced a considerable number of training films during the ground school course. The official history of the United States Navy's air war was proud of the innovatory visual aids to learning:

> Between March 1941 and March 1945, well over 2,000 training films were completed by the Training Division for use in aviation training. These have included everything from a film on the care of a machine gun to such documentary epics as *The Fighting Lady*. One film showed the use of the lathe, another gave a picture of the duties and functions of the plane captain in caring for an airplane.[25]

Looking back on their training, some former students felt that the programme was not helped by variations in the quality of instruction which British aviation cadets received. The rapid expansion of the United States Navy meant a reduction in the quality of instruction. That was partly offset by the regular rotation of instructors to ensure that the influence of the good and less good instructors was evenly spread to all trainees. Many British students would have preferred to stick with one particular instructor, but this was firmly against the policy of the United States Navy. Even with the rotation system, by 1943 the Royal Air Force, in particular, was increasingly sceptical about the value of pilots trained under the Towers scheme, but they recognised that, because of Lend-Lease, training in the USA was far less expensive than it was in Canada.

The Royal Air Force Delegation in Washington prepared a paper on the subject, which argued:

> It must be remembered that the US Navy Aviation service has been expanding at an incredible speed since Pearl Harbour. Flying instructors are for the most part pilots who themselves have only had the war training of a cadet followed by an instructor's course which is not much more than extra flying practice. There is no system of testing instructors other than by the checking of students.

It is believed . . . that, provided the check pilots are good, a high standard is assured, and bad instructors are detected. This system does not make for the survival of the fittest and RAF pilots graduating should all be good enough to settle down quickly in RAF squadrons.[26]

The problem was alleviated by supplying more Royal Air Force personnel to act as instructors, and by the slowly diminishing requirements of the British and United States Navy for pilots.

In March 1944 the United States Navy announced that it was cutting back the number of its own pilots in training from 25,000 to 20,000 annually. By mid-1944, the Royal Air Force had more flying boat pilots than it needed, and the Air Ministry decided to end the RAF's involvement in the Towers scheme.

If the United States Navy faced a shortage of first-class instructors, then it sometimes also faced a shortage of quality aircraft, since the fleet had a priority claim on all new equipment, even though in January 1942 a percentage of all new equipment was set aside for training purposes. Until wartime production could be expanded, the USN could not simply discard obsolete equipment, so the air training system sometimes used obsolescent aircraft, as did most other air forces in the world. With the fleet also having first call on mechanics and spares, the serviceability of some training aircraft was an on-going problem, even though quotas were revised in the light of experience.

Other problems that arose during the course of training were even less predictable. Seemingly insignificant differences between British and American cadets could have a major impact on washout rates. Trainee British pilots tended to have less experience with machinery such as motor cars, which might help to sharpen a future pilot's reflexes. Lack of mechanical experience also reduced their ability to judge speed, monitor dials and co-ordinate controls. Comparatively small things like this could make a large difference in determining the success or failure of a trainee pilot. The 'washout' rate for British pilots ('dip out' rate in the terminology of the New Zealand trainees) was a steady 36 per cent until mid-1944, when the bottom of the manpower barrel was reached and it climbed to over 50 per cent. Remedial action was necessary before it began to fall back to the long-term rate.

The washout rate of the Fleet Air Arm was invariably higher than that for the Royal Air Force and the United States Navy, both of which subjected potential aircrew to an initial period of testing and flight grading.

The future of those unfortunates who washed out of training lay in the hands of the senior British officers, who might decree three possible fates: further flight training, re-mustering for service as other aircrew – navigator, wireless operator/air gunner or telegraphist/air gunner for the Fleet Air Arm – or no further aircrew training. For many washouts returning to Canada or the United Kingdom for re-mustering, the process could be devastatingly disappointing.

Those trainee pilots who completed primary training faced a number of problems which the Air Ministry failed to foresee. The United States Navy drew a sharp distinction between enlisted men and aviation cadets. Both the RAF and RN placed enlisted student pilots and navigators in aircrew training. On completion of the intermediate stage of pilot training, successful Fleet Air Arm students were warranted as midshipmen or commissioned as sub-lieutenants. Initially, there were no facilities or uniforms for RAF men to be commissioned at Pensacola, so all successful cadets were promoted to sergeant. Later matters improved, and approximately one-third of each course was commissioned on graduation, while the rest were promoted to sergeant.

For trainee aircrew, insignificant cultural problems abounded, such as differences in the dress code between the Royal Air Force, Royal Navy and United States Navy. The standard British rig of shirts and shorts was so frowned upon by the United States Navy that British aviation cadets were issued with long khaki trousers to match their shirts. The US Navy was happy to supply the British in their hour of need, so RAF and RN aircrew students were provided with summer uniforms from US naval stores. In addition to such problems of immutable service customs and traditions, British cadets faced many personal difficulties while living and training in the United States.

With the approaching end of the war, the training of British flight students in the United States was cut back. By April 1944 fewer British students were being sent for training as pilots under the Towers scheme or at the four remaining British Flying Training Schools. The final draft of Royal Air Force pilots completed their training under the Towers scheme in November 1944, and on 20 November the US Navy's Chief of Naval Operations wrote to inform the Chief of Naval Air Training that the British Air Delegation wanted to end the flow of Fleet Air Arm pilots into the scheme.[27] The final draft of Fleet Air Arm personnel left England on 20 April 1945 to begin training.[28] In addition to the pilots who had been trained, 645 wireless operator/air gunners (telegraphist/air gunners), and about 545 navigators had also completed training under the Towers scheme.[29] To complement these activities, more than 6,000 Royal Navy and Royal Air Force personnel were trained on engines, propellers, and airframes for the American aircraft destined for British service. Much of the maintenance training took place at the University of Oklahoma and at factory schools in Chicago and Detroit.

Production line maintenance (PLM), which required large, less highly skilled crews, was an American innovation developed by a California civil contract primary flying school in response to the growing wartime manpower shortage. The system, which the US Navy adopted in 1943, spread to other flight schools and to tactical squadrons, including overseas units. British and American personnel, often women civilian air mechanics (CAMs), were trained in specialised aircraft maintenance, covering everything from instruments to turrets. Aircraft were lined up and moved slowly through a hangar. Within the hangar, a large number of specialists swarmed over each aircraft and inspected, repaired, or replaced critical parts. They recorded their actions in writing and moved on to the next aircraft. The PLM system dramatically improved aircraft availability.

On 10 September 1945 the training of British aircrew in the United States finally came to an end. The arrangement had lasted four years and three months. In total, according to official Air Ministry records, 16,033 aircrew completed their training successfully – 13,673 pilots, 1,715 navigators, and 645 wireless operator/air gunners. For most trainees the progression to 'gaining their wings' or specialist brevet was a tortuous journey. Even after qualifying, getting into the war at sea, despite the desperate nature of that struggle, could also prove unexpectedly difficult and slow.

3

AIRCREW INDUCTION IN THE UNITED KINGDOM

For all aviation cadets on the Towers scheme the struggle to qualify as a pilot had begun long before they boarded a ship for the United States. Potential pilots of the Royal Navy's Fleet Air Arm and the Royal Air Force had a number of shocks in store for them as they enrolled and were inducted into the ranks of Britain's armed services. Getting accepted for training often proved surprisingly difficult, and they then had to come to terms with service life steeped in tradition, routine and discipline. Despite the weakness of Britain's military position after 1940, and despite urgent appeals for volunteers to enlist in the armed services, the process of enlistment and initial training was far from slick. Many cadets were disgusted at what they saw as the stupidities of service life. While the Royal Air Force undertook a series of checks on men volunteering for aircrew duties, the Fleet Air Arm relied on first impressions at interview.

A 1943 guide to the Fleet Air Arm gave an account of the procedure and the selection methods used, referring to the process as being similar to a cricket match:

> Peters wants to be a [naval] pilot. He is alert, intelligent, with plenty of initiative. He is a hard-hitting batsman and a dashing three-quarter. He can drive a car and is fond of tinkering with its engine. He is a sound shot . . . The application forms are filled in and dispatched . . . [He] is keyed up for the ordeal and tremendously excited, determined to do his best. As he is ushered into the room by a Wren he sees a long table at which are seated a Captain RN, an Instructor-Captain, and a Lieutenant who is wearing the pilot's

badge. The President bids him good morning and asks him to sit down.

He takes the chair opposite the President and awaits the attack. He does not find the ordeal so terrifying as he had expected. It seems that the Board is not trying to bowl him out, but is sending down an over that will enable him to display his form. He answers the President's friendly queries about himself frankly and without trying to show off. Then the Instructor-Captain takes a hand. By a few shrewd questions, he is able to assess just how much trigonometry and maths Peters really knows: no chance of stealing a quick run here. But the Instructor-Captain seems satisfied and then the President hands him a list of HM ships.

'Just tell me what you think they were called after,' he says. 'Take this one – Kenya'.

'A British colony in East Africa, sir.'

'Right. And this one – Benbow?'

'A British admiral, sir.'

'Good,' says the President. 'We had someone in just now who said it was a public house.'

After a few more questions to test Peters' history, geography, and general knowledge, the President pushes towards him some small ship models and asks him to identify them. Peters has a little trouble in distinguishing between a destroyer and a corvette, otherwise all goes well. The President then hands him over to the Fleet Air Arm representative.

Peters finds this young man more alarming than the senior officers. Why does he want to join the Navy? Why does he want to be a pilot? Does he know anything about motor cars and their engines? What are the main types of naval aircraft? Can he identify them? Peters can, and does from the models on the table.

'What would you do if you were flying from London to Liverpool and your observer gave you a north-easterly course?' is the next question.

'I should tell him to think again, sir.'

'I should hope so!'

Peters is then asked to withdraw. After a few apprehensive moments, he is recalled.

'It's all right,' the President tells him. 'We've decided to recommend you to be trained as a pilot.'[1]

This impressionistic, rather than scientific, approach to the selection of aircrew was hardly a reliable way of finding the good pilots, accurate telegraphist/air gunners (TAGs) and competent observers required by the Fleet Air Arm. The procedures of the Royal Air Force also left something to be desired, especially since some trainee aircrew felt that their interview experience was an unnecessary delay in preparing them to face the enemy. Frank Robinson, 19, an architectural assistant in Manchester, eventually joined the first RAF course at Pensacola in July 1941. In the autumn of 1940, at the age of 18, he had volunteered for RAF aircrew duty. He recalled that early experience some forty years later:

> I was accepted at Padgate and sent home to await the call to the colours along with my school chum and work colleague, Harry Hayne, who was just 18. In the spring of 1941, Harry and I had heard nothing from the RAF so, having been bombed in Manchester by the Luftwaffe over the winter of 1940, ... we wrote a strong letter to the Air Minister asking how he thought he would win the war without us! After that, my feet never touched the ground, and by return [mail], I got my papers on 3 May 1941 and reported to No. 2 Receiving Wing at Babbacombe, Devon.

Attested aircrew volunteers for the Royal Air Force, like Robinson, were provided with special lapel badges, so that on the streets they would not be regarded as slackers. They were told to remain at home and continue in their jobs until called. The Fleet Air Arm ran a similar programme. Both services also conducted preparatory courses for potential aircrew. The Royal Navy's 'Y' Scheme proved to be a very effective introduction to the naval service for students and others yet too young to enlist. The Royal Air Force also attracted young men to the Air Training Corps for pre-service indoctrination and training.

Kenneth R. Blevins, who joined the third RAF class at Pensacola in September 1941, was one of the aircrew volunteers who were persuaded to enter the Royal Air Force immediately, rather than wait to be called up for training. He had joined the RAF in December 1940 at Uxbridge, Middlesex, after successfully passing the aircrew selection board for pilot training. At the selection board he was asked to make a difficult decision:

> All successful candidates were offered the choice of 'direct entry' or 'deferred service', i.e., entering the RAF there and then for ground

duties while awaiting an aircrew course (ITW) or returning to civilian life for the (probable) 6 months wait. Thus, I (in the period of elation immediately after passing the selection board) opted for direct entry. After 'basic' – two weeks at Uxbridge for uniform issue and very basic indoctrination – I was posted to Blackpool for further 'square bashing' etc., and to Morecambe, Lancashire for 'small arms' training. On completion, my unit was posted [to RAF Manston], ostensibly for 'aerodrome ground defence' duties (along with about 800 army . . . the Buffs Regiment) on sentry duty at night, and on a variety of menial 'general duties' during the day, e.g. 'coal fatigues' (humping coal – what else?), potato-peeling in one or other of the cook-houses, and one of we 22 'white flash' boys was assigned to a mysterious civilian – a Mr. Rose. That job turned out to be cleaning out toilets! ('White flash' was the designation for aircrew cadets who sported a white flash in their forage caps – a great and treasured status symbol, which put us apart, or so we thought at the time, from other low-grade airmen.) Manston was a very active aerodrome . . . the fighter squadrons flying flat out . . . Around about May 1941 I was posted to No. 5 ITW at Torquay, Devon, along with all the deferred service lads. We direct entry types were put into a squad of our own, as we did not have to be taught foot and rifle drill. We walked away with the graduation drill competition. A number of us from the ITW course were assigned to the Towers scheme (this conveyed nothing to us at the time).

David Harold Frederick Banton, who joined the fourth RAF class at Pensacola in September 1941, had a similar experience to that of Blevins. Banton joined the Royal Air Force on 24 January 1941. Before that time he had been a clerical worker at Colwyn Bay, North Wales. He completed his basic recruit training at RAF Padgate, Lancashire, after which he was assigned to ground defence duties at No. 14 Operational Training Unit at Lossiemouth, in Scotland. There he served as a gunner from March to April, before he was moved to RAF Waterbeach in Cambridgeshire as a member of the ground crew 'bombing up' Wellington aircraft for raids on Germany.

From there, he was posted to RAF Kenley, a fighter station, where he did pre-initial training wing ground school in April and May. Finally, in June 1941, Banton was posted to No. 13 Initial Training Wing at Torquay, Devon. Serving as ground crew while waiting for entry into an initial training wing formed an interesting, and perhaps valuable, apprenticeship for a trainee pilot, but most resented what they saw as a delay to their getting into action. The Royal Air Force viewed the initial training wing stage of a recruit's life as so important that in 1942 they considered setting one up in the United States to deal with residents who might wish to join the RAF.[2]

Some potential aircrew had to employ a little deception to get past the defences of the RAF or Royal Navy. Thomas H. Clayton of London, who would be one of the first RAF cadets at Grosse Ile in 1941, was eager for action. He had tried to enlist on 4 September 1939, the day after Prime Minister Neville Chamberlain's announcement of the declaration of war on Germany. When he at last got as far as an interview, however, he found that he was too old for aircrew. He soon found a solution:

> I very improperly fiddled my age, which was simple. '13.7.11' became '11.7.13', and I was granted a medical. Together with a host of others, [I] failed the mercury test (long abandoned) which called for blowing into a tube and holding up the mercury to a given point to ensure that the participant not only had lungs, but that they reached RAF standards. But I had not passed, hence – 'You are fit for Aircrew training bar a suspected hernia. Get it corrected and report for further examination,' and as I protested that I had never had such a thing in my life, I was led out by a harsh-faced Warrant Officer. And from that moment on I was confronted with a problem, described so perfectly – so much later – in *Catch 22*. All hospital beds were reserved for possible civilian casualties, whilst unimportant operations akin to suspected hernias would be dealt with after the war. I spent the next five weeks visiting one hospital authority after another, with spread hands, asking, 'So you tell me – how do I go to Adastral House after the war, and say, "Here I am, hernia free, all set to enter the war"?'

With a little help from his former employer, Clayton eventually succeeded in getting around the problem of the medical.

Other difficulties in enlisting for aircrew training faced those in certain types of employment. Jim Glazebrook, who eventually arrived at Pensacola in the tenth RAF class in April 1942, was a telephone engineer in Wallington. He was classified as being in a 'reserved occupation' and was not allowed to volunteer for military service at the outbreak of war – or until early 1941, when special release was given to those found qualified to be pilots or navigators. On 18 August 1941 Glazebrook reported to

London as ordered. Previously there had been many small reception centres, but after July 1941 a single large centre in London was the first step for aircrew candidates.

Hyde Park, a vast open space in the heart of London, was a Royal Park with several hundred acres of walkways, shrubbery, trees, and a large zoo. Lord's Cricket Ground, the national headquarters of that famous British sport, was close by. Aircrew candidates were housed in nearby apartment houses and were fed from kitchens in the zoo. On 6 September 1941, after two and a half weeks in the newly established RAF Aircrew Receiving Wing (ACRW) in London's Hyde Park and Lords Cricket Ground (called 'arsey-tarsey' by the students), Glazebrook was sent to No. 4 Initial Training Wing at Paignton, Devon.

In their efforts to enlist for pilot training, some men could offer stronger credentials than others. A good physique and solid academic abilities counted for much, but within the RAF the 'old boy network' was still influential. Going to the right school and coming from the right social background were viewed as important.

Some entrants had even stronger credentials to impress a selection board. Anthony P. Vincent, who would arrive at Pensacola in March 1944, was a university student at the time of his enlistment in July 1943. It was probably inevitable that he should enter pilot training in the RAF, because he had one of the most famous fathers in that service. Air Vice-Marshal Stanley Vincent had entered the Royal Flying Corps in 1915 and was credited with six confirmed victories in the 1914-18 war. During the Battle of Britain he had been a Group Captain, station commander at RAF Northolt, and was credited with destroying another five enemy aircraft while flying Spitfires and Hurricanes – one of the few men in the world to become an 'ace' in both wars. Anthony Vincent was assigned to an initial training wing in September-October 1943 and successfully passed flight grading at RAF Desford, Leicestershire.

For those already in the RAF, transferring to flight training had its own particular difficulties. Denis James Fry of Purley, Surrey, who later learned to fly in the fifteenth RAF class at Pensacola between September 1942 and April 1943, was one of the men who faced the difficulties of transferring within the RAF. He had made the mistake of allowing himself to be talked into entering the RAF as ground crew, even though he wanted to be a pilot. After enlisting on 5 September 1939 he had done eight weeks of basic training at RAF Uxbridge before going on to RAF Cranwell for three months' training on an accounting course. From Cranwell he joined 266 Squadron at RAF Sutton Bridge as an accounts clerk. In the spring of

1940, when the squadron moved to RAF Martlesham Heath, he moved with them. From 7 May 1941 to 15 February 1942 he remained at RAF Wittering. He volunteered for aircrew duties in spring 1941, and was found qualified for pilot training, but Fry, by now a temporary corporal, had to wait until February 1942 before remustering as a pilot under training.

Many cadets were to value the training that they received at the initial training wings to which they were sent in fifty-man flights. The RAF syllabus required more than 500 instructional hours and included intensive work in mathematics, navigation, Morse code with buzzer and Aldis lamp, meteorology, aircraft identification, RAF customs, more drill and ceremonies, physical training and a variety of other subjects designed to prepare young men for the rigours of flying. The Royal Air Force considered the initial training wing stage of a recruit's life to be very important. The system expanded rapidly; by late 1943 the number of initial training wings had expanded to twenty-three, processing 17,500 men.

J. H. Ashley, who arrived at Pensacola in May 1942 with the eleventh RAF class, was something of an exception. He had enlisted in the RAF in May 1941, after being employed in the Civil Service. He recalled his early RAF training many years afterwards:

> I reported for duty at Lord's Cricket Ground on 21 July 1941 and was billeted in the area for 4 weeks, collecting kit & uniforms, taking night-vision and other medical tests, inoculations, etc., and some four hours drill each day. I was one of 50 aircrew cadets who, on 25 August 1941, were sent as an experiment (the first of its kind) to undergo ITW training at an RAF operational station. Cadets normally went to ground schools located mainly in seaside resorts, but we had our initial training attached to RAF Turnhouse, near Edinburgh. Although we all enjoyed the 'feel' of being part of an operational group whenever we visited Turnhouse, the scheme was not particularly successful. Firstly, we lived and trained in a rather bleak and remote castle-like building (Clifton Hall) on the outskirts of Edinburgh. Secondly, the course lasted 5½ months instead of the usual 3 months at a traditional ITW. But we lived and served together as a very happy and self-reliant unit, in the charge of a Flying Officer and a regular Sergeant of some 15/20 years service. We studied the usual subjects – maths, navigation, Morse code, anti-gas, hygiene, law, armaments, and aircraft recognition, but in a leisurely, detached fashion as befitted 50 guinea pigs! We developed

a strong bond of comradeship and about half of us stayed together till the end of flight training. In February 1942 we left Scotland and, after 6 weeks at a Drafting Centre in Brighton – for intensive drill, learning the basics of military law & discipline & RAF organisation – we were all posted to No. 9 EFTS, RAF Anstey, near Coventry. Here we averaged 11 hours flying on Tiger Moths to show whether we were suitable for a full flight training programme in the USA or Canada. I might have soloed there had the weather not turned very stormy in the closing days of the course, but I was adjudged OK and my recollection is that all but four of the 'Turnhouse 50' were successful.

The Turnhouse 50 may well have been unusually successful. The biggest hurdle facing RAF cadets after the initial training wing courses was flight grading. It had been introduced in November 1941 in an effort to reduce the number of RAF failures in primary flight training.

The United States Army Air Force had looked for ways of assessing whether recruits would be suitable for training as aircrew. In mid-1941 they had urged the Civil Aeronautics Authority to use older qualified pilots to establish several hundred small flight schools near colleges and universities. In 1942 these College Training Detachments (CTDs) were re-designated the War Training Service (WTS) as a means of holding qualified USAAF, Naval, and Marine Corps aviation cadets until there were openings for them to enter flight training. These CTDs offered students 12 to 25 hours of flight time while they were enrolled in ground school courses at a college or university. Another system, the Civilian Pilot Training Program (CPTP), which had been authorized by Congress and implemented in 1939 by the Civil Aeronautics Authority, was designed to train a military reserve. The CAA also trained instructors for primary flying schools Most of those instructors were not eligible for active military service because of age, diabetes, poor eyesight or other disqualifying physical handicap. At government expense, young qualified airmen studied basic ground school courses which were designed to aid them in pre-flight and flight training, and they were also provided with 12 to 25 hours of flight training in Cessnas, Piper Cubs or other light aircraft.

In October 1941 a training conference was held in Washington DC. It was attended by USAAF training officers and by Air Marshal A.G.R. Garrod, the member of the Air Council responsible for training (AMT). The prime topic of discussion was how to reduce the terrible wastage in pilot training. As a result, RAF leaders decided British cadets must have a modicum of flying ability before the country went to the expense of shipping them overseas for training. The RAF adopted the American system of 'flight grading,' and both services agreed to designate all flight students 'cadets,' even though the RAF and the USAAF used enlisted (i.e. non-commissioned) pilots. The designation 'cadet' remained a problem with British students, who connected the label with the disciplinary 'bullshit' they had to bear, not realizing that they would benefit in the end – and not just in flying. RAF volunteers of working class origin thought officer training 'poofy' and had no thought of ever becoming officers.

Denis Fry, who had served as an accounts clerk with 266 Squadron, despite having been accepted for pilot training, was one of those men who had to face the challenge of flight grading:

> On 16 February 1942 I arrived at Aircrew Receiving Centre, London, then was posted to the initial training wing at Cambridge on 7th March and to No. 28 Elementary Flying Training School at Wolverhampton on the 10th of June. I believe that, in the early days of the war, prospective pilots were sent to various parts of the world before they had ever flown in an aircraft. Probably it was eventually found that some were not suited to flying and a wasteful procedure was amended, so that a test of approximately 12 flying hours was given to assess potential. My very first instructor was a Pilot Officer Fry! I went solo in about 8 hours, which was average. The aircraft used were the DH 82A Tiger Moth.

Getting through the initial training wing was itself a considerable landmark. A good level of education and physical fitness were important factors in surmounting this first major hurdle, which brought promotion to Leading Aircraftman (LAC). Frank Robinson, of the first Towers course in July 1941, recalled: 'At home I had been a trainee architect, high school educated, a rugby player and general outdoor man, and this helped to get me through the initial period.'

Those who opted for training in the USA now faced a journey to the coast for embarkation on a trans-Atlantic passenger vessel. Robinson reported on board the AMC *Northumberland* on July 6 for a voyage that would last eleven days. Aboard ship, RAF cadets were joined by those of the Fleet Air Arm who were destined for the same course. Their route from enlistment to pilot training was somewhat similar to that for RAF cadets, except that the Admiralty refused until 1945 to require its aircrew candidates to undergo flight grading.

Michael Price was accepted into the Fleet Air Arm on 19 September 1941, 'after a full day of medical examinations, aptitude tests, and finally interrogation by a selection board who considered not only my potential as a pilot or observer, but also my suitability to become an officer'. To his 'great disappointment' he 'did not immediately don naval uniform', but was told to 'return to civilian life until such time' as he could be 'absorbed into the system'. Later, a provisional call-up date of early 1942 was postponed to mid-1942. Incensed at the delay, he 'wrote back to the Admiralty' to complain bitterly at having his call-up deferred. He immediately received word to report to HMS *Royal Arthur*, which he did on 15 April 1942. HMS *Royal Arthur* was a shore base, like HMS *St Vincent*.

Most aircrew would be channelled to HMS *St. Vincent* for two months of initial training. *St Vincent*, a large brick-built barracks in Gosport, was entirely given over to the training of aircrew for the Royal Navy. Situated by Portsmouth harbour, it had been a centre for training boy seamen until the demands of war forced a change in its use. The primary focus of training at *St Vincent* was on naval matters. Fleet Air Arm men were sailors who flew, not airmen *per se*. This meant foot drill, boat drill, knots, physical training, navigation, meteorology, and weapons training on pistols, rifles and sub-machineguns. Beds were provided for the men in 25-man dormitories, but they were expected to place their hammocks on top of the beds, rather than use the beds in a conventional manner.

Bugle calls sounded the start of the day. At *St. Vincent*, naval airmen were supposed to learn the finest traditions of the Royal Navy, as well as the more practical aspects of 'life on the ocean wave'. Ray Gough, who passed through *St. Vincent* in early 1944, wrote to his parents: 'Yesterday we visited Pompey [Portsmouth] dockyard & harbour. We also went round the *Victory*. It was all very interesting and we saw lots of things I am not allowed to mention.'[3] Naval airmen were expected to acquire the Nelson touch, and the service demanded very high standards.

While Gough might have been rather awe-struck at some aspects of the training at *St. Vincent*, others were considerably less impressed. Gavin Waite enlisted in the Royal New Zealand Navy for aircrew training. Arriving at HMS *St. Vincent* in 1941, he found a lot that was not to his liking. He later remembered 'very basic food here & not at all appetizing'. At least, though, they were 'well past the Battle of Britain...so air raids were few'. He was surprised to find that the Royal Navy seemed in no great hurry to rush them through training. It took six weeks at *St. Vincent* for him to be enrolled on a pilot's course. The delay gave him a lot of time for leave and travelling in southern England.

The memories of Leo Ferguson, another New Zealander eager to gain his wings in the Royal Navy, were even less favourable:

[Pilot's] Course No. 66 commenced 12 June 1944 and ended 11th September 1944. Apart from the naval subjects, [it was] a complete waste of time as far as we were concerned, as we had all had over 6 months at least of ground instruction in the RNZAF before we left NZ, and to the stage that we were ready to commence flying. It would therefore be no surprise to know that our fertile minds were quick to seize on the hitherto unknown attributes of one of our Kiwis, 'Rupe'. He was an expert on locks. During an air raid, a group of us broke into the office of the infamous Chief Petty Officer Wilmot, got the safe open, and copied out the examination answers. These were faithfully learned by the Kiwis, making sure that each of us made different odd mistakes. I believe the New Zealanders in Course 66 are credited with the highest academic marks ever recorded.

Use of false dog tags to evade Sunday church parade was another escapade of the bored New Zealanders on Course 66. They were also not afraid to invoke the involvement of the New Zealand High Commissioner in their dealings with the Royal Navy. Aspects of the British class system and the rather stuffy ceremonial, class-ridden atmosphere of the service annoyed many of the New Zealanders at *St. Vincent*. As far as they were concerned, they had answered the mother country's call to the colours, endured training and a lengthy sea voyage, only to see their time being wasted by the Royal Navy. It was with a sense of relief that they received their embarkation orders.

Fleet Air Arm and Royal Air Force cadets received their embarkation orders at one of several personnel embarkation centres. The RAF said good-bye to the miserable wired-in camp at RAF Wilmslow, Cheshire, and moved to Heaton Park, Manchester. There was a sense of excitement tinged with fear, despite two weeks of ground school, square bashing and other duties while waiting for a ship out of Liverpool or Glasgow. Embarkation leave was granted, giving cadets the time to find amusements which would take their minds off the fact that they were going to be travelling across the storm-tossed and U-boat ridden North Atlantic. Mixing Royal Navy and Royal Air Force personnel was not entirely easy.

Philip Guest, who in 1943 completed the fifty-second pilot's course at *St. Vincent*, later commented:

> At the beginning of September 1943, I left with my draft by train from the little railway station in Gosport . . . and arrived at a large RAF reception centre at Heaton Park . . . It was clear that the draft was not entirely expected, since the RAF personnel also destined to go with us to Pensacola and ourselves were forced to live in half-completed barracks and use washing facilities which consisted of two or three stand pipes.

Especially in the less than salubrious surroundings of Heaton Park, the delays seemed endless. Able to accommodate 2,000 men at a time, Heaton Park saw 134,490 RAF personnel pass through between September 1941 and October 1945.[4] Hundreds of young men found themselves at a loose end as they waited for a posting. Sometimes they would be sent on temporary duties such as harvest gathering or acting as drivers. William Warner, while at Heaton Park, wrote to his wife:

> It is the most weird place I've ever seen. There are hundreds of fellows here whose 'numbers' have been lost – they've been here for months, sleeping in their beds day and night until they are mental and physical wrecks. The food would be all right if the cookhouses did not smell, and they washed the plates once a week.[5]

Warner was not the only one to find Heaton Park a disturbing place. S.R. Palmer joined the RAF on 28 September 1942, and in March 1943 he passed a flight grading course after 12½ hours dual instruction at RAF Desford, Leicestershire. He had been appalled at the delays which saw 'very keen fliers "helping" the war effort by polishing the canteen floor and keeping the gardens dug and tidy, and doing guard duty and airfield patrols with no ammunition'. While preparing for embarkation, however, the programme suddenly became more real: 'We were ordered to keep very quiet about our departure, no word to our families, but the locals told us when we were sailing; and on the 24th June we left Heaton Park for Liverpool'. After a short time, they boarded the troopship *Empress of Scotland* and departed 'in broad daylight for all on the quayside to see'.

Palmer was not the only one to experience this sharpening of the reality of training for war.

Alan Bell entered the RAF, after deferred service, in May 1943. He too was selected for pilot training after undergoing flight grading at No. 29 Elementary Flying Training School at RAF Clyffe Pypard, Wiltshire. He had spent 12 hours flying Tiger Moths before being ordered to Heaton Park, Manchester, to await an overseas posting:

> At Heaton Park there were four squadrons, each of approximately 1,000 men. We did a two-week ground school there after having two weeks embarkation leave from grading school, then were assigned to 'useful duties' until posted to the embarkation unit prior to posting to Rhodesia, South Africa, Canada or the USA. It was while I was at Heaton Park that I volunteered for the Towers scheme. We travelled to Liverpool by train, then marched through the streets escorted by a number of service police, until we boarded the *Mauretania* that had just discharged a load of US servicemen. I can remember that we got a meal of stew and little white loaves of ship's bread just after we boarded. We were hungry, having thrown away the travelling rations issued to us leaving Heaton Park, as they were inedible as usual. An RCAF [Royal Canadian Air Force] officer that was travelling back to Canada had been put in charge of us, and he apologized that he was unable to get any more stew, but we told him that was OK, just get some more bread. This was the first white bread that we had seen for some time, the British ration being of a somewhat grey unappetizing colour.

While Bell's experience of boarding a ship was reasonably positive, most aviation cadets found their trans-Atlantic crossing, on one of approximately fifty ships used for the purpose, to be an experience which they preferred to forget.

In August 1941 William Warner wrote to his parents while aboard the *Stratheden*: 'You should have seen the look of horror on our faces when we saw where one hundred and sixty of us had got to live for the trip.'[6] Fortunately, Warner and his fellow cadets made the best of the situation. He even found the hammock a 'very comfortable' substitute for a bed. A large part of the problem on troopships was that they were required to carry far more passengers than they would in peacetime. There were few stewards and other staff to ensure that life on board was at least bearable. On some vessels the toilets and living spaces were awash in faecal matter and/or vomit, as S.R. Palmer never forgot: 'Conditions on the ship left a great deal to be desired, and I recall that after a couple of days there was no toilet paper on our deck and the toilets were blocked anyway.' Despite the imperative need to make maximum use of every ship, the authorities who risked the lives and health of military, naval, and civilian personnel in filthy, overloaded ships perhaps deserved to make voyages themselves under conditions identical to those suffered by servicemen in transit.

Conditions on the trans-Atlantic troop transports eventually became so bad that they provoked a mutiny of would-be passengers. At Halifax, on 15 September 1941, some 270 Australian and New Zealand military personnel, most of whom were trained aircrew, refused to remain aboard the *Empress of Asia* in protest at the filthy conditions. In consequence, the Royal Canadian Air Force established a major RCAF Movements Group in Halifax, one of the busiest ports in the world, and its commanding officer insisted on strict rules. As soon as ships had docked in Halifax, Boston, or New York, assigned RCAF Movements Group staff used specially trained and supervised crews to ensure that vessels were cleaned thoroughly and inspected before departure. Cleaning was a particularly big issue to avoid the spread of infectious diseases. The *Empress of Asia* incident was reported to London, and orders went out to embarkation centres in an effort to help remedy sea transport problems. Beginning in September 1941, aircrew sailing from British ports were organized in 14-20-man groups, with an older cadet designated as leader. Each group would alternate duty assignments in cleaning their living and eating spaces, and in obtaining food and beverages for the group.

The aim at all times was to ensure the maximum use of all available tonnage. The change came none too soon. After 1942 a ship bound for Britain from the United States might well be carrying a full complement of American troops as part of the build-up to D-Day. On the return leg of a voyage from Liverpool, Milford Haven, Avonmouth, or Gourock, those same ships would be carrying Royal Air Force and Fleet Air Arm personnel for training in Canada and the United States. As passenger numbers increased, the chances of things going dramatically wrong with accommodation were also magnified. Large passenger vessels like the *Queen Mary* and *Queen Elizabeth* were involved in a shuttle service across the Atlantic and, despite the efforts of the authorities on either shore, resulting conditions were anything but glamorous. However, there could be hidden benefits – not least because the huge passenger vessels re-provisioned in the United States. Conditions might be crowded on board, but the food was a definite improvement on what cadets had been accustomed to in tightly-rationed Britain.

In the spring of 1944 Ray Gough, who had been on the 62nd pilots course at HMS *St. Vincent*, wrote to his parents from on board ship: 'The ship is run in proper Yankee style with coffee at every meal and the only mineral to drink is Pepsi Cola.' He had also taken advantage of the ship's cinema to see Spencer Tracey in *Boom Town* and considered overall that time on ship was 'pretty easy'.[7]

The ships carrying aviation cadets would usually, but not always, dock in Halifax, Nova Scotia. New Zealander Leo Ferguson, of the Fleet Air Arm, was one of the lucky ones who went straight from Scotland to Pier 92, New York City, in September 1944. While the declining threat from U-boats late in the war made this possible, at the height of the Battle of the Atlantic the only major year-round east coast ports with adequate safe anchorages and docking facilities were Halifax, Nova Scotia and St. Johns, Newfoundland. Of these, Halifax, with a huge harbour, safe anchorages and vast warehouses, was the most utilized, since it was the principal forming up and dispersal point for the Atlantic convoys. It also had a railhead for the Canadian National and Canadian Pacific railways. Many of the cadets felt rather worse for their ocean journey, and Halifax was not a very prepossessing city.

William Warner was one of those who found himself in Halifax waiting in camp until he could be sent forward for air training. Milling around with hundreds of other British military personnel awaiting transport to a training base, Warner felt bitter at his treatment, but there were some compensations. Shortly after landing, he recorded his amazement at the food he had received. 'This is what we had for lunch to-day: tomato and macaroni soup, pork, potatoes and apple sauce, sultana pie and custard, followed by the most delicious coffee I have ever tasted.'[8] In August 1941 Warner wrote, 'There are hundreds of "wings up" pilots here telling tales of the flying fun they have had down south.'[9] Story telling was about the only pastime to while away the hours. Warner moaned: 'There is absolutely nothing to do at the camp.' Within three days he had been able to travel a little further afield, and he was not favourably impressed by the city of Halifax:

> This place is . . . full of sailors and airmen. The former are always fighting and are picked up by special 'Naval Patrols' in large blue vans. The town is 'dry', but I have never seen so many drunks in my

life! At least three-quarters of the town consists of immoral houses of the lowest type, but the other quarter is really very fine.[10]

Warner was very glad when he boarded a train for Toronto. Already he and his fellow cadets were beginning to encounter culture shock, which was an important experience of virtually all of the British aircrew trainees. That culture shock had begun on their voyage across the Atlantic with their experience of foodstuffs, like white bread, which had been in short supply since 1940. On reaching North America, they found even fewer restrictions. 'Never seen so much food,' remembered Geoffrey Bird.

The impact of culture shock extended to even quite small matters. Robert Farrow commented: 'To be given a glass of water, serviettes on the table in drug stores was a new innovation to us.' To men accustomed to clothes rationing, which restricted the style, quality, quantity and variety of what was available in Britain, North American fashions came as a surprise. On the western side of the Atlantic, clothing was lighter and brighter than on the eastern shore. Later on, cadets would rejoice at the wearing of US Navy uniform, which Pensacola veteran Denis Fry remembered as 'so much better cut and better material than the British'.

The vastness of the North American continent also took some getting used to. Robert Farrow later recalled: 'Everything was on such a vast scale – your scenery (the vast landscapes).' Enormous landscapes concealed hidden frustrations. A ten-hour train journey in Britain would be sufficient to traverse the length of the country. In North America, British servicemen found themselves undertaking train journeys that might last for two or more days across the Canadian prairies or from Grosse Ile, Michigan, to Pensacola, Florida. Thus, even before beginning training or continuing it at a higher level at a new location, British aircrew experienced some sense of disorientation. It must be remembered that, in a highly intensive training programme, they had little time to adjust to new surroundings.

William Warner was undoubtedly glad when he received his orders to board a train to Toronto, but it was on that first journey that many aviation cadets began to learn the awesome scale of the North American continent. The journey would last approximately thirty long hours. Coming on top of a lengthy sea journey and inactivity at Halifax, the effects of the rail journey were hardly likely to boost morale. Typically, at Truro some sixty miles west of Halifax, cadets received sandwiches, milk, and fresh fruit from groups of Canadian citizens recruited for the purpose by the RCAF No. 1 Movements Group. The journey through rural

Canada was immensely pretty, but most of them only remembered its duration. However, the train journey could offer other attractions, as Warner was later to describe: 'The train we are on is very queer – very large with hard seats and bunks on springs. The main idea of fun at the moment is to release the spring and the bed shoots back and the unfortunate sleeper finds himself upside down in a coffin-like box. I must say the efforts of these fellows . . . trying to get out head-first is pretty entertaining.' Warner survived the journey and found Toronto much more to his liking than Halifax: 'Toronto is a grand place. Everywhere is so clean, spacious and modern.'[11]

Securing the orderly movement of hundreds of Royal Air Force and Fleet Air Arm personnel in Canada was nightmarishly difficult. The rail movements of the first Towers scheme cadets were coordinated by the Royal Canadian Air Force's No. 1 Movements Group from its headquarters in Montreal. That city was the location of the central offices and workshops of the Canadian National and the Canadian Pacific Railroads, so it was an ideal base from which to control the rail movement of aviation cadets. RAF Flight Lieutenant Paul Goldsmith arrived at Toronto on 24 May 1941, as the first commander of the RAF detachment there. By 19 June, three other British officers had arrived. The unit was now called the RAF Transit Section, and its commander was Squadron Leader J.F. Houchin, a veteran pilot of the 1914-18 War and of the 1940 Battle of France.

After September 1941 and the *Empress of Asia* incident, it was clear that No. 1 Movements Group was no longer able to handle the volume of aircrew passing through Canada, and this prompted an administrative reorganisation. On 1 October, RCAF No. 2 Movements Group was formed with headquarters at RCAF No. 1 'Y' Depot at Halifax. Group Captain Frank S. Magill of Montreal, a 46-year-old former Director of Postings and Records at RCAF Headquarters, was appointed commanding officer of the Movements Group. From Halifax, Magill directed an enlarged staff to inspect facilities (including ships and trains), and to analyse the details involved in transporting troops by land and sea. Within one month, major problems had been identified, and solutions had been proposed and implemented. Co-ordination of land and sea movements improved as No. 1 Port Transit Unit was set up, and closer liaison was established between the Canadian, British, New Zealand and Australian air forces.

Naturally, the aviation cadets were unaware of the vast administrative enterprise that was necessary to support their training. They merely griped about delays and poor facilities. At least conditions at Toronto were much better than at Halifax. The Royal Canadian Air Force's No. 1 Manning Depot was located on the vast grounds of the Canadian National Exhibition, on the south side of the city. It served as RCAF Recruit Depot for that part of Canada and as an aircrew processing station for trainee aircrew for the RCAF, RAF and Fleet Air Arm. During the course of 1941, the facilities available for trainee aircrew in Canada would expand.

Although new 'Y' depots to receive or quarantine arriving aircrew were opened at Halifax and Debert, Nova Scotia, in the spring and summer of 1941, it was apparent that the growing influx of trainees would overstretch the available accommodation. As a result, the authorities decided to build two huge depots near the railheads at Moncton, New Brunswick. By mid-October 1941 four barrack blocks, which could sleep 800 men, had been constructed, but other facilities were still under construction. On 18 October, Squadron Leader Houchin arrived from Toronto to assume temporary command of the new station. On 20 October, by Secret Organization Order No. 22, dated 3 October, No. 31 RAF Personnel Depot was formed, with the establishment of 'personnel and mechanical transport' on the site. The temporary RAF Transit Unit, which had been established as part of the Royal Canadian Air Force's No. 1 Manning Depot at Toronto's Canadian National Exhibition, had closed by 25 October. On the same day, 56 airmen arrived at the new station in Moncton to continue their duties.

4

LIVING AND TRAINING IN THE USA

From Canada, the aviation cadets would begin the last leg of their long journey to training stations in the United States. Most were filled with a sense of excitement mixed with foreboding. An apprehensive William Warner told his wife: 'I know I'm generally pessimistic, but don't be surprised if I do not get through this course. We've been told that only about 20-30% get through, so the chances are against it.'[1] The hundreds of young men arriving in the USA under the Towers scheme had little real understanding of Canada or the United States in which they were to train. Their induction to the Royal Navy or the Royal Air Force had been designed to give them a thorough introduction to the traditions and duties of their respective services, but it had done little to prepare them for what they would find in North America.

Even the best educated aviation cadet in 1941 had only a passing acquaintance with the major landmarks of American history, and only to the extent that they concerned the development of the British Empire. The physical, historical and human geography of the United States was a closed book to most of them, and few had ever met an American. With the huge influx of American military personnel into the United Kingdom from 1942, later cadets on the Towers programme showed an increasing familiarity with America and American ways. This came about in part from increased face-to-face contact and in part from a campaign of public education through the British media. That campaign was designed to ensure good relations between the American expeditionary forces and their British hosts, but a collateral effect was an enhanced understanding of the United States by British sailors and airmen undergoing training over there.

The BBC devoted some of its programmes to the cause, and public talks on America were organised in many British cities. A rash of books explaining aspects of American life appeared in 1942 and 1943. Typical amongst them was John Gloag's *The American Nation* and Alicia Street's *USA at Work and Play*. Advertised as 'What America is Really Like, by an American', Street's book looked at everyday life in the United States. The work of Street and others highlighted the fact that most British people in the 1930s and '40s based their expectations of America and Americans on what they had seen on 'the movies'. Hollywood provided an essential – if distorted – introduction to American ways and, most importantly, American English.

Professor Arthur Newell, President of the American Outpost in Great Britain, addressed a meeting of British Women's Institute members, only to be asked whether all Americans lived in penthouses and went out to clubs to eat. In the opening of her book Alicia Street was at pains to challenge the Hollywood image: 'Not even the most avid reader of Wild West fiction or gangster stories believes that the United States of America is inhabited entirely by hard-riding bronco-busters or baby-faced gunmen. The days of the gangster are over, and the cowboy in reality is seldom a figure of romance.'[2]

Many cadets were keenly aware of the cultural adjustments that life in the United States would force them to make. One of them later wrote a particularly reflective piece for a cadet newspaper:

AMERICANA

Before the War, many of us had ambitions to visit America to see for ourselves the cities and sights we had come to know so well on the screen. I was often stirred with an eager longing to experience the traveller's emotions on beholding the skyscrapers of New York, the busy industrialism of the North, the desert lands of the West, the song-fabled cotton plantations of the South, and I was vaguely ambitious that some day these thrills would be mine.

I can remember, when I was even younger, that the very name of America was enough to conjure up a semi-mythical vision of a land of wealth and plenty, of hustling, hard-living people who lived in towering cities of steel and concrete, of physical and artificial phenomena, which I could only associate with that country of gangs and gang-fights, brutal murders, sensational happenings, and general lawlessness. Life was cheap over there, I used to think, but it was certainly colourful . . . and my notions of the glorious West and its nomadic, glamorous cowboys, if not original, were certainly rose-coloured.

As for the South! Why, that was a veritable enchantment of cotton and corn plantations where kind-faced old Negroes and their shiny, black, fat 'Mammys' sat on the steps of their shanties and crooned mournful, yet pleasant, numbers to a gloriously tinted sunset.

Whenever I met a citizen of this wonderful continent, I would look him over with half awe, half wonderment, and seek an opportunity for our better acquaintance. This accomplished, you may be sure he was subjected to a completely exhausting 'quiz' on his home, his native habits and customs. Little by little, through association with many Americans with whom I was fortunate enough to come into daily contact, my beautifully illustrated dream-picture was altered, its perspectives modified, its pattern changed, the flaming splashes of colour softened into more harmonious tints, and its highlights dimmed to more natural tones.

In addition to the cultural challenge offered by living and training in a strange country, cadets also had to measure up to a political challenge. The high and the low politics of British aircrew under training in the USA required considerable adjustments.

The men who arrived for training before 7 December 1941 faced diplomatic, as well as military, responsibilities. The training of British airmen compromised American neutrality in a war in which a majority of Americans desired no involvement. Exemplary conduct on the part of cadets was of considerable importance in a battle for 'hearts and minds'. Likewise, it took considerable diplomatic skill to respond to the many generous offers made by American citizens to welcome these guests of the American government. Most Americans may have wanted to preserve their non-belligerent status but they were far from neutral in their thoughts and attitudes.

Hitler's repeated acts of aggression in Europe from 1935 onwards, his destruction of democracy in Germany, his racial politics and militaristic posturing had made many Americans believe that Britain had to be supported on both a collective and an individual basis in her fight against Germany. Following the RAF's successful defence of Britain after the fall of France in June 1940, British pilots enjoyed a glamorous image at home and in the United States. American newspapers, radio reporters like

Edward R. Murrow for CBS, and newsreels like *Time Marches On* were happy to play their part in glamorising British pilots.

Some of the first British aircrew trainees were given Hollywood-style profiles by the American press. In April 1942 the *Pensacola News Journal* profiled Corporal Leonard Johnson, one of the RAF trainees at the local base. It told how he was a Dunkirk veteran who had fought for days on the beaches: 'On the afternoon of the fifth day Johnson discarded his equipment and with hundreds of others entered the water. Alternately he swam or was towed by a row boat for the three quarters of a mile to the French destroyer. Often enough he would dive to escape machine gun fire from swooping planes.'[3] It was not surprising that Royal Air Force and Fleet Air Arm aviation cadets seemed imbued with almost mythical qualities in the eyes of some Americans.

Efforts were made to prepare RAF and FAA cadets for the complexities of the political situation into which they would be thrust. They were advised that their 'primary job' was to 'fly well as quickly as possible', but that Americans would judge 'the value of helping the English to the limit' by their conduct.[4] They were urged to ignore the propaganda line in the British press that 'every citizen of the US, except for a small minority, [is] already convinced that England is well worth fighting for.' The reality was that the majority of Americans hoped they could avoid involvement in the war, and that there was a danger of inflaming this section of opinion by insensitive behaviour, which might lead to such negative thoughts as: 'You see how these young Britishers behave here. They act very badly and carry on as if they owned the place. If they are a fair sample, I don't think it is worth fighting a war to help them.'[5]

The cadets were warned about speaking to American newspapermen, who were to be referred to the commanding officer on all issues. If pressed to give an answer to the question 'When should America enter the war?' they were to answer that this was a question for the American people. They were also told to avoid criticism of their instructors and the quality of their course, which they were assured would be good.

Interestingly, their briefing extended beyond a statement of the obvious diplomatic pitfalls which they might encounter. Differences in the British and American ways of war were highlighted as a potential source of difficulty. Flippant comments about the war, born of the 'stiff upper lip', were to be avoided. Questions about the bombing of British cities were not to be met with a jocular response. While the British might choose to regard the war as being like the second half of a deadly soccer match which had kicked off in 1914, Americans who chose to regard it as a crusade against Fascism, totalitarianism, German militarism or barbarism were to be left to their beliefs. Further cultural differences identified as potential pitfalls for cadets on their diplomatic mission included adverse comments on unfamiliar food and the complexities of American English. 'Do not think that American is merely English mispronounced and with a few odd words introduced into it. It is in fact a different language with varieties of its own, like the dialects used in different parts of England, and there is nothing in the least humorous about it. Americans are rightly annoyed at their language being regarded as an inferior brand of English.'[6]

Unsurprisingly, cadets occasionally found it difficult to combine military training with personal diplomacy. The pessimistic William Warner, who arrived at Grosse Ile in September 1941, found himself in an awkward position on a visit to Detroit. Feeling somewhat harassed by the hustle and bustle of the city, he and some other trainees visited a local bar. He explained what happened next in a letter home: 'We bought one drink, then things began to happen − the bar sprouted drinks, the boss brought a tray full of drinks over to us; unknown people bought us drinks, and within a short while, we were collecting invitations for week-ends by the dozen.' Warner found himself in the embarrassing situation of wanting to get back to the base, but without offending the generous hospitality of so many ordinary Americans.

Not everyone in the bar, however, was pleased by the appearance in the city of British service personnel: 'I met one educated man who was against England. I asked why, and he said he wasn't going to fight for a system where everybody had to walk round raising their hats to the village squire. When I explained things, he was all pro-British, shook hands, and ordered another drink.'[7] Aviation cadets were called on to render service to their country in many forms, but Warner's diplomatic efforts for the hearts and minds of Detroit's citizens appear to have been amongst the more unusual and rewarding.

As Warner's experience shows, few aviation cadets met real hostility from American citizens, and this became still rarer after the Japanese attack on Pearl Harbour. Misperceptions about life in Merry Old England, such as the belief that the English still imprisoned and executed prisoners in the Tower of London, were comic rather than deadly serious. J.F. Brown, a Fleet Air Arm cadet who was at Grosse Ile from May to September 1942, recalled: 'I very occasionally met civilian hostility from people who recognized my British uniform and went out of their way to be objectionable. This was rare, however, and the offenders were promptly scolded or reprimanded by other US citizens.'

Most cadets quickly adapted to the American way of life, but some aspects of it were almost beyond their comprehension. They could only marvel at the immense wealth of some of America's eminent citizens. Royal Air Force cadet Leonard Trevallion, who arrived at Pensacola in time for America's entry into the war, was one who remembered the opulence enjoyed by some Americans:

> We decided to visit Palm Beach and, on the way, we bathed and played on deserted, but wonderful, beaches, played football with large coconuts still in their husks, and swam in the sea until we were exhausted. We were amazed at the quality of life there and took many photographs of the sumptuous residences, which must have been the homes of millionaires. We were told of the Woolworth and Dodge family residences being there.

A further problem that most British students had with living in America was difficulty with US naval jargon. Denis Fry, of the fourteenth RAF course at Grosse Ile, explained: 'We had minor troubles with Navy phraseology. "Get your sneakers on and get outside for calisthenics", "open that porthole!", "get away from that bulkhead!" and "liberty boat" we came to realise meant "Get your plimsolls on and get outside for PT", "open that window!", "get away from that wall" and "bus".' The linguistic differences between Britain and America were a rich source of amusement and trouble for aviation cadets.

Those cadets who had family connections in the United States settled into living and training very quickly. Dennis Coupe of the Fleet Air Arm trained at St. Louis and then Bunker Hill in 1944. He went to visit a distant cousin in Perry, Missouri, population 801. Within five minutes of arrival in Perry, he was in the back of a drug store drinking whiskey 'with the boys'. Within a few hours, he was 'walking down main st[reet] with [a] sheriff's six-gun down my blouse on our way to do a bit of shooting'. Their Lordships of the Admiralty would undoubtedly not have approved of such unorthodox gunnery training for a Fleet Air Arm pilot. However, as a means of fitting in to small town rural America in 1944 and demonstrating that not all the British were stand-offish, public school educated gentlemen, the young pilot's diplomatic sense was probably impeccable.

Some aspects of American life caught cadets by surprise. S.B. Hanson, on the wireless operator/air gunner course at Jacksonville, decided to hitchhike to Hampton, Florida, to see some relatives. He later recalled with some horror: 'I remember one lift – near Pomona – where the driver was a boy of 10, sitting on a cushion, and with his mother sitting beside him.'

As Hanson's experience shows, the Southern United States posed their own special problems for the British cadets on the Towers scheme. They soon realised that they were entering a very different world. William Warner 'was surprised . . . [by] the social/political impact of the Mason Dixon line. If asked how we had been treated "up North," we had to be very careful. We had to infer "quite well" but nothing compared with the South!'

One of the major problems was the humid climate in which insects proliferated. David Large, Fleet Air Arm trainee at Pensacola and Miami, remembered without affection the 'appalling numbers of insects in Florida – huge cockroaches (called palm bugs by natives) especially'. The humid climate was also responsible for an altogether more dangerous phenomenon that British cadets had never encountered before – subtropical thunderstorms. Richard Allen, who arrived at Pensacola in 1942, had the misfortune to encounter one while flying over the Everglades:

> We were recalled suddenly to base because a violent thunderstorm was developing. Unfortunately we couldn't work our way round or over it and were buffeted unmercifully by the vertical air currents to the extent that we could only control the aircraft by one of us exerting full force on the stick and the other on the rudder pedals. During that same exercise one aircraft crashed killing both student pilots.

The tropics also threw up the still worse meteorological danger of hurricanes. In a letter home one cadet gave an interesting account of what it was like to be under threat from the kind of weather unknown in Britain:

> We're in the midst of another hurricane warning just at the moment, Barney. You'd be amazed at the activity that goes on when they think the hurricane might strike them. We were going on peacefully at ground school when all of a sudden, about three quarters of an hour before time, we were told to secure and get back to our

buildings. We hurried back & found that we were in what they call 'condition 2'; that is no one allowed off the station. Later we went on to 'condition 1', when everyone is confined to the building. However, when we got back we found that everything movable had been lashed down . . . All the furniture in the office was lashed under a tarpaulin & all the windows were closed. All the flying boats were flown away to another station & all the rest of the 'planes [were] battened down in the hangars all night, but after this preparation . . . the hurricane has veered off somewhere else.[8]

In addition to hurricanes, the Florida climate also offered the chance to experience the joys of sunlight in quantities unequalled in Britain. In a letter of 23 August 1941 Frank Robinson, more used to the cold climate of Lancashire, felt compelled to apologise to his fiancée for the shakiness of his penmanship: 'Forgive me if this letter is a bit wobbly in parts darling, but I caught a bit of the sun today & my head feels a bit achy. One has to be quite careful of the sun here or it knocks you off your feet. I'd been out swimming for about 3 hours; that's why I've got it – silly ass aren't I?'[9]

The warm sun could tempt the cadets into other dangers, as Robinson had previously told his fiancée in a letter of 9 August:

I'm afraid I've got a bit of bad news . . . Well, did you ever hear me talk of Jock Shearer? He came over with us from Paignton, he was in 2 flight. Well, we went on a bathing parade on Monday the 4th at approx 12.45: Jock came down with us to the beach & bathed as we all did, but he was missing at the muster taken at 2.00. Action was taken to find out whether he had met with an accident or whether he had deserted. On Tuesday morning they found his body on the beach: he must have been swept away by the strong undercurrent which was running. The funeral is today & he is to be buried with full military honours here at Fort Barrancas. Poor kid. It's going to be mighty hard on his folks back home, they'll be awfully upset; he was a real decent chap.

Robinson's letter highlighted the dangers of the strange new land in which he found himself learning to fly. It also, in its expressions ranging from a very American 'its going to be mighty hard on his folks back home' to a very English 'decent chap', showed the extent to which the cadets were swiftly influenced by the society which surrounded them.

The challenges of the South to British aviation cadets extended to the local food specialities. To some, Southern cooking with its delicacies like grits and chitterlings was the downside of Southern hospitality. Spicy food was then almost unknown in Britain. Fred Fish, who trained as a wireless operator/air gunner at Pensacola, obviously acquired a taste for it: 'I personally adjusted quite readily to the heat & food, though many of my colleagues did not like the "Southern" food & found the hot humid climate almost unbearable at times.' Fish was sometimes the beneficiary of the reluctance of his fellow cadets to get to grips with Southern cuisine. Few of his colleagues would touch the oyster stew that he found 'delicious', so 'naturally [he] benefited by having several helpings. This applied to a lesser degree to the pumpkin pie & sweet potatoes.'

Later in life, William Warner reminisced in great detail about the physical strain of living and training in an unfamiliar climate:

> The mounting strain plus the heat and humidity broke many chaps. Many of us contracted very serious and painful heat rashes in all the worst places. We used to find distant beaches, post sentries, and expose to the sun . . . but to no avail. By August the air was like a hot wet blanket, over 100°F with over 95% humidity. You went to the pictures not for the film, but because it was one of the only air-conditioned places. The rest had fans. After a few minutes you were shivering with the chill air and many developed near pneumonia. One dreaded leaving and coming out into the unbreathable atmosphere. Food was over-indulgent . . . Unlimited coffee with horrible tea-bags as an alternative. No alcohol on the station, just cokes and ice cream. We were awakened at 5 a.m. 'Hit the Deck!' We were on the flying line waiting for dawn to break. Flying and courses all day. Swotting in the evening. Then I used to do about three hours on the *'Limey'* magazine and to bed about 11 p.m. Sleeping nude with only a sheet was difficult and the mattress was sodden in the morning. We were given loads of salt tablets but many suffered from heat exhaustion. Only about 25 of us finally survived the course, I think. I eventually got through, mainly by pleading with my instructors. One said, 'I'm doing you a favour mister . . . for the sake of your wife, give in!!' Another said, 'You nearly killed me!' But I talked them round.

The Southern climate was beyond the understanding of many in the Royal Navy and RAF. Early Towers drafts arrived equipped with tropical pith helmets, but their RAF flying gear was appropriate only to the cold of western Europe. In a sympathetic gesture, the US Navy gladly issued them with khaki uniforms and lighter flying togs.

In addition to the climate, the issue of racial segregation was one of the most difficult aspects of living in the South to trouble British servicemen. One Fleet Air Arm cadet, Norman Hanson, set down in his memoirs how he fell foul of the segregated bus system while training at Pensacola:

> We boarded a bus in Pensacola town one afternoon – five or six of us – to go out to some beauty spot on the coast. We clambered in, saw the back seat . . . completely unoccupied and, naturally enough, parked ourselves in it. Departure time came and went. No activity. Then one of us asked a passenger in front of us what was the cause of the hold-up. 'The driver's waiting for you to get off that seat,' said the lady addressed. 'This seat? Why? What's wrong with it?' 'That seat's for black folks.' 'Well – there aren't any on board.' 'Don't matter. That seat's for black folks and that driver ain't gonna go 'til you boys get off it.' Sure enough as soon as we stood, the bus departed. We called that just plain bloody ridiculous![10]

William Warner also observed segregation at first hand and contrasted the black experience in the North with that in the South: 'Down South they are made to keep their place, but up North they compete with the white man and work in defence jobs and so earn pots of money. I was talking to a woman in a shop at Detroit the other day, and she said it was quite a problem: "They make a lot of money and they insist on going into the expensive shops where there are white assistants".'[11]

After moving from the North to the South, some cadets were shocked at the severity of the treatment handed out to black Americans. One night Richard Allen was returning to the Naval Air Station from Pensacola town:

> A black moved from the rear of the bus (where all seats were already taken) and slid into the furthest back row of the main section reserved for whites. The white driver saw him in his mirror and told him to move to the rear. Either the black did not hear him or chose to pretend that he hadn't, whereupon the driver diverted the bus to the Police Station where he was manhandled off the bus by two white policemen. When we arrived at the Air Station I asked the

driver what would happen to the black and he replied that they would keep him in the cells over night to 'cool him off'.

Other cadets, like Leon Armstrong, saw bus drivers refuse to allow African-Americans to board their buses if all the 'coloured' seats were taken.

William Warner was shocked at his encounters with segregation in the South: 'We were surprised and appalled at the treatment of the coloured people. I was thrown off a Greyhound bus for insisting that I offered my seat to a very pregnant coloured girl who was nearly passing out in the heat. The "reserved for coloured" back seat was full.' Warner was particularly incensed by what he saw as the inequality before the law between black and white Americans. He heard a story one day that 'a young negro was jailed for life for stealing three pounds of apples'.

Warner was not alone in attending services at African-American churches. He thought he saw signs that a new generation of black Americans was perhaps ready to challenge their inferior place in society. While some trainee aircrew brought with them attitudes towards race which one might expect from belonging to an empire that covered vast swathes of Africa and Asia, the majority regarded segregation as an affront to human dignity and contrary to the principles of liberty, freedom and democracy on which the United States had ostensibly been founded.

One further aspect of American life that gave some cadets considerable difficulty was the relationship between the sexes in the United States. To most 'green as grass' British aviation cadets American women seemed strange and exotic. Well dressed and seemingly more glamorous than their wartime English counterparts, American women were naturally attractive to British men far from home. For their part, American women were attracted by the politeness, youth and glamour of British trainee pilots. Some of the students welcomed the new social environment in which they found themselves, but perceptions that American society enjoyed a greater level of sexual freedom were often misplaced.

If America was a strange and difficult land, then, perhaps inevitably, British trainees on the Towers scheme tried to maintain some of the outward signs of British culture. *Pin Feather*, the magazine of Naval Air Station Bunker Hill, revealed on 6 August 1945 that the wireless in the cadet lounge was set to the BBC; rugby was one of several organised sports that could be played on the base; and a team of cadets had recently beaten the Chicago Cricket Club by 123 runs to 99, with Henderson taking a match-winning 4 wickets for 14 runs. At a personal level, cadets tried hard to maintain their links with home. Some of them were letter writers on an epic scale, as were their friends and family.

On 3 November 1941 trainee Frank Robinson wrote from Pensacola to his fiancée to express his feelings: 'Oh thank you so much Barney, you've saved my life once more. This morning salvation came in the form of 3 letters from you. I was so happy to get them.'[12] Robinson's letters to and from England exemplify the importance of links with home for most of the cadets. He frequently reminded his fiancée of the good times that they had had together and reassured her that better times were still to come. The pain of separation was present in every letter. He wrote to her on 25 August 1941: 'I'm so sorry you feel . . . a bit weepy over us, darling, but please don't think I don't understand. I do so very well. I know you only have a little weep when you are on your own & I don't blame you for it 'cos I know I often feel like it myself but I just daren't.'[13]

Maintaining the links with home had to be mediated through the official censor, who scoured each letter for careless revelations of military secrets. Robinson assured his fiancée: 'Don't let's worry about the chappie who opens these letters of ours – don't lets worry one bit. I mean after all he is sworn to secrecy and he's only after any gen which we may unwittingly unleash. I bet when he comes to the private parts he sighs jealously 'cos he's probably a nice little old gent with a baldish head & a little tash, 3 children & a past.'[14]

The censored letters formed a vital link with a man's home and with Britain, but it was not the only link. Robinson occasionally got through on the telephone. Other students spoke to their friends and families in Britain via a British Broadcasting Corporation hook up with a local Florida radio station. Frank Robinson's father wrote to him in August 1941 to say that a group of Pensacola cadets had been shown on a newsreel in the local cinema in Britain. Robinson's father had been told that it seemed 'to be a very big place' with 'nice quarters' and 'lots of chance of recreation'.[15]

Some cadets disliked the brashness of the ordinary American. William Warner wrote home to his parents on 5 July 1942: 'I must say I prefer the Canadian to the American. The average American is always so sure of himself. They are always telling us how dumb and slow we are.'[16] Students compared – some very thoughtfully – every aspect of British and American culture. Despite the initial culture shock, some found much to praise in the ways of the old country. One of the articles that appeared in the student newspaper, *The WAG* in 1942 was based on exactly such a comparison:

TRIPPING THE LIGHT FANTASTIC
OR
JIVING AT THE JUKE JOINTS

One of the things that deeply interested me before coming to the States, which has been the sum of numerous discussions back home, is the supposedly natural ability of the American to jitterbug. So it was that when I first came here I decided to spend part of my spare time (if any) in seeking out and attending the various dances held locally and by dropping in at some of the 'juke joints' where there are nearly always to be found a couple of 'swingcats' cutting a rug. There, over a glass or two of the liquid that cheers, I hoped to gain a first hand impression to take back home with me, should that time ever arrive. Well, anyway, to get down to the point, as the monkey said as he sat on a tintack: Is your dancing so very much different from our own? I think not. It is true that we have a much greater variety than you have, for besides the tango, conga, and rumba, we also have the Lambeth Walk and the Palais Glide, with of course, the waltz always an established favourite. But, it is an entirely erroneous idea that English girls still run around in bustles and gingham gowns and only dance the old fashioned waltz. We, too, have our 'jitterbugs' as any of the boys who have been to the Astoria, Charing Cross Road, The Ritz, Manchester, or other such dance palaces will tell you. In our own flight alone we have 'jivemen' Quin, Smith and Smallridge, who can cut a rug with the best.
A.G.P.M. (It's That Mann Again)

While the trainee aircrew of the Royal Air Force and Fleet Air Arm had to get used to the new environment in which they would be training, the American public and press had to come to terms with the British presence in their midst. The training of British aircrew in the United States called for changes all round to establish a harmonious working relationship. The pages of the *Pensacola News Journal* offer an insight into the process of adjustment on the American side. The newspaper's editorial column on 27 July 1941 featured a formal welcome to the 130 British student aviators who had recently arrived: 'We welcome the British here with all our hearts and are glad that the Pensacola station, as a part of the immense defense force of the United States, can play this lead role in support of Democracy.'[17]

In subsequent issues the newspaper reported the kind of entertainment that had been put on for these visitors from England – a tea party at the

San Carlos Hotel, courtesy of the Municipal Advertising Board.[18] The *Pensacola News Journal* also passed on a request from the Chamber of Commerce for local people 'to entertain these RAF men in their homes when they have leaves. The Chamber will be glad to place anyone's name on the list and make arrangements for such entertainments.'[19] From this point on, sections of the paper were routinely devoted to the activities of the British students, which were reported surprisingly fully.

The *Detroit Free Press*, by contrast, found British censorship a considerable impediment in reporting the activities of Towers cadets at Grosse Ile. One report commented on the arrival of the first contingent of pilots: 'British censorship makes it impossible to report the number in the party beyond saying that it contained 80 to 100 youngsters, averaging about 23 years old.'[20] Cadet achievements and local dances attended by British personnel featured regularly in the Florida newspapers.[21] It was with a sense of pride that one newspaper revealed on 4 January 1942 that two Fleet Air Arm men, J. Large and G. Symons, had become the first British students to pass the course and would now go on to further training at Miami.[22]

The warm relationship between the cadets and the local Pensacola newspaper was such that it felt able to go beyond reporting the superficial aspects of the British presence in Florida. It sometimes ran articles probing attitudes or revealing certain aspects of that relationship. By December 1941 one reporter felt emboldened to ask a group of cadets about their likes and dislikes so far as the United States was concerned. The reporter told the readers of the newspaper: 'The opinion among British students seems pretty general that our beer is not very palatable, as compared to the brand of draught beverage fresh from the barrel that they consume in England.'[23]

The first death of a British trainee – drowned while swimming off the enlisted men's beach – was reported sorrowfully by the paper on 6 August 1941. It also carried an account of the first British fatality in flying training on 29 March 1942.[24] On 29 November 1942 the newspaper told its readers of a letter that had been sent to a Pensacola couple by the parents of one of the trainees who had graduated. He had been killed during further training in England, but his parents wanted to thank the couple who had befriended him while he was at Pensacola. The relationship between the trainee aircrew, the American press, and the American public was remarkably close. Without a doubt, the press in Florida, Michigan and the other places where men were trained under the Towers scheme did an important job in mobilizing the American public to extend their hospitality to the strangers in their midst.

The press and public were important, but perhaps the most crucial American reactions to the training of British aviation cadets came from within the United States Navy. The Royal Navy and the United States Navy had intertwined and distinguished histories. The American War of Independence and the War of 1812 had bred a healthy rivalry between the two navies. That rivalry had sharpened in the early twentieth century, especially after the First World War when American naval building plans threatened to give the US Navy a battle fleet far larger than Britain's. Ever since the wars against Napoleon, the basis of British naval policy had been the two-power standard. By that criterion, the Royal Navy aimed to be big enough to defeat the next two largest naval powers combined. At the Washington Conference in 1921-2, however, the British government had recognized that the two-power standard was no longer tenable.

In the aftermath of the First World War, Britain could not afford a naval building race with the United States, and at Washington both nations agreed to accept parity with each other while ensuring supremacy over the Japanese, French and Italians. From that point on, naval relations between the two powers had been relatively harmonious. By 1937 the first significant contacts paving the way for possible wartime co-operation were being made. The 'destroyers for bases' deal in 1940 and the birth of the Towers scheme in 1941 were further significant events in a deepening relationship. However, while relations at the highest level between the British and American navies were good, the Towers scheme ensured that relations would be tested at an altogether less exalted level. The way in which ordinary American sailors and naval instructors would react to their British students was more problematic.

At such levels, grand strategy and world alliances did little to colour the face-to-face relationships between men from the two navies. Some Towers cadets were ready to ascribe a failure in training to the anti-British bias of a particular American instructor. What was perhaps surprising, however, was that almost all cadets quickly appreciated that, whatever the personal views or family origins of individual instructors, United States Navy personnel regarded themselves as one group of professionals working with another group of professionals, albeit from a different country. The particular rights and wrongs of the war hardly entered into the training, although the sympathies of most instructors were plainly with Britain rather than with Germany.

What mattered to United States Navy instructors were the orders they had been given. They were going to ensure that as many British cadets as possible learned to fly as quickly and as well as they could. Some of the instructors were mavericks who had made reputations for themselves as barnstormers in the 1920s and '30s. Some of their training methods were also a little unorthodox. Geoffrey Bird, who left HMS *St Vincent* in May 1941 for training on the Towers scheme, recorded that he had 'never known anybody to curse & swear and be as foul-mouthed' in his life as his instructor. However, there could be no doubting the skills of most of the instructors and their determination to turn out good aviators by whatever means they felt necessary.

Inevitably, United States Navy instructors had expectations of the pupils whom they would teach. Some of those expectations were not necessarily correct or entirely beneficial. In 1942 *The WAG*, the newsletter of the wireless operator/air gunner students at Jacksonville, carried an article which placed this aspect of training into sharp relief. Headed 'What an American Instructor Thinks of the RAF,' it recorded the impressions of one United States Navy instructor:

> When I accepted this job and was told that I was to teach the RAF students here in America, I formed many opinions of them, as all others would when they were about to meet someone they had heard about but never seen. I had formed a mental picture of their moods and outlook on life. I had expected to find men deep in their study, seldom smiling or saying much about back home. But indeed I found a group of men who were always smiling, joking in their own way with no gloom or dread of going back to the war-torn cities of England . . . One of the outstanding differences between the American and British student is the great co-operation, which exists among the latter. The American desires to get ahead, to out-do the other fellow. The Britisher will go out of his way to help the others.[25]

Meanwhile, British aircrew had their own expectations of the kind of training that they would receive. All expected their training to be of the highest order, while some wondered about whether the politics of particular instructors might interfere with their decisions on whether to pass or fail British students. It was suspected by many Towers trainees that instructors of German descent were, in the words of Richard Allen, 'prone to down-check British students'. Many of the differences between

British and American practice could be laughed at, but some were cause for more serious complaint. The system of demerits was a cause of real friction between British students and their US Navy superiors. Demerits were awarded for breaches of regulations – even for the smallest offence – up to a maximum of fifty per week, at which point more serious sanctions would be invoked.

Philip Guest remembered: 'On the back of a door . . . at Main Base in Pensacola was pinned a notice listing all the offences one could commit in room cleanliness. Thus, the list started with "Deck – dust on, dirt on." Whilst agreeing that it was essential for a military body to pay attention to room cleanliness, it was difficult not to have a sense of being unfairly treated when 5 demerits were incurred for say "Deck – dust on, dirt on," the dust having accumulated in the period from 6.45 a.m. when we left the room until 11.00 a.m. when the O[fficer] o[f the] D[ay] carried out his inspection.'

The perceived pettiness of the system upset almost every cadet. Leon Armstrong was one of those who fell foul of the system: 'One could return to the barracks after having been flying, only to find a chit on the bed advising that 3 demerits had been awarded because the blankets had not been folded in the regulation manner.' On one occasion, Armstrong and a fellow cadet earned five demerits for failing to halt at a stop sign on the air station at Pensacola. The time was 5 a.m. and the only observers to the incident were the men of the Navy patrol who stopped them. To trainee British aircrew the demerit system seemed entirely alien.

The rigidity of the demerit system surprised many British aircrew. Richard Allen was one cadet who was left aggrieved by the way the system operated:

> Soon after having gone solo on the Harvard at Pensacola, I tried to land in a particularly strong cross-wind and ended up by doing a ground-loop at the end of the landing run, thereby damaging one wing-tip – a not infrequent occurrence particularly for 'rookie' pilots in a cross-wind. I was hauled before the Commander (Flying) next morning who immediately awarded me 10 demerits. I remonstrated that there were extenuating circumstances in that the Control Tower realised their error and immediately changed the duty runway to one facing correctly into the wind. The Commander was, indeed, most understanding but invited me round to his side of the desk to inspect the typed list of 'Offences and Corresponding Punishments' displayed under the glass top of his desk. 'There you are, son, in

black and white,' he said, pointing to my particular offence. 'There's nothing I can do about it.' I couldn't help feeling that I would have had a more sympathetic hearing from an officer back home.

In addition to demerits, further tensions arose from British expectations of shore leave, which conflicted with those of their hosts. Dennis White, who arrived at Grosse Ile in early 1942 after completing the course at HMS *St Vincent* in December 1941, recalled his shock at 'trigger happy sentries' who fired on him as he climbed over the fence after a late night excursion. At one point in 1942 there was a potentially serious confrontation between the British students and their hosts over shore leave, as Michael Price, who finished his course at HMS *St Vincent* on 9 August 1942, relates:

> Two British students who had overstayed their leave one evening by about half an hour persuaded one of the American personnel at the base who had an automobile to conceal them in the back and get them into the base. Although this operation was apparently successful, the guardroom was alerted to the fact that the number of British students who had checked out that evening exceeded the number checking in by two. An investigation was immediately carried out to find the names of the two who had smuggled themselves back in, and although they were known to the senior British student . . . it was decided at a mass meeting of the students that their identities should be concealed from the authorities for fear of the ultimate retribution – being thrown off the course. The CO then handed out the ultimatum that, unless the two culprits owned up, the whole body of British students would be confined to camp. As Christmas was fast approaching and most of us had invitations out to dinner, the situation looked fairly serious. However, a deal was negotiated between the CO and the Senior British Naval Officer . . . that, if the culprits owned up, their punishment would fall short of dismissal from the course. This was put to the student body on 24th December, whereupon the two offenders owned up, and the rest of us were able to accept our Christmas dinner invitations. (The two guilty ones were never allowed to leave the base for the remainder of the course.)

The collision of expectations between guest and host could arise over comparatively insignificant matters. In Florida, the Royal Navy's standard tropical white shorts were frowned upon as being offensive to local tastes and so, unless cadets were in their formal whites, they spent most of their time in khaki trousers and long sleeved khaki shirts. British trainees were unable to understand the nature of the offence to which shorts could give rise. They expected Americans to behave and think like British citizens and were surprised when they did not.

Despite minor difficulties in the relationship, its basic strength was underpinned by a rich vein of humour. Differences in Anglo-American English were treated as a source of comedy that was exploited to the full by both sides. Fleet Air Arm student Geoffrey Wright, who trained at Grosse Ile in early 1943, remembered one particularly good example of this kind of comedy. It took the form of a notice by one of the hangars: 'Students - Gas your own Planes: English Pilots – Gentlemen, kindly replenish your petrol supply.' Publications like *The WAG* and the *Limey*, magazines of the British flight students, were particularly good exponents of this kind of trans-Atlantic comedy.

Much of the comedy was unintentional and sometimes the humour took a while to break through. Even the names of particular students could present problems, as Pensacola cadet Richard Allen was to find out:

> My full surname is Fleischmann-Allen, which was used throughout my service career. When I arrived at Pensacola our first day's flight schedule involving dual-student exercises was read out by the duty instructor. When he came to my name he said, 'Fleischmann, you are flying with Allen.' When I replied, 'I normally do, Sir,' he at first thought I was 'taking the mickey' until I explained that we were one and the same person.

Such language comedy became a source of rich entertainment to Towers cadets. *The WAG* edition for October 1942 featured a short feature headed 'Sayest Thou'. It argued that various modern American sayings did not originate in the United States, and gave some examples: '"Step on it Baby" – was the invitation extended by Sir Walter Raleigh to Queen Elizabeth, referring to his cloak . . . "Oh Boy, What an Eyeful" – what King Harold said when an arrow went through his eye at the Battle of Hastings, 1066.'[26] The humorous element intensified after sizeable numbers of US servicemen began landing in England in 1942 and 1943. Now aviation cadets could contrast their own experiences of America with American experiences of Britain.

In October 1942, *The Wag* ran a spoof story headed 'Sez You?' It foretold the forthcoming annual report of the Chief Constable for Wallasey: 'I cannot refrain from commenting adversely on the pernicious and growing habit of youths to use Americanisms, with nasal accompaniment, in order to appear, in their vernacular, "tough guys". On one of my officers going to search him, a young housebreaker told him to "lay off cop". "Oh yeahs" are frequent in answer to charges.' The reason for this was ascribed to 'the ever-increasing influence of sound-films, cheap fiction, and the unprecedented wartime exchange of population'.[27]

The ability of Americans and British to make jokes at one another's expense was important, but what could be turned into a joke could equally become a source of major irritation. Comedy was a means of defusing potentially tense aspects of the training programme. It was a means of getting along. Humour eased the wheels of training and masked the reality of preparing to fly in a conflict that, by December 1941, had spread around the globe. It was a deadly serious business, and a little light relief was part of the coping mechanism for most of the cadets.

5

PRIMARY AND INTERMEDIATE FLIGHT TRAINING

Primary Training

In primary or elementary training, an airman had to acquire a basic understanding of how an aeroplane flies, how it is constructed and how it is controlled. Student pilots had to reach the stage of being able to take off, fly, and land an aircraft unaided (that is, to 'go solo'). After six weeks of intensive instruction on the ground (known as ground school), they would take to the air in N3N two-man open-cockpit biplanes to learn the basics. Flying training was divided into six parts:

1. Initial dual instruction in taxiing, take-off, climbs, turns, spirals, glides, landings, stalls, spins and emergency situation recovery – 10 flying hours.
2. Primary solo/dual instruction, practising further the initial work, but solo; learning steeply-banked turns and spirals, spins and advanced emergencies, doing precision landings . . . and applying this technique in small field approaches. Learning small field work, emergency landings and slips, then practising slips to landing. Then came the 20-hour check.
3. Advanced solo, learning and practising splits, loops, wing-overs and eights, rolls, and precision spins, Immelmann turns, falling leafs, cartwheels, and inverted spins, finishing with emergency landings with a dead engine in small fields. Then followed the 33-hour check.
4. Formation flying, learning 3-plane formation, simple V, formation take-off, formation V to echelon, position shifts and formation landing in V.

5. Finals included general reviews of the syllabus ending with a front-seat check-out and solo.
6. Night-flying instruction, night flying with a safety pilot and night locale flying with landing practice.
A total of approximately 85 flying hours were logged in primary training.[1]

In just 85 hours, a pupil had to learn the basics of flying, formation flying and night flying. In primary training cadets usually developed a love-hate relationship with the aircraft. This was usually dependent on the type of aircraft they flew. Bryan Noel Edwards, a member of the RAF class at Grosse Ile and Pensacola, described the NP1 as 'flying like an agricultural tractor and [with] the gliding qualities of a brick; only to be expected of an aircraft reputed to have been built in a shipyard'. He also described the N2S Stearman as 'a beautiful airplane'. In such aircraft the students placed their careers and their lives.

Learning to fly was terrifying enough but, before they had completed primary training, they were expected to be able to put their skills into practice in the dark. John Bazalgette was one of those who went on to advanced flight training at Pensacola in September 1941. He particularly disliked the experience of flying at night for the first time: 'I thought that the first "go" solo-at-night flying was a risky business. It was difficult to orientate oneself the first time aloft during the nocturnal hours.' Inevitably, on a highly pressurized and intensive course, there was a steady stream of casualties. A number of aviation cadets were killed, and over 50 per cent could expect to 'wash out' of flight training for a variety of reasons. There was a black comedy about the process, which helped to mask on-going tension and strain. Pensacola cadet E. C. Sheppard recalled one illustrative incident:

> On one occasion during my time there, six RAF students were picked to attend a military funeral at Barin Field . . . As Barin Field was some distance away, the six-man RAF squad was collected with a pick-up truck, an empty coffin, and a Union Jack. As a pick-up truck is not the best means of transport for six men, they decided to sit on the coffin.
>
> When they arrived at the main gate, the Marine Guard took one look at this, with one of them actually sitting on the flag, and had the lot off the truck, and into the guard room in no time at all. Insulting the flag seemed to be the main complaint, and to the USN

this was, it seemed, close to a capital offence. It was all sorted out a few hours later, but so far as I know, they were never allowed to attend the funeral.

The first cohort of Towers students reported to Pensacola on 24 July 1941. They would remain together through primary and intermediate flight school, where they learned more complex techniques such as flying on radio beams. The US Naval Air Station at Pensacola, Florida, had been commissioned on 11 February 1914. The British cadets who went through primary training there before 7 December 1941 had the status of civilians learning to fly in a neutral country. Their situation was, indeed, bizarre; and they were effectively guinea pigs testing out an intensified version of the United States Navy's training programme. Inevitably, that programme needed to be steadily refined in the light of experience.

The first Towers drafts went to Pensacola but, after a re-organization of training, further drafts would go through primary training at more northerly Naval Reserve Air Stations. Primary training was shifted to Grosse Ile, Michigan, where the United States Naval Air Station on the Detroit River had been used as a flying base since 1925.[2] Then it had been used for seaplane training by a naval reserve unit and by other groups. During the latter part of 1941, under the command of Lieutenant-Commander R.C. Young, it underwent a major expansion to give it three runways of 4,000, 4,500 and 5,000 feet.

The first British students arrived at the base in late 1941, as American aviation cadets shipped out. For a time the base was used purely for the training of British airmen until, in early 1943, over 600 Royal Air Force and Fleet Air Arm servicemen were in flight training there. A delay to the flow of British students early in 1943 resulted, however, in the placing of 156 American airmen for training at the base. One year later the numbers of British students were stretching the resources at Grosse Ile to capacity once again.

Overseeing the training of British students at Grosse Ile were Squadron Leader Briggs, Royal Air Force, and Lieutenant-Commander P.B. Jackson, Fleet Air Arm. Both were distinguished pilots. Briggs had flown the Catalina, with a USN co-pilot, which spotted the German battleship *Bismarck* in May 1941, and Jackson had flown a Fairey Swordfish in torpedo attacks against the same ship. Jackson later recalled his experiences at the base for the journal *Michigan History*. 'I found myself in charge of some 180 to 200 British student pilots at Grosse Ile . . . I had to be the shoulder upon which the British lads wept, their paymaster, father confessor, wet nurse, and final word if they failed their US flying check or were found unsuitable.' Jackson's job also extended to diplomacy:

> The most important part of my duties was to be as diplomatic as possible with the US Navy and also with the splendid people of Detroit. Their great hearts and kindness made this an easy task. However, there were a few in the Midwest who had strong associations with Germany and possible sympathy with Ireland. I might add that in the latter case my first name (Patrick) and my Irish Catholic grandmother really came into her own.[3]

The British students who trained at the base found the course unexpectedly tough. The demerit system and tight security caused a little unease, and the discipline imposed by the United States Navy was considered heavy-handed by many of the British servicemen. Royal Air Force cadet R. Palmer recalled this aspect of his training without much affection:

> After a pep talk by a Chief Petty Officer (who chewed tobacco) and a cold shower, we settled into very comfortable barracks. It soon became very obvious that US Navy discipline and certain members of the RAF were not going to get along 100%, and it was obvious that life was going to be tough and many a budding hero was to find himself on the train back to Canada at various times on the course, because his shaving brush was not 1.5 inches from the edge of the shelf or the hospital corner of his bed was 44 instead of 45 degrees.

Palmer was not the only one to remark on the culture clash between English humour and American discipline at the base. About his joining the Grosse Ile course on 13 September 1943, Joe Winandy remembered: 'On our arrival we were asked to complete a questionnaire. One of the questions was, "What would you do if you saw someone stamping on the American flag?" One English student mistakenly used his English humour and suggested that he would give them a helping hand. The sensitive authorities had this student out of the country by midnight.'

At least Winandy and Palmer could take comfort in the quality of life at Grosse Ile. William Purdon thought that the food was 'good, varied, [and] plentiful'. Stanley Duxbury never forgot his first meal on arrival: 'We collected a metal tray with depressions thereon [for] various kinds of food ... The stipulation was "Eat all you Take". A US Navy ensign stood close to the trash bin to see that the stipulation was complied with. Coming from wartime rationing in Britain, airmen found it comical that they were expected to eat up the generous servings on offer at Grosse Ile.' Students also found the accommodation surprisingly pleasant. Duxbury noted that his dormitory 'was fitted with wireless, radio to the Americans, and the local station WXYZ plugged along with advertisements throughout the day with accompanying jingles'.

William Warner, who arrived at the base in 1941, pronounced it 'an absolute winner'.[4] Later students, such as Alan R. Bell who entered the Royal Air Force class at Grosse Ile in March 1944, shared his favourable opinion of the facilities:

> We seemed to settle down fairly quickly at Grosse Ile, for this was a station that had been dealing with [the] RAF for a number of years, and I rather think that our predecessors had done a spot of brainwashing. Anyway, the only unpleasant thing that I can think of at Grosse Ile was that the food was too rich for us after stringent wartime rations. We would delight in eating chocolate cream pie etc., and then throw it up again as our stomachs rebelled. It would have been better, I think, if they could have broken us in a little more gently. The thing I do remember about the meals was the marvellous salads, especially the Waldorf salad with peanuts, and the choice of entree, and the availability of 'seconds'. At the same time, I remember the terrific waste of food that we would have given our eyeteeth for back in Britain. One day, while we were flying from Lambert Field, three of us were delayed in landing, due to a crash on the field, and when we got to the Mess Hall, lunch was over, and the entire contents of the serving trays had gone into the garbage. I can remember that there was cold ham on the menu that day, and it, along with all the salads, had been thrown out. We got chits from the CPO in charge of the Mess, which enabled us to get steaks at the coffee shop in the Ship's Service. While we were at Grosse Ile, there was a USO set-up in a large house not far from the station, and it was like a home away from home. We were very welcome there, and transportation was laid on to take you there and bring you back. If the ladies knew that you were having a birthday, then you could be sure that there would be a cake for you.

In addition to the facilities at the base, the bright lights of Detroit beckoned and local families were eager to provide entertainment and hospitality. William Warner wrote home in 1941 with his impressions of the city: 'Terrific skyscrapers, millions of cars, street cars, and people – all rushing, pushing, and shoving, as if they were being prodded from behind.'[5]

The British students were primarily at Grosse Ile to learn to fly, however, and for many it would not be a happy experience. The geography and climate of Michigan, with its own micro-climate generated by the Great Lakes, could conspire to produce stern challenges for inexperienced aviators. On one occasion in December 1941, shortly before Pearl Harbour, a cadet flying solo became lost in a snow storm. Eventually landing in a field, he enquired at a nearby farm house about his location, only to be told that he had landed in Canada. The diplomatic complications of a British pilot landing an aircraft in the markings of a neutral United States in belligerent Canada were rendered academic by Japan's attack on the US Pacific Fleet.

Climate was also to cause problems for Lindsay Todd, who was in the RAF Class at Grosse Ile from July to October 1943. He eventually washed out of flight training at Grosse Ile, only to gain his wings later in Canada. Perhaps part of his problem at Grosse Ile is summed up in his overall thoughts on the base: 'Summer '43 was very hot in Michigan. Being a Northern Englishman, I particularly suffered from the heat. Our sleeping barracks, especially, rarely got under 90 degrees overnight and ventilation was poor.' He did find some aspects of life on the base appealing: 'recreation was very good – virtually a new "free" film every night, excellent "ships stores," all A-OK. Detroit was "out of this world". It had a superb USO and hospitality facilities.' As someone who eventually washed out, his comments on flight training at Grosse Ile are particularly revealing:

> My instructor was an Ensign Palmer, and I did my compulsory 12 hours flying dual, then was transhipped by Liberty bus to one of several airstrips on the mainland for 1st solo. The Flying Programme used these, mostly unmanned, for various different practice routines [stages of training]. One, between Wyandotte and Ann Arbor, was used for 'slips and circles' landings, and the circuit pattern was changed to wind direction via a ground smoke pot. The various changes of airfields had made me late on the 'roundabout' this day, so, noticing a second Stearman N2S 75 ahead of me on approach, I didn't waste time identifying the circuit and followed it in, noting that the second plane had two occupants. Just after this, I was 'shot

up' by this plane, and on return I was charged with incorrect procedures and, despite protesting that I'd followed in the instructor/pupil who'd also 'gone the wrong way', was given 10 demerits, the instructor informer not being reprimanded in any way. My demerits meant my giving up 4 nights of study time to march with a wooden rifle around the base with mostly 'gobs' who were doing likewise for being AWOL and the normal service offences. The base USN Liaison Officer, a captain, was most sympathetic and agreed that I had had a rough deal, but urged me to accept that the instructor informer in one plane, and the other soloist, never checked by the informer, were getting off 'scot free'. Although the captain was a nice, gentle and civilized man, he couldn't or wouldn't 'stir the system up'. Rumours obviously reached the flight instructors, and from then on, at even 100 hours, half of it solo, and 'UP' checks all the way, I was virtually 'at risk' from my own instructor and the other 'check stage' instructors. I was even accused of freezing on the controls during an inverted spin, and was finally given two 'DOWN' checks. On the subsequent 'ECT' check, which my log book tells me was Stage DXI, I felt I must have done 'OK'; my sole question to the instructor on our walk in was 'How did I do, Sir, please?' Nothing was said until we walked through the pupils' crew room and through to the instructors' room where all heard him say, 'That guy has just talked himself into a DOWN & washout!!'

Todd went to see the RAF Liaison Officer, who declined to intervene. Despite the pain of 'washing out,' Todd was impressed with the quality of his flying instructors at Grosse Ile, whom he found 'pleasant, courteous, very friendly and efficient in whatever they did for us'.

Learning to fly was an inherently difficult thing to do, especially in the context of an intensive course compressed by the demands of wartime. Ground school offered few terrors for most of the students, except for the boredom factor. British students were more willing to express their boredom openly than were their American counterparts, who were governed by a strict honour code. Richard Allen witnessed one revealing incident: 'During a particularly boring lecture . . . a number of British students (who generally sat at the back of the class) decided to abscond by climbing out of the back windows of the lecture hall whilst the instructor was writing on the blackboard. Although a number of American students saw the incident, none of them reported it to the lecturer which, of course, they would have been bound to do if was one of their own.'

The boredom of ground school served as an uneasy preparation for the difficulties of flying. The levels of skill required to pilot a plane were more demanding than some Towers hopefuls had imagined. William Warner did his best to explain one of the challenges of flying in a letter home in September 1941: 'The thing that amazes me is the delicacy required on the controls. You have only to move the stick an eighth of an inch to do a steep turn – if you move it half an inch it apparently turns the plane on its back or something.'[6] Cadets with poor co-ordination skills, airsickness, or depth perception problems would rapidly be weeded out as instructors at each stage of the course carried out checks. An up-check, and they were free to move on to the next stage: two successive down-checks, and they washed out of training. A considerable responsibility was placed in the hands of the instructors, especially those who flew as check pilots.

Not every instructor was highly regarded by the British students. John Jones, who had left HMS *St. Vincent* in July 1943, was profoundly unimpressed by the quality of the instruction he received. His first instructor 'did not teach me anything but showed me what he could do! He did not want to be an instructor – just wanted to get back to operations.' Jones complained and got a new instructor, and a second chance at the course as he was on the verge of failing it. Those who did not have cause to complain still considered that the course was extremely hard.

That toughness extended to every aspect of life and training on the base, especially the emphasis on physical training. David Large, who had left *St. Vincent* in October 1941, hated the American style PT that they were forced into: 'At Grosse Ile we had to go in the dark, first thing in the morning on rising, to an aircraft hangar full of petrol fumes, to do violent physical training. We managed to get an RAF sergeant PT instructor, re-mustered for aircrew, to lead us in "Swedish drill" – none of those explosive punches required by the brutish big blonde Swede who so enjoyed putting us through it in the American way.' The course was undoubtedly tough, but it was so for a purpose.

The ultimate test of a developing pilot's skills came when he flew solo for the first time. Joe Winandy, who flew solo after collecting one down, one up, one down and two up checks, described it as 'something special'. It was a tense moment all round, as one pilot explained in a letter: 'That front cockpit looks awfully empty when you are up there on your own with no guiding hand to help you out of difficulties.'[7] Students noticed that their instructors were just as nervous as the students, as the latter embarked on their first solo flights. William Warner wrote: 'Most of the instructors are queer fellows – whilst they are teaching you, they are as tough as eggs, but when you go solo they daren't watch you.'

By 1943-4 Grosse Ile was functioning effectively as a base for the training of British airmen, but it had taken two years to reach this stage. Kenneth Blevins, who joined the third Royal Air Force class at Grosse Ile in September 1941, remembered his initial reactions to the base and some of the difficulties that were encountered in the early days:

> And so to Grosse Ile, Michigan . . . the forbiddingly accurately named 'Elimination Base'. We were the first British cadets to pass through this centre and, as a result, received full press coverage. Remember, this was 15 August 1941 . . . before Pearl Harbour, so we were issued gray civilian suits to wear off the camp, and, of course, had to do US Navy drill on camp. At first, we were confined to camp totally, as the Commandant, a Marine, was scared of the big hospitality that we would get, which would affect our flying progress. We rebelled (a strike!). We were allowed out. Some of us were eliminated. If you didn't go solo on the N3N navy trainer in 10 hours, you were washed out. The survivors went to Pensacola. Many of our course were Royal Navy (Fleet Air Arm) lads, mostly New Zealanders, I recall. They were destined for carrier training eventually.

Most aviation cadets enjoyed their experiences at Grosse Ile. J.H. Ashley, who joined the tenth RAF class in May 1942, certainly had appreciative memories of his training there:

> The next three months was the most marvellous period of my RAF career. We covered a wide range of additional ground school subjects – meteorology, engines, physics, and physical training (none of which were exactly enjoyable but proved of value later) – and 78 wonderful hours of elementary flying on three types of USN landplanes, the NP-1, N3N, and N2S4 (Stearman), all biplanes. The Stearman was a particular delight to fly, and I was extra fortunate in having the most experienced instructor on the base, a craggy-faced, utterly dedicated character with a tough manner, but lots of patience. His name was Lieutenant John Van Bruggen, who had spent several pre-war years in 'barn-storming', and could practically make an airplane talk. All the instructors were USN or USMC officers, apart from a few civilian teachers at Ground School, and we had an RAF

Liaison Officer on the base, a very strict disciplinarian named F/Lt Cullum. We had some 6 hours of Ground School every weekday and, as I said earlier, none of us really enjoyed the heavy emphasis in US Navy training on 'academic' subjects such as physics and maths. We naturally wanted to be flying all the time! We were housed in excellent two-story barrack blocks and greatly enjoyed all the food (such abundance!). I found the staff uniformly pleasant and highly efficient at their jobs. The climate was much hotter than in England (Detroit recorded some 117 degrees in the sun during our stay), but there were no complaints, particularly during 'liberty' weekends, which we usually spent in Detroit enjoying the wholehearted hospitality of so many civilian friends, who loved to entertain servicemen, particularly the British, who never ceased to be overwhelmed with kindness and consideration. We stayed in private houses, went on picnics, and to cinemas and theatres, and during this period we all formed a most favourable impression of the Americans and their way of life which, speaking for myself, never left us.

My first flight in the USA was on 3 June 1942 and I soloed after 11 hours on Stage 'A', after receiving an 'UP' check at first attempt. The rest of the elementary (the USN called it 'primary') flight programme consisted of Stage B: emergency landings, carrier-type landings, advanced turns, glides, side-slips, and spins. I completed this stage in 46 hours. The reason for the longer hours under Stage B was because I failed 4 consecutive 'B' checks, and after a Special Board, was given additional instruction time before successfully passing to the next stage. Quite a few of us had difficulties with B Stage, notably the emergency landings (the instructor would suddenly 'cut the gun' and you had to land wherever you could) and carrier-type landings. The latter involved landing the wheels first time in a 25-foot diameter circle. Neither appeared in the RAF syllabus, but both proved useful at later stages, certainly in two incidents reported. Stage C, aerobatics and night flying, I completed in 22 hours; Stage D, night flying, low flying and more aerobatics encompassed 10 hours; and Stage E, 10 hours of formation flying, had to be flown from a satellite field at Pensacola because the weather prevented completion at Grosse Ile. So far as I recall, most of the lads passed the elementary flying stage – [but] certainly at least two were sent to Trenton in Canada for re-mustering.

The Link trainer was loathed by many students, including Norman Hanson. 'We sweated for hours and hours under the hood of a ground-based link trainer, practising flying on radio beams, making timed approaches to "airfields" and controlled let downs in simulated bad weather.'[8] It was at the end of the intermediate stage that Fleet Air Arm aviation cadets qualified for their wings, but RAF students were not promoted until they had completed advanced flying training.[9]

In the middle of 1944, as the resources at Grosse Ile were stretched to the limit, it was decided to relocate the primary flying training of RAF and Fleet Air Arm cadets to Lambert Field, St Louis, Missouri. For some airmen the changeover came as a most unwelcome disruption. Alan R. Bell, of the Royal Air Force, was among the unlucky ones who were transferred in the middle of their training. His experience at St. Louis proved to be very disappointing, as he 'washed out' before re-mustering as a bomb aimer in Canada:

> We had a special train to take us to St. Louis, and I can always remember that when we were in the dining car, and asked what was for lunch, the dining car steward said, 'Whatever you want, you can have. We've got to give you anything you ask for!' Such a pleasant change for wartime travel! When we arrived at St. Louis, the US naval cadets were waiting to get on the train that we got off. When we got up to the field, they made a great fuss over us. The naval band had learned to play English tunes etc., and I'm afraid at the beginning they thought we drank nothing but tea and ate nothing but roast beef. The civilian population of St. Louis were very quick to issue invitations to come to dinner, and one or two nightclubs, I regret to say, used the RAF and FAA boys as a sort of freak show. After inviting them to the club, they would keep putting the spotlights on them. As newcomers to the city, there were one or two embarrassing moments. I had gone to the movies downtown, and put my money down at the cashier's cage. When she asked for more I pointed out the price, and she said that was only for servicemen. I asked her what she thought I was, and she said she thought I worked for Western Union, and refused to accept the fact that I was an Ally. We flew Stearmans at St. Louis, and I was awarded an instructor by the name of Lt (jg) Armstrong – 'Down Check' Armstrong, as he was called. He was one of the check pilots and had never been known to give an 'up' check. He certainly didn't give one

while I was there. He was somewhat embittered, wanting combat duty instead of his present assignment.

Bell's reference to 'Down Check' Armstrong shows the extent to which pilots in training at St. Louis and elsewhere were gripped by suspicion and rumour. For every 'Down Check' Armstrong there was another instructor who was judged to be generosity personified. Ray Gough wrote home from Lambert Field on 5 August 1944: 'I regret to say only one of [us] got through. He had "Santa Claus", the easiest check pilot on the station.'[10]

Gough's course found St. Louis rather uncongenial. The weather was a problem for one thing, with summer temperatures reaching over 100 degrees Fahrenheit. Gough required extra time on the 'B' stage before he was successful. Many of his comrades were not so fortunate. He wrote home on 22 August: 'Another ten of our course went back to England yesterday, leaving us with a meagre twenty-five only, twelve of whom are on the 'C' stage. The others are either on extra time or are still on 'B' stage. I believe our course holds the record for eliminations here.'[11] For Gough, and for his fellow students, the fear of failure had a depressing effect and led him to view his surroundings and the men around him in an understandably jaundiced way: 'The 59th course came in today and some of the chaps I knew at *Vincent* were on it. They were awfully thrilled at the prospect of flying; poor fellows; they don't know what they are in for. It seems a shame to see them come in here so keen to fly and yet, within a week, thirty per cent of them will be heading back to New York.'[12]

In August 1944 the primary training of British aviation cadets on the Towers scheme was transferred once more – from St. Louis to Naval Air Station Bunker Hill, Indiana. That site had been selected for a primary flying training school in February 1942. The Naval Air Station consisted of a main field, with four 5,000 feet runways, and nineteen outlying fields at distances of six to fifteen miles from the main base. The base would close in February 1946, after training almost 6,000 Americans and over 700 British aviation cadets.[13] The reasons for relocating the training of British students to Bunker Hill were highlighted in a letter from one of the students, Ray Gough, to his parents: 'The field is a pretty large one and consequently the course rules are a lot more complicated. There is one good thing about it, however, and that is that there are no civilian airway liners coming in to land all the time, and you [are] not liable to get mixed up with Corsairs, Helldivers, Wildcats, Avengers etc. I nearly got cut in two by a Dauntless at Lambert.'[14] The skies of Indiana offered good, and less cluttered, flying conditions. Indiana had open spaces, and trainee pilots were less likely to collide with other craft than was the case over industrialized St. Louis and its environs. The move to Bunker Hill also coincided with growing concern at the drop-out rate in the Towers scheme. Commander S.H. Suthers, the new SBNO (Senior British Naval Officer) at the base, attempted to work out why the drop-out rate appeared to worsen. While at Lambert Field he had formed a very favourable impression of the United States Navy and its methods of training air cadets, something he experienced at first hand. 'I made a point of being shown by a USN instructor all the flight manoeuvres taught to the US and RN students. I was impressed by the precision approach to all manoeuvres, the careful testing of students at each stage of their training, and the air traffic control, which enabled the mass training of pilots to take place in safety.'

By talking to instructors, students and 'washouts', Suthers was quickly able to identify a number of problems, which might be contributing to the drop-out rate. He came to the conclusion that:

(a) The shortage of young men available in the UK by 1944 had led to a lowering of required standards for selection of flight training material. For example, we received some young men who were below the minimum height and had difficulty, therefore, in reaching the Stearman's rudder pedals.

(b) USN flight instructors taught both American and British students. This tended to leave the British at a disadvantage. Their American counterparts had mostly driven/owned cars, all had had some 25 hours pre-flight training on light aircraft and in general were 'easier' to teach.

(c) I obtained firm evidence that some USN instructors were anti-British, and as a result, some British students were treated unfairly, became demoralized and understandably failed to make the grade.

(d) Many of our students were learning to fly with nagging worries about their families at home. The UK was being heavily bombed, and the doodlebugs were also becoming a serious and worrying threat to UK civilians. Furthermore, the majority of RN students were away from home for the first time in their lives and homesickness played its part.

Whether or not certain flight instructors were anti-British is open to question. In view of the drop-out rate and the sympathies of some in the mid-West, however, it was perhaps understandable that Suthers should put the failure rate of British students down to more than points (a), (b) and (d) above.

He responded in various ways to the problems which he had identified. Firstly, he secured his own involvement in the decision whether to terminate a particular student's place in flight training. Secondly, he arranged with the American squadron commanders for instructors to volunteer to teach only British students in order to eliminate those with potential anti-British bias. Thirdly, the base appointed a trained psychologist to its staff to monitor student problems, particularly accident proneness. The psychologist provided counselling to those with worries about training and life back home. Fourthly, Suthers made representations to the British Admiralty Delegation in Washington to tighten up requirements on the selection of individuals for aircrew training. Lastly, some American flight instructors gave generously of their free time to teach their students how to drive. Some old cars were purchased just for this purpose, and a large field was set aside for this unorthodox extension to training. The resulting improvement in the ability of students in the air to co-ordinate controls, estimate speed and distance, and read instruments quickly made itself felt, and the washout rate improved as a result.

The students at Bunker Hill were appreciative of the base's facilities, which included an Olympic-size swimming pool, gymnasium, and a large PX. In August 1944 one cadet, Ray Gough, wrote to his parents: 'There seems to be plenty to do on the camp here, including a large canteen, swimming pool, arena, tennis courts and a large gymnasium, where you can play almost anything you wish. In the canteen you can get hamburgers, hot dogs, sandwiches, milk shakes, sundaes etc.'[15] Despite the excellent facilities, some students found grounds for complaint. Small towns like Kokomo could not offer off-duty cadets the same kind of delights that St Louis or Detroit had offered to those at Lambert Field and Grosse Ile, but the small towns around Bunker Hill did their best to outdo the citizens of St Louis and Detroit in their hospitality. Soon Commander Suthers found himself employing one member of his staff as a social secretary for the British trainees under his command.

On 21 May 1945 the final class of British students arrived; and, as the history of NAS Bunker Hill records: 'It was on 2 September 1945 that the last of the British boys took off for the East Coast and home. Over 800 had taken training at this station since their arrival in August of 1944.'[16] The base had grown phenomenally. In 1942 it had three N2S Stearmans for training. By December 1944, this had grown to 419 aircraft, and almost 6,000 American aviation cadets were being trained alongside 701

British students. In less than three years Bunker Hill had grown from nothing to become a major training centre. It was a good example of the way in which the war was transforming the economy and geography of the South and mid-West. In the words of the base history: 'Its growth among the prairies of Indiana is typical of the mobilization of our democracy to fight this war!'[17]

Intermediate Training at Pensacola

For most of the students who survived primary training, the next stage of their journey lay south to Florida and the delights of Pensacola. Men of the Royal Air Force and the Royal Navy's Fleet Air Arm would continue training at Pensacola until November 1944, when RAF flying boat training came to an end there. On 16 December 1944, intermediate and advanced flying training of Fleet Air Arm pilots was transferred to the US Naval Air Station at Corpus Christi, Texas, where it would continue until September 1945.[18]

Although the first cohort of British aviation cadets under the Towers scheme had been taught at Pensacola, most received their primary flight training further north at Grosse Ile, St Louis, or Bunker Hill. The journey down to Florida offered British servicemen a chance to see more of the United States. As E.C. Sheppard described, it was some journey, taking them through Toledo, Dayton, Cincinnati and Louisville:

> We had been given meal tickets for use in the dining car, so we all had a good dinner and a breakfast somewhere along the way near Birmingham, Alabama. We changed locomotives at Louisville from a monster steam engine to a noisy L & N diesel engine, which took us the rest of the way. Each time the train stopped at the main cities along the way it was invariably a long stay. It was at least half an hour and more than that at times.

Sheppard loved travel. He was certainly one of the more adventurous aviation cadets during his stay in the United States and travelled quite widely, but one can see his frustration at the length of time taken by the journey from north to south. Since troop trains had the right-of-way, delays to ordinary services often occurred.

At least, though, on arrival at Pensacola, Sheppard was impressed by the facilities at the enormous US Naval Station: 'The barrack blocks were two-storey, white clap-board buildings with wide steps up to a rather grand entrance in the general style of the Southern Colonial estates. The accommodation was very much better than we had ever enjoyed in the past. We were housed in rooms for two, with individual clothes lockers, a table and chairs, plus a chest of drawers. This was luxury indeed.' The barrack blocks were near to the beach, and Sheppard and his classmates welcomed the warm climate. He quickly found other attractions in the vicinity. The base offered considerable sporting facilities. These were put to good use to keep the trainee pilots at a high level of physical fitness, and to improve their abilities as pilots. One serving American naval officer wrote in 1942: 'The emphasis in all athletics is on balance, rhythm and co-ordination – not muscle building. For this reason, fencing is under consideration as an addition to the athletic program. Boxing, while tolerated, is not encouraged . . . eyes are too important.'[19]

The facilities also offered the chance for the occasional exercise in good public relations. New Zealand cadet John 'Jack' Sisley remembered: 'On February 6th 1942 the RAF and FAA flight students decided to support President Roosevelt's polio fund appeal. We played rugby and soccer in the Pensacola Stadium before 1000 people who paid £300. The FAA won both games before an appreciative and rather bewildered crowd.' Such endeavours were typical of the expatriate British community which developed at Pensacola. The *Limey* magazine, which had been founded in 1941 by RAF Cadet William Warner, also helped to foster that sense of community by 'reflecting in a mirror of laughter, the life of the RAF and FAA cadets in training'.[20]

Although most students loved the facilities at the base, few had any high regard for the town. A port city, Pensacola could boast its fair share of prostitutes and drunken brawls. Most British flyers preferred to stick to the well-patronised delights of the San Carlos Hotel and not probe too deeply into the nightlife of Pensacola. A further downside to life in Florida for British cadets was the weather. On 25 October 1941 Warner told his wife that it had been 'terrifically hot lately, and I feel half-dead. Studying under these conditions is pretty trying, although every first-class room has shutters and about a dozen fans. The worst part, so far, has been the drill – 1½ hours a day in the sun.'[21] Others, however, would revel in the tropical climate. D.A. Souray, writing a piece for the *Limey*, was captivated by nightfall at Pensacola:

> With tropical rapidity the shadows lengthened, the sun set behind the trees, and it was dark. Little details on the planes along the line became more discernible. Then, like an army of glow worms emerging from their winter quarters, hundreds of little lights flashed

on all around the drome and then, as if the generals had appeared in all their glory, the floodlights lit up with startling brilliance and completely dominated the scene.'[22]

The area beyond Pensacola offered other attractions. Frank Robinson and Richard Wakeford, who arrived at the base in July 1941, bought a car with another cadet and took up one of the many invitations to visit ordinary Americans in their own homes – in their case the LeCorgne family in New Orleans. E.C. Sheppard also explored the area quite widely. With a friend, he hitch hiked to Milton, Alabama:

> This was like a journey into a Hollywood set. The row of shops were not that much more than timber shacks, with the sidewalk raised above the road as a timber walkway and a sloping canopy over. What really made the scene was the saloon in the middle of the few shops, which could have come straight out of a John Wayne Western. It was complete with double swinging half-doors. The impression of being on a film set was increased by the gaol, a white, roughcast, square block complete with barred, unglazed window and an inmate who talked to us through the opening. We left him with a part-open pack of 'Lucky Strikes'.

Sheppard may have been lucky enough to see part of the real United States but life at the base on the intermediate and advanced courses was, for most of the time, one of sheer hard work. The training system was reinforced by the demerit system and by strict discipline. RAF cadet J.C. Winandy observed: 'After a number of demerits were awarded, it was necessary to cancel these out by one or more evenings on the parade ground with a pack on the back.' He added, 'For some strange reason, the majority of students on these marches were British (it must have been the criminal element among us!).'

William Warner told his wife that the base at Pensacola comprised 'dozens of landing fields, spreading for miles, seaplane bases, catapults etc'.[23] Cadets would rotate from field to field, through each stage of their training. In addition to flight training, there would be further work in ground school where students would be required to deepen their understanding of a range of subjects. The following sample questions, from the Aerology and Navigation examinations sat by the cadets, give a good impression of the challenging nature of ground school:

Aerology
If a wind is blowing in your face you would expect the low pressure to be to your ....
The gradient wind would be that one measurable between the surface and 1500 feet. True/False.
To make the best time you would normally choose a west to east route. True/False.

Navigation
Construct a small area plotting sheet of lat. 18°N to lat. 22°N and long. 41°W to long. 45°W.
You depart lat. 18°25′N; long. 41°10′W at 0800 for lat. 20°50′N; long. 42°05′W. What is course? What is distance?

Given the trying climate and the challenging nature of the syllabus, ground school held few attractions for most cadets. J.H. Ashley, who was at Pensacola from May 1942 to January 1943, found 'discipline was very strict. Though it proved easy and popular to dodge lectures, the examinations ... were unavoidable!'

Intermediate flight training at Pensacola consisted of two separate elements. At Chevalier Field pilots would learn and practise formation flying on SU-2 Scout planes. The SU-2, which had only recently been retired from front-line service, offered a number of technical challenges to trainee pilots, and they would have to learn the secrets of mixture control, manifold pressure and trimming the aircraft. Operating in flights of 9 aircraft, the training was very tough, as illustrated by one accident that befell RAF pilot Peter Tipple, who would later earn a Distinguished Flying Cross after a lengthy tour on Beaufighters in the Mediterranean with 272 Squadron.

In February 1942 Tipple was formation flying when he drifted out of formation and came into collision with the chase plane, which was supposed to monitor and advise on the flight's formation. Incensed at the waywardness of Tipple's flying, the instructor had tried to cut in between Tipple's aircraft and the rest of the formation to highlight the problem. Tipple managed to bale out of his aircraft at 1,500 feet, only for his parachute to fail to open properly. By some miracle, the half-open parachute snagged the branches on the only tree for hundreds of yards. Tipple lived, but the instructor and student in the other aircraft did not.

The second part of intermediate training saw trainees refining their use of instruments and learning to fly blind on radio beams. Much of the work could be done in Link Trainers on the ground. These basic simulators, located in air-conditioned facilities, allowed aviation cadets to practise and hone their skills in complete safety and relative comfort. Simulated night flying involved trainees going 'under the hood' to shut out all light. On the ground in summertime, that experience could be particularly unpleasant because of the heat, but at altitudes above 500 feet the air was cooler. For work in the air, the cadets transferred to the SNJ3 Harvard. This fast, low-wing, all-metal monoplane was a delight and a challenge to fly. It was reliable, rugged, and free from many of the aircraft vices that could kill. At the end of intermediate training, pilots would have to undergo a two-hour check flight on the SNJ3 Harvard. If they passed the check flight, there would come the parting of the ways as American, Fleet Air Arm and Royal Air Force aviation cadets went on to different forms of advanced training.

6

WASHOUTS AND OTHER AIRCREW

Several of our group faded out soon after flying training commenced . . . There were various reasons, of which one was persistent airsickness, diagnosed by the US Navy instructors not as something which would disappear in the fullness of time, but rather as a firm indication that the sufferer had a subconscious phobia about flying which would prevent him 'making the grade'. The other was 'depth perception' . . . It is the quality and breadth of depth perception, apparently, which enables one to judge one's height from the ground whilst steadfastly watching the horizon.[1]

These words from Norman Hanson's memoirs describe two of the major causes for washing out of flying school, but there were other ways of failing. Officially, little was said to incoming students about what happened if one failed, but the 'grapevine', even though often exaggerated, provided more than enough worrying information. The following figures show that it was possible to fail at any point and for a variety of reasons:

Washouts: Primary Training: Bunker Hill [2]
Failure to Reach Flight Standards

Stage	British	USA
A	20	15
B	19	5
C	11	7
D	1	2
E	1	0
Totals	52	29

Failure for Other Reasons

	British	USA
Fail to meet ground school standards	6	14
Physical Problems	4	4
Own Request	6	4
Disciplinary	6	7
Totals	22	29

Aircrew students who failed these courses were returned to the Royal Canadian Air Force No. 1 Manning Depot at Toronto until they could be posted to RCAF Trenton, a flying boat station some 50 miles northeast of Toronto. At Trenton they would be interviewed by RCAF officers and assessed for re-mustering to other duties.

By September 1941 more than 1,000 RAF trainee aircrew had been eliminated from pilot training in the United States alone and, because of their numbers, no one knew what to do with them. The RCAF's Toronto Manning Depot did not have enough accommodation to absorb all of the washouts in addition to the new drafts regularly arriving from Britain. By 15 September the personnel depots at Toronto and Trenton had become bottlenecks. The overwhelming numbers of RAF aircrew brought movement through the training pipeline to a halt.

According to men who were there, westbound students eager to begin their training were crowded in with large numbers of embittered washouts waiting to be re-mustered. Tempers flared, men 'gave tongue' to their feelings, and a minor 'rebellion' was in the making. Letters home to parents and to officers in initial training wings (ITWs) described chaos. Military censors of personal mail, ever mindful of rules to report morale problems, regularly reported discontent to commanding officers, and the complaints made their way up, or evaded, the chain of command. Influential parents were the source of most complaints which reached the ears of British politicians. At RCAF Trenton some 'washouts' were reported to be sleeping in a flying boat hangar. Moreover, a near-riot was reported to have occurred among eliminated airmen at the RCAF No. 1 Manning Depot in Toronto. High-ranking staff officers were sent from London to Toronto and other Canadian and American air bases to carry out inspections and sort out the problems.

The 51-year-old, Canadian-born, Air Commodore A.C. Critchley, CMG, DSO, Officer Commanding 54 Group, arrived 'to inspect RAF training in Canada'. Critchley's responsibilities included the recruitment and training of instructional staffs, and the organizing and administering of air crew receiving wings (ACRWs) and initial training wings (ITWs) in resort hotels, university facilities, and on active air stations in Britain. Critchley and his staff had already handled the formidable organizational and logistic problems common to all military services. While in Canada Critchley may well have inspected training stations, but he also met in Toronto a large number of disgruntled airmen in efforts to sort out remustering and other problems. He arrived in Toronto during the evening of 16 September 1941 to tour No. 1 Air Training Command.[3]

A picture of Air Commodore Critchley in the *Toronto Star* showed a grim, stocky figure in uniform. In a brief article below that photograph, Critchley was reported to have said, 'The men I have talked with, men sent from overseas after their initial training, can't speak too highly of the training they get here.' If the aircrew under training in Toronto's RCAF No. 1 Manning Depot at the time are to be believed, their reaction was not quite as contented as the newspaper reported, and as Critchley might have wished.

Though these may not have been the precise orders given by Critchley or staff officers for dealing with the 'bolshie' airmen, the effect of their directives was the same: 'Break 'em down into smaller groups, move 'em, send them to air stations and get them off their duffs . . . keep 'em busy!' 'Washed-out' airmen at Toronto were separated quickly from aircrew students newly arrived from Britain. Divided into smaller groups, the failed aircrew trainees were posted on general duties assignments to air bases scattered about Canada. They arrived at these stations just in time to pack or to remove a few thousand tons of snow from runways and aerodrome streets and to peel a few tons of potatoes. Inevitably, many of these washed-out airmen were forgotten or 'lost' . . . or at least they believed that they were an example of 'out of sight, out of mind' as far as the RAF was concerned.

Since all Canadian aircrew training schools at the time were crowded, and the training pipeline was blocked at Toronto and Trenton, those who were 'lost' wondered if their transfer had been done accidentally or on purpose. Given the distances and complexities of wartime travel, the difficulty of record keeping, and the possible loss of documents in ships sunk by U-boats, some dislocations were perhaps inevitable. Regardless of cause, these administrative problems were beyond either the interest or concern of the young airmen. They wanted to fly; and many of them demanded another opportunity to do so.

Critchley's official report of these developments has not been located, and his autobiography oddly fails to mention his September 1941 visit to Canada (his birthplace). There is no doubt that he and other RAF officers were sent there with the urgent task of finding solutions to the problems which had created embarrassing bottlenecks in Canada and elsewhere. By autumn 1941 the major culprit appeared to be the American training system, which was much more rigid than that of the RAF. Significant problems were also uncovered in the existing system of Canadian transit camps, and steps were taken to remove the Toronto bottleneck and to reduce aircrew wastage.

In October 1941 a four-week acclimatization course in the USA was introduced for Arnold scheme cadets.[4] It was badly needed because the washout rate for Arnold scheme cadets was running at between 42 and 45 per cent. That was almost twice the rate at the British Flying Training Schools and slightly above the rate for men in training under the Towers scheme. Meanwhile, the Admiralty stubbornly refused to assign RN aircrew volunteers to either acclimatization or flight grading courses in preparation for training under the Towers scheme.

In order to tackle problems within the American system, other high-ranking RAF officers were sent out to inspect training stations in the United States and to meet American air officers in training conferences. As a result of Air Commodore Critchley's mission to Canada and Air Chief Marshal A.G.R. Garrod's visit to Canada and the United States, the officers of all three nations learned much about the early experiences of British aircrew students. In the United States, agreement was reached about posting some of the RAF's best new pilots who would graduate from the Arnold scheme and British Flying Training Schools in 1942 to regional instructors' schools, from where they could later be assigned as flight instructors to many USAAF primary, basic and advanced flying schools. In addition, hazing – pointless chivvying and bullying – was stopped, the curriculum in each phase of flight training was reviewed and improved, and regular training conferences were instituted. In addition, a drive began for the standardization of aircrew training, while the amount and quality of supervision was significantly improved.

The introduction of flight grading in November 1941 also helped to reduce the number of washouts. Under flight grading, trainee aircrew in the RAF were subjected to some basic tests in the United Kingdom to investigate their aptitude. Those with depth perception and airsickness problems could be expected to fall at this hurdle. Grading 'consisted of up to 15 hours dual instruction and normal . . . ground instruction in a three -

week course. Pupils who showed promise of making satisfactory pilots could be taken off the course at any time after five hours of flying and passed as fit to proceed for flying training overseas. Pupils not considered promising enough to be sent overseas went either to United Kingdom schools, if they appeared to be slow starters, or were transferred to other training.'[5] Although the Royal Air Force introduced flight grading as early as 1941, the Fleet Air Arm continued to resist it. In a letter of 15 November 1943, Air Commodore D.V. Carnegie, Director of Flight Training at the Air Ministry, described the advantages of flight grading:

(i) The wastage rate at EFTS has now been stabilised at 10 per cent.
(ii) A noticeable proportion of the pupils who would never graduate at EFTS are weeded out at an early stage, and can consequently be put into alternative training without the long delays which are inevitable when a double crossing of the Atlantic is involved. These delays had been found to have an adverse effect on the keenness and morale of the men being sent back for re-classification.
(iii) Since the wastage in pilot training is much higher than in any other aircrew category, it is recognised that the pilot is the most difficult member of the crew to find. Coupled with the latter problem is the known fact that 90 per cent of aircrew volunteers hoped to be pilots, and it is considered an advantage, from the point of view of recruiting, if the 90 per cent already mentioned know that they will be given the opportunity, by means of the Grading course, to show by their own efforts that they are suitable for subsequent training as Service pilots. In addition, the men who are not classified as pilots are far more willing to adopt an alternative aircrew duty.[6]

Carnegie, who had directed UK aircrew training in the United States for more than a year, had been promoted and assigned to the Air Ministry in London. As the Director of Flight Training, he urged the Fleet Air Arm, which had rejected flight grading in April 1943, to follow RAF practice. For the moment, the Fleet Air Arm continued to select its aircrew by the 'impression' method at a short interview, although it had been shown by that stage to be unreliable as a device for selecting good aircrew.[7] At least, the Admiralty had agreed to include more instruction on the theory of flight, airmanship and engines in the programme of instruction at HMS *St Vincent*.[8]

It was only reluctantly, in the closing months of the war, that the Fleet Air Arm was persuaded to introduce grading. In April 1945 Carnegie wrote: 'The first [RN] course to have been fully graded is now undergoing instruction, and a very considerable improvement has been noted, in that the pupils have already developed a sense of airmanship, can orientate themselves, and are not suffering from air sickness to the same degree as previously.'[9] His satisfaction was tempered by some of his other findings on a return trip to North America. With the war in Europe drawing to a close, he found a number of aviation cadets willing to admit that they had only chosen aircrew training in the hope of delaying their entry into combat. The extent of this attitude, as a problem within training, is impossible to estimate. Few were willing to own up to their intention to work the system in the 1940s, let alone half a century after World War II.

Some of those who washed out of pilot training were re-mustered for further aircrew training as wireless operator/air gunners or as navigators. In the early days a man might wash out of pilot training in Florida, and be sent back to Trenton or Moncton in Canada, only to find himself sent back to Florida once more for further training in some other aircrew role, still under the Towers scheme. In Florida, disappointed pilot hopefuls would be trained alongside men who had been selected for non-pilot aircrew duties at the initial training wing stage.

At 10 p.m. on a mid-July night in 1941, 30 young RAF men dressed in grey flannel double-breasted suits arrived outside the headquarters building of the sprawling United States Naval Air Station at Jacksonville, Florida. They had travelled from the Jacksonville railway station by US Navy bus, and their baggage followed them on a large truck. The purpose of their being sent to the air station was to enter the US Naval Aviation Radio School. Within a relatively short time they were escorted to their barracks. Immediately after their arrival there, a truck delivered their kit bags from the railway station, and they busied themselves unpacking and questioning some US naval personnel about their new home. Since it was late and they were disturbing men who needed to be on duty early the next morning, they showered quickly and went to bed.

The RAF students were to be trained as wireless operators and air gunners (WOp/AG) under a two-phase programme. Some of the men had failed to make the grade as potential pilots and were now being recycled within the North American training area. At Jacksonville they would receive their radio and radar theory and practice on the ground. Upon completing their course and qualifying as Radiomen, they would be sent on to the US Naval Air Station at Pensacola, Florida, to receive training in air gunnery and some in-flight radio work aboard PBY-5 and PBY-5A Catalina flying boats. On completion of this American training, the RAF would send the men back to Great Britain for operational flying duties in Coastal Command aircraft. Each individual group of WOp/AG trainees sent to Jacksonville or Pensacola trained alongside US Navy and Marine Corps personnel, but their separate identity was maintained as British flight students and they were housed together in billets designated for that purpose.

The numbers of British airmen admitted to WOp/AG training remained small as the RAF, distrustful of the quality of the American training, was reluctant to use the full training capacity available to them at that station. The training began in July 1941, five months before the United States entered the war, and ended after ten classes of varying sizes had passed through the school. Flight No. 1 began training at Jacksonville in July 1941 and completed the course there on 3 December 1941. On 3 January 1942 that same class completed their air gunnery training at Pensacola and was sent to Moncton, New Brunswick, for return to the UK. Following graduation of that initial WOp/AG class, however, the system for posting RAF students from Jacksonville was apparently modified so much that records of the period are unclear as to precisely what procedure was followed.

Output of RAF men at the radio school at USNAS Jacksonville totalled 286, while only 251 RAF men graduated from the air gunnery school at Pensacola, Florida. It is likely that the extra 35 graduates of the Jacksonville radio school were simply not sent on to Pensacola for the air gunnery course. Either, they were retained by the RAF as radiomen for service in operations rooms at various levels, or they were given additional training in US Navy or RAF schools for other communications duties.[10]

A few of these men may well have become sonar operators on Coastal Command aircraft or radar observers, either for ground or air duty, wherever American equipment was being used. Another possibility is that the 35 unaccounted-for graduates of the radio school at Jacksonville could have been Fleet Air Arm personnel. Serving in the Royal Navy, they might well have been excluded from RAF statistics. Perhaps the best way to determine numbers trained is to use the American separate-course system, rather than the combined-course designation used by the Royal Air Force. In American terms, 537 men were trained: 286 as radiomen and 251 as aerial gunners; in RAF terms, 251 were trained as wireless operator/air gunners (WOp/AG's), and 35 men were trained only as wireless operators (W/Ops). However, RAF records indicate that, in all, 645 WOp/AGs were trained in the United States.

The training of WOp/Ags in the United States lasted a comparatively short time – from July 1941 until November 1942. Their average age was 18-24, but some were older. Some had previously been in the army. One of them, Peter Kennedy, who had been evacuated from Dunkirk with the British Expeditionary Force in 1940, had 11 years army service under his belt before volunteering for the Royal Air Force. Another trainee, Harry Smith, was a professional soldier who, as a commando, had taken part in the raid on the Norwegian Lofoten Islands in 1940.

The Aviation Radioman School's 20 week syllabus for WOp/AG's comprised the following elements: theory, code, semaphore, radio procedure, maintenance, watch standing, blinker signals, ordnance and practical work. The gunnery course, which they also had to take, required them to become proficient in gunnery (fixed and free), maintenance of equipment, and air combat. Shooting at ground and aerial targets was combined with work in ground school. The Royal Air Force was not entirely happy with the training syllabus, and in early 1942 a Squadron Leader Woffindin was asked to report on the training programme.

Group Captain Carnegie, Director of United Kingdom Air Training, raised the issue with the Superintendent of Aviation Training at Pensacola in the most diplomatic way possible. Expressing pleasure at Woffindin's findings 'that the Officer-in-Charge of the Radio School and his staff are trying hard to give the British pupils as good a course as is possible', he drew attention to 'the shortage of instructors' and the lack of 'air experience for the men under training'. He also held out the possibility that four graduates of the programme would be retained at Pensacola to help train further cohorts, and that the Royal Air Force might be able to provide more equipment for use in training.[11]

Ben Cecil's experiences of WOp/AG training are illustrative of the process. He completed his training with Flight No. 7 at Jacksonville and Pensacola. He would later complete two tours with bomber command on Stirlings and Lancasters. During pilot training he had washed out in Canada because he failed

> to fly solo in the specified time, and was posted to Trenton, Canada. This naturally was a terrific disappointment, since the dream of most teenagers at that time, following on the Battle of Britain, was to be a fighter pilot! However, I had to concede that, while I could fly the plane in the air, I did have this problem of landing, and since the RAF laid great store in both men and machines being returned to earth in one piece, undamaged, I could not quarrel with their

decision. There had been quite a large failure rate at Caron, so, upon being posted to Trenton, I met up with several people I had known at Caron, and one of these, Reg. Hunt, told me that he was down for a Wireless Operator/Air Gunner Course at Jacksonville, Florida, and suggested that I go with him. Accordingly, when I went before the panel for a re-assessment of aircrew duties, I mentioned this course and was accepted for re-training as a WOp/AG. Consequently, 28 of us were accepted for the course, and we set off by train, certainly disconsolate and disappointed, and yet at the same time, looking forward to seeing Florida, well known to us as the millionaire's playground, and a place that we had never dreamed we would visit, having been brought up in the depression days of the 1930s. Upon arrival at Jacksonville we were introduced to Chief Petty Officer Quimby of the United States Navy, who was to be responsible for discipline, cleanliness, and general behaviour of the British Flight Students for the next six months, and with whom we were to have various clashes during that time. On reflection, the fault may well have been mostly with us, since we were all disappointed, a bit fed-up, and some, who had failed pilots' courses for reasons unconnected with flying, such as having dirty lockers etc., were positively bitter, so we couldn't have been an easy bunch to handle. However, as I remember it, we felt that we had done our quota of square bashing when we joined up, had been through the drills and disciplines of ITW, and now wanted to get on with the job of learning our aircrew trade, so that we could get back to Britain to continue the battle. This feeling of wanting to join the battle was not confined to the RAF. The US forces training there were also clamouring for action. Little did we realize how much we were all to see before the war was over!

Cecil's experiences of training were not uniformly positive. The demerit system proved particularly onerous, and the camp was a long way from the town. In any case, they were only allowed out at weekends.

Monday to Friday consisted of very concentrated sessions learning Morse code, radio theory, practical radio, and even, since it was a Naval Station, the Aldis lamp and semaphore. Being restricted to the camp was no great hardship, however, since it was equipped with cinemas, swimming pools, sports pitches and canteens where, to our great delight, we were able to purchase unlimited supplies of chocolate, a luxury denied to us in war torn Britain. The sports fields were in constant use and, once we were able to obtain a soccer ball, we amazed the Americans by chasing around the field playing soccer in the middle of a Florida summer . . . There were so many on the camp at that time that training was done on a two-shift basis, one lot starting early in the morning, and the others starting in the afternoon. We were not allowed out of camp between Monday & Friday, but we were free every weekend. Civilian instructors were brought in to help teach us Morse code, and since this was their peacetime occupation, the standard was very good. In fact, a higher speed was required in Morse code to pass out in the US Navy than in the RAF at that time.

[WOp/AG's were made just as welcome by American families as any pilot.] We were at that time living in the reflected glory of the Battle of Britain pilots but, although the Americans were well aware that we had no part in that, since we were still training in 1942, they could not have made us more welcome if we had been Group Captain Bader himself . . .

I completed my course at Jacksonville at the end of August 1942 and received a certificate as 'Radioman', which I still have. We then had two weeks leave, which most of us spent in New York, having a fabulous time as everyone in the city seemed determined to make sure that all servicemen enjoyed themselves there. We then reported to Pensacola, where we received gunnery instruction and put into practice in the air the radio training which we had received. The flying was mostly done in Catalina flying boats, and it was also from these that we did our air gunnery, firing at drogues towed by other aircraft.

The course there lasted about 10 weeks, at the end of which time we were promoted to sergeants, which was the aircrew rank which we would have attained after RAF training. Incidentally, it is interesting to note that the early RAF WOp/AGs trained at Jacksonville/Pensacola were not promoted to sergeant until after they returned to England and had satisfied the RAF that their training was of a sufficiently high standard, but by the time that we had completed our training (and we were Flight 7) there was no longer any question of waiting, as the course had proved more than satisfactory, and we returned to Moncton in Canada as sergeants. We returned to England in the ship *Queen Elizabeth* in December

1942, and I was home on leave by Christmas Eve, having been away almost exactly a year.

[Cecil was highly appreciative of the training he had received.] When we completed our course, we felt that our training was at least equal to that which we would have received anywhere, which was undoubtedly true, since [the] USA were still maintaining their peacetime standards of training. After returning to England, and being posted to an Operational Training Unit, we were told to sort ourselves out into aircrews. US-trained WOp/AGs had no difficulty finding a crew, and in my particular crew, apart from myself, both the pilot and navigator were US-trained.

Robert Farrow, of Flight No. 9 at Jacksonville and Pensacola, was another who had washed out of pilot training and been sent back to Canada to be re-mustered to other aircrew training. At Moncton, Farrow and 18 other RAF aircrew were re-mustered for wireless operator/air gunner training and were sent by train to Jacksonville. They travelled via Boston, New York, and Washington, and while in New York, 'saw the French Liner *Normandie* burnt out & lying on its side'. On 30 May 1942, they reported to the US Naval Air Station at Jacksonville, and found the station so crowded that classes were scheduled in two shifts, morning and afternoon-evening, which were alternated between classes a 'month about'. They found restriction to the base onerous and different at first, but soon discovered that American military installations had phenomenal recreational facilities of great variety. On completion of their training at Jacksonville in November 1942, the RAF contingent was posted to Pensacola for a two-month air gunnery training course on Catalina flying boats. On 15 January 1943, with training completed, Farrow and his classmates were promoted to sergeant and received the RAF WOp/AG brevet before entraining for Moncton, New Brunswick, and transport back to the UK aboard the troopship *Andes*.

RAF WOp/AG students came from pilot trainees who had washed out of Canadian elementary flying schools and from the British Flying Training Schools and the Arnold scheme schools in the USA. For most of the men it was a stern test of personal strength in surmounting grievous disappointment and applying themselves to achieving success in an alternative ambition. Joseph R. Johnson, for example, travelled across the North Atlantic in early November 1941 and south to Montgomery, Alabama. On completion of the acclimatization course at Maxwell Field, Johnson was posted, with approximately 170 classmates, to Darr Aero

Tech Inc., Albany, Georgia, a civil primary flying school under contract to the United States Army Air Force to train pilots. After a few hours of flying, Johnson was eliminated from pilot training, returned to Maxwell Field for a short period, and then posted to Canada for re-mustering. He was sent to Jacksonville and then on to Pensacola for training as a wireless operator/air gunner.

In the form of *The WAG*, WOp/AG's at Pensacola had their own magazine in which they recorded their frustrations.

R.I.P.
Let me tell you the story of 8-42,
Who are going at last, but alas, how few.
We started this WAG.'s course thirty odd strong,
But whitewashing some didn't take very long,
And as weeks rolled by I'm sad to relate,
That more and more names were rubbed off the slate.

And the few that were left, felt horribly queer
From taking Morse code 'til it rang in their ear;
The boys that have 'Had it' we honestly say,
Were some of the best, and we'll remember the day
They left here forever, all laden with kit,
No more to be 'cursed' with 'Dit dahs' and 'Dit dits.'
But although they are washouts they left with a grin
And a cheery word to those still left in.

They're crossing the border to try hard again
And we know when they enter the Trenton-bound train
They'll be thinking of us, as we are of them,
With one thought united till we meet again,
Of Somehow, Someway to finish this war
And return to the country that we all adore.

The Towers scheme for WOp/AG training came to an end in February 1943. Four months earlier, in October 1942, Pan-American Airways and the Towers scheme had wound up their training of RAF navigators.[12] In total 545 navigators were trained under the Towers scheme at Pensacola, and 1170 (at a rate of 150 per course from July 1941) at the Pan-American School. Navy-trained navigators went through similar training to that experienced by the cadets at Coral Gables. Dennis Burgoyne's story was typical. He had washed out of pilot training in July 1941 and was stationed at Montgomery for six weeks while others were gathered for training as navigators. He was sent to Toronto and Trenton before being assigned to navigator training at Pensacola. Thus, it was after a long delay and much travel that Burgoyne finally got back in the air in January 1942. Training began early in the morning and finished in the early afternoon each day.

In addition to classroom training in aerial navigation, navigator cadets practised in PBY-2 and PBY-5 flying boats. Peanut butter sandwiches would be supplied as provisions for practice flights over the Gulf of Mexico. During flights lasting five to six hours, positions would be plotted using fixes on the sun and by the taking of radio bearings. RAF navigator Hilary Jarvis recalled:

> We crewed up an American skipper, a British co-pilot, American flight engineer, radio officer, as the flight crew, and four trainee navigators. We were to be flying ten-degree segments with three-hundred-mile main legs, lasting six-hourly trips. Collecting sandwiches every morning, we were lowered into the water, the engines fired for checking, followed by a revving up, casting off, the nose turned seawards, the engines opened to full throttle; it was like being in the largest speed boat, the wake getting wider and wider, suddenly ceasing, [and] we were airborne. . . . [to] the throb of the engines. The smell of the oil was not conducive to eating sandwiches, especially those containing peanut butter, which on dry land was greasy enough; but in the air, being bounced around, it became a ritual to open the blister canopy, making sure we were secured by the safety straps, to drop all peanut butter sandwiches over the side to feed the fishes far below.

After a flight in which they covered over six hundred miles of open-ocean, using only the sun as a navigation point, training aircraft would re-cross the coast. If they were within twenty miles of their estimated position, the instructor would rate this as a 'very good performance'.

Richard Bartlett was another who washed out of flight training only to be re-mustered as a navigator:

> Pensacola!! Well, from Moncton three or four days on the train. Once there – Excellent!! Usual American food etc. I was put straight into hospital with ear trouble. Diagnosed as Otitis Media. The Quack gave me a local anaesthetic in the ear and told me to go and

lie on his operating table in an adjoining room. This I did and found I was looking straight at a clock and, if I remember rightly, I lay there for about an hour, getting more windy all the time in case the anaesthetic wore off. ... I was [in hospital] sixteen weeks.

I would think our first month [of training] was spent in the classroom getting theory. You must remember we were going to fly over the Gulf all the time. There are no church steeples, villages, rivers or railway lines to follow. One wave top does look rather like the next, no matter at what height you fly. So, we learned stars by night. Navigation at night was far easier. You could pick up the constellation of Orion and then you had ten stars from which to take your pick. Having taken the shot with your bubble sextant on your chosen star, within minutes you took a shot of the Pole Star. You know your speed – hopefully – you advance your first star shot as if it had been taken simultaneously with your Pole Star shot, and where those two lines crossed is where your are. No messing!! We flew 250 miles out into the Gulf, turned and did a second leg of 50 miles, and then flew back to base. We always got there. Whether the pilot cheated and had some homing beam we didn't know, but I do know we were good. We didn't need church steeples and rivers and railways. We just wanted to get above any overcast, and we could find our way wherever our skipper wanted to go.

Once again, just like Camden, confined to barracks all week; only the weekend free, but Pensacola was a vicious place. You dare not go out on your own. If you did, the local Marines would get hold of you, and three or four of them would beat you up just for the hell of it. There was a very good USO Club in Pensacola, which, with others, I used to patronise and, for several years, I kept in touch by Christmas cards with three or four of the organisers. Pity I can't recall their names. I seem to have mislaid my old address book.

We had three or four trainee observers on each plane – P2Y2's I think – and we'd be out for about six hours. Each of us had to keep our own log etc. as if we were the only ones up there. We realised very quickly it was no use at all cribbing from each other. You could either do it, or you couldn't. Within months we'd be doing it for real on our own. Therefore, the time to flop was on our course, not over Germany.

Alongside navigator training for the RAF, observer training for the Fleet Air Arm was set up in 1941 with the aim of providing 150 observers.

While the duties of a pilot and a navigator were fairly obvious, those of an observer require some explanation. As one former observer has explained, it was his duty to:

> (a) captain the aircraft, (b) do the navigation, (c) code and cypher signals, (d) sometimes operate the radio in Morse code, (e) aim bombs for high-level bombing, also fire rockets, (f) be rear gunner sometimes, (g) report movements of enemy ships when in contact, (h) spot the fall of our shot in gunnery engagements of the Fleet, (i) take aerial photographs, (j) drop leaflets to civilians, (k) report on weather conditions.[13]

The Fleet Air Arm observer was a jack of all trades. Training was consequently difficult. The Royal Navy was seriously short of pilots and facilities that it could use for observer training. Hector Mackenzie trained as an observer at HMS *Goshawk* in the West Indies in 1940-1. He found 'the pilots were a funny lot; the Navy were so short of them that, for unimportant work like training observers and TAGs (telegraphist /air gunners), they recruited middle-aged men who could fly small planes, contracted for strictly non-operational service. Most were from the pre-war idle rich who had learned to fly, and a nice comfortable war they had in Trinidad.'[14] Under the Towers scheme the intention was to give the observers three months experience with the American Fleet. Pearl Harbour made that impossible, and in April 1942 the programme was closed to make extra space and resources for the WOp/AG courses.[15]

The numbers of navigators, observers and other aircrew trained by the United States Navy on the Towers scheme was comparatively small, but the importance of these training programmes cannot be measured simply in terms of the number of aircrew trained. A large part of their value has to be assessed in terms of the recycling of washouts from pilot training. Bitterly humiliated and disappointed at failing in flight training in North America, their problems of morale could be aggravated by lengthy delays in re-training. If aviation cadets washed out of flight training, the sooner they were re-trained for some other role the better. The administrative process for recycling washouts from North America improved during the war, but it was never truly speedy or efficient.

Through the Towers scheme, hundreds of failed pilots were recycled rather more swiftly than would have been the case if they had merely been returned to Great Britain. Few trainee pilots drew any comfort from the idea that, if they failed, they could be recycled for other aircrew duties;

but, in terms of re-building and maintaining the morale of men who would later fly one or more tours with RAF Bomber Command or Coastal Command, the opportunity to train for other aircrew roles under the Towers scheme made considerable sense.

7

ADVANCED, CONVERSION AND OPERATIONAL TRAINING

Upon completion of intermediate training at Pensacola or Corpus Christi, the Fleet Air Arm cadet won his wings. If under 21 years of age, he would become a midshipman; those over 21 became commissioned officers. These midshipmen and commissioned pilots were then posted to advanced flying training at a number of different airfields close by the US Navy's main stations at Pensacola or Corpus Christi, where instructors evaluated the abilities of each of the young pilots. Those instructor assessments and the recommendations of RN liaison officers determined how the pilots were assigned to operational training on fighter, torpedo bomber, reconnaissance or dive-bomber aircraft. American and British trainee pilots, who had been kept more or less together until completion of advanced flying training, then went their separate ways.

The US Marine Corps aviators, who until this time had trained with navy cadets, went to their own operational training course at Cherry Point, North Carolina, or to stations on the west coast, where they learned tactics likely to be useful in their future combat assignments. US Navy ferry pilots and NATS (Naval Air Transport Service) pilots were separated from the programme at this point and were sent for specialised training. Still others were posted to instructors' schools where they could learn the skills for teaching in primary or intermediate flying training. British students also left the programme at this stage. RAF flying boat pilots continued at the Pensacola main station in the advanced and operational phases of flight training.[1]

Whereas approximately one-third of each course of RAF pilots trained under the Arnold and BFTS training schemes in the USA were commissioned, the RAF pilots trained in the Towers scheme were only promoted to sergeant when they completed advanced training. Not surprisingly, this caused ill feeling between the two groups. RAF commissioning policy became such an issue that in 1942 the matter was discussed at an Air Training Conference at Ottawa. Although soon after the outbreak of war the RAF had agreed to commission up to 50 per cent of pilots, it found itself out of step with the United States Army Air Force, which commissioned 80 per cent of its pilots and 100 per cent of navigators. It was also contrary to the wishes of the self-governing dominions.[2] As a result of the Ottawa conference, a compromise was agreed to commission a third of pilots at the end of training, but with no upper limit on the numbers who could be commissioned on active duty. Thus, able pilots would find themselves in line for a commission. Those completing a full tour of operations were virtually certain to finish it commissioned or as warrant officers.

Some Fleet Air Arm pilots found their own change to commissioned status inconvenient. Ray Gough announced to his parents in February 1945: 'I am now a midshipman of the Royal Navy – the lowest form of officer life.'[3] Later, at Corpus Christi, he complained:

> Living in BOQ [Bachelor Officers Quarters] is not bad, but in my opinion is no better than cadet quarters, the food being definitely inferior. So far since moving over, I have got to pay over fifty dollars for various things – twenty-five for mess bill, ten as a deposit, ten for a party the officers held, and the other for laundry etc. At this rate, it is going to be pretty difficult.[4]

In advanced training, Fleet Air Arm pilots were divided into squadrons according to their instructors' recommendations about their suitability for further training as fighter, dive-bomber or torpedo bomber pilots. Although the instructors' assessments and the needs of the service had the final word, pilots had an opportunity to express a particular preference. The reasons which might lead a pilot to prefer one type of training to another were often very personal. Ray Gough explained his motives to his family back home in Britain in May 1945:

> I went down to the Navy office and had my name put on the list of TBR [Torpedo/Bomber/Reconnaissance] pilots. This means that, if I get TBRs, I shall be coming home when I finish here . . . It took a long time to make up my mind, as I definitely wanted fighters. However, I also want to get home and, after hearing about all the

VE celebrations and hearing the King's speech, I went straight over and volunteered for TBRs. It will probably mean training up in Scotland on Barracudas.[5]

Advanced Fighter Training for Carrier Duty

Although some pilots preferred the sedate life of the bomber pilot, many set their hearts on the more glamorous world of the fighter pilot. Advanced fighter training, based at Naval Air Station Miami, was an extensive operation. First commissioned in August 1940, NAS Miami eventually consisted of three separate fields: Mainside at Opa Locka, plus Miami Municipal airfield and Masters airfield, both purchased from the City of Miami in 1942. It took an enormous staff to run the station: 675 officers, 7,139 enlisted men and 3,136 civilians.[6] In the course of eight weeks, student pilots were required to undertake over 93 hours of flying time, as the following flight syllabus shows:

Phase A	Familiarisation	9 hours
Phase B	Formation Flying	6 hours
Phase C	Navigation	6 hours
Phase D	Gunnery	
pt 1	fixed and free	7.5 hours
pt 2	anti-submarine bombing	4.5 hours
pt 3	glide bombing	9 hours
pt 4	torpedo	15 hours
pt 5	low level bombing	3 hours
pt 6	rocket attack	4.5 hours
Phase E	Night Flying	10.5 hours
Phase F	Instruments	10.5 hours
Phase G	Carrier Landings	8 hours

The training was intensive and tried to reflect the realities of combat. The instructors, who acted as squadron commanders, briefed their pilots before each 'mission'. The student pilots learned to work as a combat team. They trained together and graduated together. To complement the flying syllabus, pilots also had to complete 170 hours of ground school. The Miami ground school was designed to develop a pilot's all-round abilities. The most difficult aspect of the course was that student pilots would have to master the transition from the relatively simple and rugged aircraft of earlier training to more modern machines.

Early on, the Brewster Buffalo was the type of aircraft available at Miami for single-seat fighter training. Considered a front line aircraft in 1941, its marked lack of success against the Japanese led to its withdrawal from combat squadrons and relegation to a training role. Obsolescent it may have been, but for training purposes it provided useful experience half-way between the primary training aircraft and the tactical types which students would later fly in operational training and combat.

The ground syllabus reflected the emphasis on familiarising students with increasingly complex aircraft:

Pre-flight Familiarisation	30.50 hours
Engineering	6.75 hours
Gunnery	16.00 hours
Ordnance	7.50 hours
Torpedoes	12.25 hours
Night and Instrument Flying	8.50 hours
Radar	6.75 hours
Navigation	15.75 hours
Communications	18.50 hours
Recognition	11.50 hours
Air Combat	17.00 hours
Aerology	2.50 hours
Special Subjects	16.50 hours

In addition to the ground school curriculum, a rigorous physical training programme was designed to ensure that crews remained in peak physical condition.

For most students, gunnery training at Miami was the most exciting aspect of advanced training. Norman Hanson noted in his memoirs: 'By day we covered all aspects of fighter training: ground strafing on half-submerged rocks off the coast; air-to-air firing on drogues towed over the Everglades; gun camera attacks on individual aircraft or simulated bomber formations, flown by our own classmates.'[7] Partially submerged rocks were not the only target for the guns of British students. David Large later admitted: 'We were dreadful despoilers of the environment – we used to shoot up alligators in the Everglades if we had ammunition left in our aircraft guns.'

At the advanced level, discipline was a little more relaxed than in the early stages of training. Maurice Shippey found 'discipline [at Jacksonville] was not too strict. One pilot returned to Jax from Lauderdale along the beach at 100 feet without authorisation.' He was reported to the American authorities, and they asked Commander Gibson, the senior naval officer, to take action against him. 'Gibson lectured approximately thus, "If you are going to fly low, fly at 10 feet not 100 . . . Don't be caught . . . again".'

That some of the advanced training aircraft they were flying were virtually worn-out provided further excitement. New Zealander Ben Heffer, who went on to fly Corsairs with 1833 Squadron, recalled the perils of flying Brewster Buffaloes. Faults with the landing gear were a frequent occurrence, so that a pair of wire cutters was usually left in the cockpit to allow a student to free the landing gear in flight by severing a control cable and allowing gravity to lower the undercarriage and lock it into place. On one occasion he was in the air when Jimmy Wong, a fellow student, developed a problem with the undercarriage of his aircraft:

> I heard him call the tower in his very aristocratic English accent, 'I say, I do not seem to be able to get my wheels down.' Silence for a while, then from the tower, 'Have you used the goddam pliers?' Wong really is a good engineer, (still is) and felt insulted, 'Of course I have tried the remedy that must have been filched from the Wright brothers and it certainly does not work. Have you any sensible suggestions?' Again some waiting, then, 'Well you can hit the silk, or put her down in the grass. Your choice, buddy.' Wong's reply was, 'I shall land this aeronautical engineer's nightmare on the grass. Please, have all the emergency equipment at the ready.' He did a perfect landing in the grass and vacated the cockpit promptly.[8]

While undergoing the carrier course at Corpus Christi, James T. Wells observed an incident with a similarly fortunate outcome:

> Headley Radford's engine failed over the sea. I took over the lead while he followed agreed practice, ditching with cockpit canopy open. As soon as the plane stopped, he was out, onto the wing and into the sea. The water came up to his knees; he was on a sandbank. So he climbed back in and read a Readers Digest until help arrived. (He always carried a book; not sure why...)

Carrier training at Miami and Corpus Christi was beset by the dangers of an over-stretched training establishment in which well maintained, reliable, and safe aircraft were sometimes at a premium. As qualified pilots pushed their skills to the limits demanded by air combat training, their aircraft were occasionally found wanting.

Torpedo Bomber Training

After advanced training at Miami, Torpedo Bomber [TBR] pilots would then move on to the US Naval Air Station at nearby Fort Lauderdale, Florida, for conversion to the popular Grumman Avenger. At Miami early flight training had been done with obsolescent machines, but at Fort Lauderdale trainee pilots would get to fly the latest operational aircraft. Morley Wheeler, who was stationed at Fort Lauderdale in early 1943, remembered: 'The Avenger was much the largest and most advanced aircraft any of us had flown, but we soon recognised its outstanding qualities of power, strength and handling.' Fort Lauderdale meanwhile offered other attractions. A small holiday resort city of some 20,000 people on the edge of the Florida Everglades, it was a pleasant place to train. Wide, clear skies and open ocean offered the perfect environment in which to train torpedo bomber pilots, and the Everglades offered considerable scope for bombing targets and gunnery ranges.

The airfield was new, construction having started in April 1942. The station was commissioned on 1 October. It had four runways with linking taxiways and two satellite airfields. On 7 October training had begun with the arrival of 17 Avengers. The first group of British pilots arrived on 7 February 1943. The TBR course there was somewhat experimental. The war diary of US Naval Air Station Fort Lauderdale proudly records: 'Ground school training was established October 5, 1942 in the simplest way possible. Lt. Comdr. Taylor said to Lt. (jg.) John Sims, as the latter reported for duty, "We don't have a Ground School Officer yet – you are Officer-in-Charge of Ground School – organise a syllabus".'[9]

The wider syllabus for the training of torpedo pilots, developed by Lieutenant-Commander Taylor, placed an emphasis on learning the basics of carrier operations, glide bombing, torpedo bombing and anti-submarine bombing. James T. Webb recalled how the emphasis on bombing and gunnery meant that one particular island in the Bahamas took quite a pasting, being bombed almost every other day and later strafed on several occasions. Although students were to have four weeks of practice in the air, there was no flight syllabus that a student needed to complete with the attendant need for up-checks. Indeed, there appeared to be no attempt to standardise and teach a doctrine of torpedo attack.

In the United States Navy, each squadron might operate on a different doctrine. Taylor was happy for his instructors to show Fleet Air Arm pilots the methods employed by the squadrons which those instructors had recently left. Until the officers of a Royal Navy vessel complained, torpedo attacks were practised against any suitable ship sailing off the coast of Florida. Thereafter, the space between two boats anchored 300 yards off-shore was used as a mock target for the dummy torpedoes made out of concrete and plywood.

There were inevitable refinements to the syllabus during the course of the war, but it remained relatively open. A 93-hour flight syllabus was introduced in February 1944. Aerology was also given an enhanced part in the ground school syllabus to enable pilots to predict more accurately the kind of weather which they might encounter, including thunderstorms and icing.

In May 1944 special 'dunking parties' were introduced to enable crews to practise ditching in the sea. They involved loading the fuselage of an Avenger on a barge, taking it out to sea and immersing it in the ocean, with all three crew members inside. In being made to practise ditching procedure at sea, Avenger pilots seem to have been singled out for especially realistic survival training.

Torpedo bomber pilots were not alone in their misery, however. All pilots in training had to practise escaping from an aircraft after ditching in water, even if it were only in a swimming pool. The procedure was indelibly impressed on Philip Guest's memory:

> We were instructed in routines for the escape from aircraft in the event of 'ditching'. Thus we were taught how to keep afloat by blowing air into one's shirt, bringing one's cap smartly down on to the surface of the sea so as to trap air inside and keep one afloat. By far the most frightening experience, especially for those who could not swim, was the visit to the Dilbert Dunker. Ensign Dilbert was a legendary character depicted in the US Navy publications in cartoon form; he was always doing things wrong. For instance, he would be shown dropping his parachute pack in oil or pulling the ripcord whilst getting into his aircraft. The RAF equivalent was, of course, Pilot Officer Prune. The Dilbert Dunker was located just up the road from the barracks in Main Base, Pensacola, towards BOQ. It consisted of a high slipway, perhaps it was originally the high diving board of the swimming pool where the structure had been placed. The slipway led downwards into the swimming pool; the idea being that the Douglas Dauntless fuselage (minus wings) was released down the slipway into the swimming pool. The unfortunate student

Advanced, Conversion and Operational Training 111

pilot was strapped in the cockpit, hood slid back, of course, in a most realistic effort to re-create what would happen if one had to 'ditch' in real life. Immediately the fuselage entered the swimming pool the water closed in over the unfortunate student and most frequently it turned over. The student was expected to release seat straps and escape from the cockpit and swim to the surface, (and) thereafter inflate the 'Mae West' life jacket he also wore. The whole affair was quite frightening, even more so in anticipation, for stories abounded of students being trapped in the cockpit unable to escape. In practice, however, the clear water enabled the lifeguards surrounding the pool to see whether or not you were in difficulties and dive in to assist in your rise to the surface.

Training of Avenger Pilots:
US Naval Air Station, Fort Lauderdale, Florida

	British pilots received	Washed out	Killed	Completed course
1943				
Feb	9			
Mar	9			8
Apr	15			10
May				
Jun	12			15
Jul	14			12
Aug				
Sept				14
Oct	3			
Nov	20			3
Dec				
1944				
Jan	13			
Feb	6			11
Mar	4			13
Apr	11	3	2^{10}	2
May	10			2
Jun	7	1		12
Jul	2			8
Aug		1		
Sept				8
Oct	15			

By August 1943, 113.5 hours were required to complete the TBR syllabus; in February 1944, 93 hours were required; and in August 1944, 96 hours were needed. Although training was dogged by the problem of unserviceable aircraft – in September 1943 some 35% of the aircraft at Fort Lauderdale were unserviceable as the needs of front line squadrons drained the pool of experienced mechanics – increasing deliveries of new Avengers offset the difficulties. The original 17 Avengers allocated to the base had grown to 135 by March 1945.

Other kinds of difficulty were troublesome, however. In May 1943 the Assistant Chief of the [British] Naval Staff complained that the 'air training of reconnaissance and striking forces [was] suffering' because of a lack of vessels against which mock torpedo attacks could be launched. That particular problem was never properly solved.[11] In September and October 1944 training was disrupted when the base had to be evacuated following hurricane warnings.

The working up of British squadrons in the United States for service aboard aircraft carriers was dogged by a lack of suitable training facilities. Owing to the expansion of US naval air training and operations, it was not possible to designate particular stations for British use on a permanent basis, so the Royal Navy was informed that their carrier training operations would have to be shifted to whichever US naval air stations could be made available. Initially the US Navy opened stations close by busy Portsmouth, Virginia, for further Towers scheme operational training. Later, some training for carrier operations was shifted to Quonset Point, Rhode Island, and Squantum, Massachusetts. Finally, stations for organising Fleet Air Arm squadrons were established on a more settled basis at Lewiston and Brunswick, Maine. Several of the American-built escort carriers (called 'Woolworth carriers' or 'Jeep carriers' by the British) were used for training as well as for transporting newly-formed squadrons to the United Kingdom.

Dive-Bomber Training

While the Royal Navy had considerable experience of torpedo bombing in the early years of the war, it had underestimated the significance of dive-bombing. Arguably, the Royal Flying Corps had developed dive-bombing on the Western Front in 1917. The Royal Navy did not use the method, but extensive trials were carried out at the Orfordness testing station in 1918. During the inter-war period, the Americans, Japanese, and Germans perfected dive-bombing, but the British virtually abandoned it. In 1931 however, Lieutenant-Commander St. John Prentice of the Royal Navy visited the United States and witnessed the dive-bombing techniques which the United States Navy was then developing. Full of enthusiasm, he returned to the United Kingdom and argued the case for the Fleet Air Arm to develop a dive-bomber element. The Air Ministry, which was then responsible for naval aviation, did not share his enthusiasm and declined to allocate funds for the development of new airframes and a new bombsight for dive-bomber use.

The first Fleet Air Arm dive-bomber training unit was formed in 1933, but World War II broke out before a modern dive-bomber, the Blackburn Skua, was operational. Skuas proved the value of the dive-bomber by sinking the German cruiser *Königsberg* during the Norwegian campaign in 1940. The Skua was too slow, however, and it was vulnerable to enemy fighters. Following the Germans' 1940 victory in the West and the publicity given to their Stuka dive-bomber, sections of the British press pressed the government and the Royal Air Force to develop the dive-bomber as a close support weapon. The Royal Air Force preferred the flexibility of the fighter-bomber (especially the Bristol Beaufighter), but the Royal Navy persisted with the dive-bomber concept in replacing the Skua with the Fairey Barracuda in 1941. The Barracuda was a versatile aircraft which could serve as either dive-bomber or torpedo bomber.

By mid-1942 the RAF and the FAA both began to take more interest in what the US Navy could offer in the training of dive-bomber pilots. Twelve Royal Air Force pilots, drawn from six British Flying Training Schools, arrived at Miami in May for training in dive-bombing.[12] After the success of the US Navy's Dauntless dive-bombers at the Battle of Midway in June 1942, the Royal Navy decided that some FAA pilots should also be trained in dive-bombing techniques in the USA. At first it was believed that fifteen hours of instruction would be sufficient to turn out dive-bomber pilots; in fact, it needed more than double that for the best pilots to be passed as satisfactory.

Part of the problem arose from inadequacies in the pilots' earlier training at British Flying Training Schools. G.F. Brogan, Commanding Officer of USNAS Miami complained: 'None of these pilots have had any formation flying, fixed gunnery, or solo spins; and in fact several of them had never spun an airplane, even with an instructor aboard.'[13] The deficiencies were quickly diagnosed. The unanticipated length of time that it would take to train dive-bomber pilots and the growing strain on facilities at Miami forced a change in the programme.

On 5 July 1943 ten British pilots under the command of Robin Grant-Sturgess reported to the US Naval Air Station at Vero Beach, Florida, for training as dive-bomber pilots. The base, which included four paved runways, taxiways, and supporting facilities, had been constructed in 1942. After following a revised and extended syllabus, the new contingent completed training on 13 September 1943.

Flying Boat Training

While Fleet Air Arm pilots learned to fly advanced carrier-type aircraft, some Royal Air Force pilots destined for service in Coastal Command learned to handle the big flying boats at Pensacola. During the course of the war the value of these flying boats had been demonstrated again and again – in ocean reconnaissance, in escorting convoys, in anti-submarine attacks, and in air-sea rescue of 'ditched' aircrew or survivors from torpedoed ships. To narrow, and eventually close, the mid-Atlantic air 'gap' where convoys could not be provided with any air cover, RAF Coastal Command badly needed longer-range, American-built aircraft, like the PBY Catalina – and it needed the pilots to fly them. The Air Ministry had purchased an aircraft for trials purposes before the war, and in 1939 an order for thirty Catalinas was placed in the United States.[14] The British Purchasing Commission in Washington later increased the order to 109 aircraft, with the first 50 being delivered to Great Britain by May 1941.

Piloting the big flying boats was less glamorous work than the world of carrier operations but, in view of the U-boat menace, it was vital work all the same. Many pilots found the process of converting from single-engine aircraft to twin-engine flying boats quite a challenge, but they also developed a genuine love of this form of aviation. Flying boat training was initially done on Consolidated P2Ys. With fixed floats and a sponson, they were the forerunner to the higher performance Catalina.

William Warner and J.H. Ashley both trained on flying boats in 1942. Warner was enthusiastic about the experience when he wrote home on 7 June:

> I like flying boats very much – when it is terribly hot on the ground it is a grand feeling to take off and in a few seconds feel perfectly cool. The edge of the bay is pure white sand, then, as you get further out this turns to a beautiful emerald green and the sea and sky an intense blue! From several thousand feet and through binoculars you can see fish swimming about. We often watch sharks attacking a shoal of fish, and one day last week saw two enormous monsters well over twenty-five feet in length!

Such sights could enliven long trips over the sea in more ways than one. Trainee flying boat pilots were organised into groups of three who would stay together, even though they might fly with different instructors, engineers and other flight crew for each trip. Flights would last for approximately three hours, during which a range of procedures would be demonstrated and then practised. J.H. Ashley later recalled that flying boat training was not too arduous. It consisted of 'largely learning landing and taking off from the sea, mooring, instrument flying and landing, night flying and some bombing and gunnery practice'. With two exceptions, everyone in Ashley's class passed the course. Despite the reliability and strength of the aircraft on which they were training, two Royal Air Force cadets in Ashley's group were killed in training.

Richard Bartlett, who qualified as a flying boat navigator under the Towers scheme, recalled one eventful training flight:

> We [had] guns & ammunition on board because it was after Pearl Harbour & America was in the war. One day, returning to base, the skipper spotted something in the water so we reduced height & he ordered us to man all guns – the 2 waist guns, one nose gun & one under the tail. We then launched an attack on the suspected submarine only to discover it was a whale. One could see where the bullets hit the water but I don't think any part of the whale was at risk. Thank goodness we weren't attacked by the Japs.

From 1942 onwards, US Army Air Force squadrons arrived in the UK and occupied numerous RAF airfields. Air Ministry officials felt that the single Coastal Command operational training unit (OTU) at Blackpool, Lancashire, was inadequate for putting the finishing touches to the training of all flying boat aircrew then under training in Canada and the United States. As a result, two new general reconnaissance (GR) schools were established at Summerside and Charlottetown on Prince Edward Island, Canada, and another was established in the Bahamas.

Once pilots and other aircrew completed further training at one of these general reconnaissance schools, they would typically be posted to Elizabeth City, North Carolina. That small southern town was home for the Douglas Aircraft Company's modification plant, which fitted out and armed new PBY5-B Catalinas built under contract for British and Russian service.

Towers scheme graduates were perceived to be weak in radio telephony procedure and code, so emphasis on these skills at the new GR schools would better prepare flying boat crews for ferrying and operational service before they returned to the United Kingdom. Another solution lay in assigning more experienced RAF personnel to act as instructors at Pensacola and other stations. In the midst of war, finding the necessary qualified pilots, WOp/AGs, navigators and others to serve as instructors was no easy task, but they were found, as reports of weaknesses continued to reach the Air Ministry and could not be ignored.

One telegram from the RAF Delegation in Washington put its criticism very bluntly:

> Pensacola pilot graduates are deficient in navigational flights, instrument, and night flying. We may get the night flying, if the instructor position improves, but other deficiencies will always exist. To reduce intakes or increase the length of course would not help beyond easing present tension at Pensacola. With a GR course in Canada, navigational deficiency can be covered, and pilots will be suitable to join squadrons as second pilots without OTU training. We will never make first pilots here.[15]

From the very beginning in 1941, Royal Air Force and Royal Navy air officers were convinced that the British system of aircrew training was superior to that of any other nation. They failed to realise that American air officers also held similar beliefs about their own aircrew training system. National pride made it impossible for either air force to imitate a system, which grew out of a different culture.

British air officers were critical of American training systems, because the United States did not maintain a Central Flying School such as the British used to certify instructors and to standardise methods of flying instruction. The RAF Delegation in Washington was critical of US Navy flight instructors because they deplored the inadequacy of the training which British students were receiving in the USA. They believed that part of the problem came with the rapid expansion of the United States Navy's training establishment to cope with the demands of war. From the American perspective, the US Navy found it very difficult to increase the numbers of pilots in training without reducing the quality of their training. Indeed, in September 1942 the United States Navy formally asked the Air Ministry to consider ending the training of British pilots on the Towers scheme in order to be able to train more US Navy flying boat pilots.

Although the RAF Delegation continued to snipe at the programme, the Air Ministry preferred to continue training in the USA. In a report of

March 1943, the RAF Delegation, obviously concerned with the training of pilots who might have to serve eventually in Bomber Command, summed up the perceived deficiencies of Towers-trained Catalina pilots:

> The average pilot who is passing out of Pensacola these days, (i) can take-off and land a Catalina flying boat safely by day. (ii) He can fly well by instruments. (iii) He cannot fly by night. In elementary and basic, his night flying has been on flood-lit airfields with conditions not unlike daylight. In the flying boat stage, he has only spent time in the air at night with a USN instructor flying. . . . (iv) He lacks initiative, since he has not been allowed it . . . (v) He lacks appreciation of how to use and treat his engines . . . (vi) Except for one six-hour flight out to sea, he has never been away from the local flying area of his airfield. His map reading is therefore nil and his practical navigation almost nil . . . (vii) In all he is a pilot who has survived a rigid system of checking and re-checking. He can fly, but needs introduction to the finer points of the game.[16]

Continuing these criticisms in the following month, the RAF Delegation telegraphed the Air Ministry:

> Quality of flying instructors in expanding USN is so low that in flying boat stage much of instruction is valueless. Flying boat pilots being turned out are poorest ever. Small contact of RAF cadets with RAF instructors does not offset deficiency of the bulk of boat training by young inexperienced USN instructors. Position is still deteriorating and USN, recognising difficulty of making boat instructors from inexperienced graduates, have formally requested an increase of RAF flying boat instructor staff at Pensacola. Recommend that Pensacola flying boat instructor staff be increased from 6 to 22 to enable bulk of RAF boat training to be undertaken by RAF instructors.[17]

The RAF Delegation's continued hostility towards the Towers scheme provoked a debate within the Air Ministry. Air Commodore D.V. Carnegie, a World War I flying boat pilot, had visited the United States often and had spent 1941-2 establishing joint USA-UK aircrew training. On returning to the UK, he became Director of Flying Training (DFT) at the Air Ministry. Carnegie was annoyed at the RAF Delegation's attitude and by what he saw as the service's squandering of a resource given to it by the sacrifice of the United States Navy. He wrote in April 1943:

> I am not . . . satisfied with the use that is being made of the Pensacola products. This capacity was given to us by the US Navy before they became involved in war, and we only got it because Admiral Towers, who was at that time Chief of the Bureau of Naval Aeronautics, is an admirer of the RAF and wanted to help. He has since been severely criticised for giving us the capacity which the USA themselves urgently require. If we had put all our products on to flying boats, then we would be above criticism. I know that the allocations have been changed since our original requirements were estimated at 60 per month, but the fact remains that, of the last 435 graduates, less than half have gone on to flying boats. The figures are as follows: 184 posted to flying boats; 181 posted to GR land planes; [and] 70 now at PRC [Pilots Reception Centre], of whom only 25 were recommended by the GR [School Of General Reconnaissance], Charlottetown, for flying boats. Assuming, therefore that the last 25 will in fact go to flying boats, only 209 of the 435 [pilots] trained at Pensacola will have been used in the role for which they were trained. If the US authorities become aware of this, they will naturally insist on cutting down our training capacity, but what is more important, the training given at Pensacola is very largely wasted if the product goes on to GR land planes.[18]

Investigations within the Air Ministry established that Coastal Command was unwilling to release any of its Catalina pilots to serve as instructors, but that it was willing to transfer some of its Sunderland flying boat pilots, who would than have to undergo conversion to Catalinas.

It was hoped that tour-expired pilots from 209 and 240 Squadrons, who had been serving in the Indian Ocean, might be induced to become instructors at Pensacola. Raiding Ferry Command for flying boat pilots offered another possible means of securing the necessary extra instructors. The situation was partly alleviated by finding some extra instructors and by the RAF's decision to decrease the numbers in the pilot training programme. In November 1943 the Air Ministry telegraphed the RAF Delegation that, as from December, it would need the United States Navy to train only 45 flying boat pilots each month, instead of 74.[19]

There can be little doubt that, in the employment of trained flying boat pilots, the RAF priority policy favouring Bomber Command was wrong.

Coastal Command remained short of flying boat pilots, and it also remained short of Catalina aircraft. Under the Arnold-Towers-Portal agreement of 15 June 1942, the RAF was promised 175 Catalinas in 1942, and 260 in 1943.[20] Aircraft deliveries were delayed by production difficulties, however. With the Battle of the Atlantic at a critical point in early 1943, and American participation in anti-submarine warfare increasing, it is easy to understand Carnegie's exasperation at the misuse of Towers-trained flying boat pilots and at the RAF Delegation's sniping.

The problem lay at a higher level than Carnegie, however. At that stage of the war, Bomber Command had priority for aircraft and pilots. With losses of both running at a high level, it was inevitable that Bomber Command should prosper at Coastal Command's expense. By 1943 Air Marshal Arthur T. Harris, Commander-in-Chief of Bomber Command, had convinced many British political and military leaders that only his command was capable of taking the war directly to the enemy, thereby avoiding the needless slaughter which had occurred in the 1914-18 land battles. Harris firmly believed that massive numbers of heavy bombers armed with huge bombs could achieve victory in Europe by ruthlessly prosecuting the strategic air offensive against Germany. As a result, Bomber Command claimed a large number of flying boat pilots and converted them for service on heavy bombers.

Helicopter Training

While flying boats were a long-established part of the aviation scene in the 1940s, helicopters represented the cutting edge of technology. In the 1920s and '30s the Royal Air Force had experimented with autogiros, primarily in the role of army co-operation aircraft. Two C-40 autogiros went over to France with the British Expeditionary Force in 1939, but both were lost to enemy action.

In the 1930s the United States Navy also experimented with autogiros, but found their usefulness sharply limited. During operations in Nicaragua in 1932, the US Marine Corps found that its OPI autogiro was of little more use than as a taxi for VIPs or the lightly wounded. By 1940, however, some individuals in the US Coast Guard and in the aviation industry began to evaluate the design and use of helicopters. For air-sea rescue operations the helicopter's vertical takeoff, hovering, and landing capabilities were promising. In 1941 leaders of the US Coast Guard, which became an element of the US Navy during wartime, were convinced that the helicopter could be useful in search and rescue work.[21]

Wing Commander Reginald Brie, the Royal Air Force's expert on autogiros, was invited to the USA in early 1942 to view a demonstration of the new Sikorsky US-300 helicopter.[22] In the inter-war period, Brie had pioneered the development of autogiros in Britain, landing one on the deck of a warship in 1935. Officers of the Royal Navy were unimpressed, however, by the display. Brie was an unconventional airman. He had been a sergeant in the Royal Field Artillery during the First World War, until he transferred to the Royal Flying Corps as an observer in 1918. From 1930 to 1939 he was the chief test pilot and flying manager of the Cierva Autogiro Company. He joined the RAF in 1939 and he was posted to America in 1941 to work on the development of rotary aviation. In 1941 he landed an autogiro on the deck of a merchant ship, the *Empire Mersey*, but both the Royal Navy and the Royal Air Force remained sceptical of the autogiro, primarily because of its inability to hover.[23]

The demonstration of the American US-300 helicopter in 1942 was to change that. Brie was sufficiently impressed to conclude that the helicopter would be far more useful than the autogiro. Brie later persuaded Igor Sikorsky to let him fly the successor to the US-300, the YR4. By this stage, Brie had been seconded to the Admiralty, which was in the process of considering how the helicopter might be used for anti-submarine work. Flying from the deck of a ship, the helicopter could become the eyes of a convoy. Brie was convinced by his test flight that the YR4 could fulfil an anti-submarine role. He went straight to Air Marshal Sir Roderic Hill, head of the British Air Commission in Washington, and asked him to place an order for the YR4 on behalf of the Admiralty.

In the meantime, experiments in using helicopters at sea were carried out in Long Island Sound. The US Coast Guard cutter *Cobb* was eventually converted into the first helicopter carrier, and in 1943 helicopter landing trials were held on the merchant ship *Daghestan*. In the same year, orders were placed for the successor to the YR4, the R5, which was larger, and could carry a pilot and observer, as well as two hundred pounds of weaponry. By this time, the US Navy was also convinced of the anti-submarine potential of the helicopter. On May 4 1943 a joint board was formed to consider the use of the 'Ship-Based Helicopter in Anti-Submarine Warfare'. The joint board consisted of representatives of the US Navy, the Bureau of Aeronautics, the Coast Guard, the Royal Navy and the Royal Air Force.[24]

While there was a considerable measure of agreement on the technology and potential employment of helicopters in the war at sea, the training of aircrew to operate them resulted in some disagreements. When

ADVANCED, CONVERSION AND OPERATIONAL TRAINING 121

the Director of the Naval Air Division turned his attention to the question of training helicopter pilots for the Royal Navy in late 1942, he raised awkward questions on a number of issues. Were helicopter pilots going to be fully qualified Fleet Air Arm pilots, who would undertake conversion training onto helicopters? Would the Air Ministry control the training of both Royal Air Force and Fleet Air Arm helicopter pilots? He believed that helicopter pilots should not convert from fixed-wing aircraft, but should be specially trained. He also favoured setting rather lower requirements for helicopter pilots than for pilots of fixed-wing aircraft. They would also be paid less. In effect, he favoured a form of apartheid in the training and career development of Fleet Air Arm pilots, according to the type aircraft they flew.[25]

This provoked a fierce debate within the Admiralty, who envisaged deploying helicopters on specially prepared merchant ships. In view of the experimental nature of the helicopter, the Director of Personnel Services felt that rotary wing pilots should be paid exactly the same as any other Fleet Air Arm pilot, while the Director of Pre-Entry Training attacked the notion of a separate entrance system for helicopter pilots.[26] Despite opposition from various quarters, the Director of the Naval Air Division pressed on with his determination to ensure that helicopter training did not draw the best pilots away from duties with the fleet.

In November 1942 he specified that individuals would be accepted for helicopter training up to age 35 and with a lower standard of eyesight than pilots of other aircraft.[27] It was noted at the same time that the delivery of two YR 4 helicopters was scheduled for March 1943 and two XR 5s would follow in May. Full production was expected to begin early in 1944, leaving the Fleet Air Arm and the Royal Air Force with little time to resolve their debate about helicopter training.

Even so, in early 1943 a considerable number of issues were still outstanding. Training of helicopter pilots was not yet under way in the United States, and the Admiralty was concerned that the Air Ministry had lost sight of the matter. The Director of Air Warfare and Flying Training made a telling contribution to the on-going debate about whether to accept lower standards for helicopter pilots when he wrote: 'There is at present no knowledge of the skill required to operate helicopters from ships. Taking this into consideration . . . it was generally agreed that initially no relaxation of medical flying qualifications could be accepted.'[28] Thus, the first group to undergo helicopter pilot training in the United States were standard entrants to Fleet Air Arm flight training. At a meeting at the Air Ministry on 8 March, the Air Council had left open the question of standards for RAF helicopter pilots.[29]

British policy on the training of helicopter pilots developed slowly during 1942 and 1943. In part, the Royal Navy's resources were being spent on the fighting in the Atlantic and Mediterranean. It was not surprising that a compromise had to be made on the training of pilots for a new weapon in the anti-submarine campaign in the very month that fighting in the Battle of the Atlantic reached new heights. On the day after the meeting of the Air Council on 8 March, the British Admiralty Delegation in Washington telegraphed: 'The helicopter situation has undergone a radical change.'[30] The United States Navy had finally accepted the helicopter for Coast Guard use, and it seemed likely that they could be prevailed upon to provide training for British pilots.

Despite the turn around, it was not until March 1944 that the first six Royal Air Force and Fleet Air Arm pilots began their training with the United States Coast Guard at Floyd Bennett Field, Long Island, New York. Maintenance ratings began a course of instruction there somewhat later. Floyd Bennett Field was far from being a perfect location for helicopter training. Until 1928, it had been the site of a garbage dump and glue factory. The island was only just above sea level, and considerable sums were needed to raise the level to 16 feet above sea level. Dedicated on 23 May 1931, the much improved airfield was named after Floyd Bennett, a naval aviator who had accompanied Admiral Richard E. Byrd on his 1926 flight to the North Pole.

Originally it had been intended to serve as a municipal airport for New York. The site of what was later to become La Guardia airport was deemed better, however, so in 1936 the US Coast Guard was given a fifty-year lease on Floyd Bennett Field, and a Coast Guard Air Station opened there in 1938. In May 1941, as the Coast Guard expanded its operations, all private activity at the field ceased. US Naval Air Station Floyd Bennett Field was re-commissioned on 2 June 1941, and it was put to use as a base to support the ferrying of aircraft from Grumman aircraft assembly plants on Long Island. Many FAA pilots were assigned to Ferry Command and used the airfield. During the course of the war, Floyd Bennett Field was extended by reclaiming land from the sea. On 19 November 1943 the U.S. Chief of Naval Operations directed that the base be assigned to helicopter training.

Some difficulties in the training of helicopter crews revolved around the experimental nature of the technology, and questions as to whether either the United States Army Air Force or the Royal Air Force wanted to make use of it. In February 1943 the Royal Air Force Delegation in Washington had concluded that the USAAF could not be relied on to provide helicopter training. They suggested approaching the manufacturer, Vought-Sikorsky, to teach the fifty pilots the RAF hoped to train before April 1944.[31] The RAF Delegation considered that 40 hours of primary training and 30 hours of operational training would serve adequately.

The development of training was critically restricted, however, by the shortage of helicopters and, as hostilities in Europe were drawing to a close, by concurrent Admiralty efforts to relocate helicopter training to the United Kingdom. In the summer of 1944 two pilots, from the first group of six who had completed training at Floyd Bennett Field, were transferred to the United Kingdom under orders to organise a Royal Navy Helicopter School. The four pilots remaining at the US Naval Air Station were assigned to assist in training the second group of pilots. Thus, in June 1944 the Royal Navy Helicopter School at Floyd Bennett Field became officially operational, with 8 aircraft and 30 ratings.

On 14 December 1944 eleven American R-4 helicopters left from Floyd Bennett Field for Norfolk, Virginia, where they were loaded on board HMS *More*. Although she was torpedoed in the Irish Sea, she made it into port with her helicopters undamaged. The December departure from Floyd Bennett Field marked the end of operational training for British helicopter pilots in the United States, as the Royal Navy Helicopter School relocated to the United Kingdom. In total, four courses of helicopter pilots and two courses of maintenance ratings were trained in the United States during 1944. This was not very much in terms of the numbers trained or, indeed, their immediate operational effectiveness, but it marked the advent of a new weapon destined to play an important role in the future of naval aviation, in addition to providing an invaluable air-sea rescue capability.

Operational Training

Once a pilot had been trained in a particular branch of flying, it was necessary to complete his flying education with a short period of operational training. Most of the operational training of Towers pilots took place through Fleet Air Arm operational training squadrons based at four naval air stations in the northern United States. Operational training for Corsair and, later, Avenger pilots was provided at USNAS Quonset Point, Rhode Island, in 738 Squadron, which formed at that station on 1 February 1943. The squadron moved to USNAS Lewiston, Maine, on 31 July 1943, and on 14 February 1945 it relocated again to USNAS

Brunswick, Maine. 738 Squadron was disbanded five months later. Operational training on Corsairs was also carried out at USNAS Brunswick in 732 Squadron, which had been formed there on 23 November 1943. At Brunswick, carrier landings could be simulated on land until they were perfected. 732 Squadron was eventually disbanded on 1 July 1944. USNAS Squantum, Massachusetts, provided another location for the training of Avenger crews.

After experiencing the excellent facilities at vast permanent air stations such as Pensacola and Jacksonville in the southern United States, many pilots were not enthralled by their stay at the less comfortable and more basic fields far to the north. Quonset Point, Rhode Island, situated between Providence and Newport, had been constructed around massive runways of 4,000 and 6,000 feet on reclaimed land in Narragansett Bay.[32] It was a busy station, housing schools for Naval Reserve Officers and Air Combat Information, as well as being home to anti-submarine aircraft which patrolled out into the Atlantic.

Some of the FAA pilots who were based at Lewiston, Maine, loathed that station. Clifford Singleton, who had left Miami in September 1943, was stationed at Lewiston from October to December 1943. He was not favourably impressed with the facilities:

> Lewiston, Maine, was our next destination, and this could not be judged a great success for anyone. The aerodrome had been bulldozed out of an area of small hills, so that gullies remained between the runways, the runways being relatively narrow. The facilities were entirely new and the place had to settle down in a number of respects . . .
>
> [Learning to fly a difficult aircraft only added to Singleton's woes.] The Grumman F4F was our next aircraft, after a couple of flights of familiarisation with the runway and the countryside. My first so-called flight in the Grumman was about 50 yards, the customary swing on take-off completely fooling me, so that I put the aircraft into the adjacent ditch.

Singleton was lucky to walk away from such a crash, for conversion to tactical aircraft and operational training continued to take a steady toll of lives. Part of the problem was the difficulty of adjusting to the more powerful aircraft they now had to control. Most pilots quickly learned to enjoy their new aircraft, however. This encouraging response was also found among the telegraphist/air gunners reporting for duties on the

Avenger aircraft. Most of them had trained in Canada on Fairey Swordfish open cockpit biplanes. Their initial impressions of the Grumman Avenger could be quite enthusiastic:

> What a pleasure it was to fly in the Avenger. For the first time, TAGs had real equipment – a big .5 Browning machine gun. Mounted in a powered turret, it seemed like a cannon after the .303 machine gun to which we had become accustomed. There was an additional .300 Browning mounted aft, under the tail of the Avenger, and a crystal frequency controlled radio with a long range.[33]

Sub-Lieutenant Frank Stovin-Bradford, who had trained at Grosse Ile and Pensacola, arrived at USNAS Lewiston, Maine, in February 1944 to train on Avengers with 738 Squadron. He would then go on to Squantum, Massachusetts, to join 857 Squadron. He recalled how his training at Lewiston prepared him for life in 857 Squadron: 'We now learned British formation flying led by a British instructor, British ADDL [Aerodrome Dummy Deck Landings] with a British Deck Landing Control Officer (DLCO), British anti-submarine tactics – glide bombing, and how to do navigation with an observer giving the orders.'[34] The training remained intensive and was designed to prepare pilots for the rigours of life in a front line British squadron. Bar Harbor in Maine provided another location where Lewiston-based pilots could practise ADDL.[35]

Squadron Formation

Once operational training had been completed, the pilots could be formed into front-line squadrons for embarkation on carriers which were being built or repaired in the United States. The US Naval Air Station at Norfolk, Virginia, was the initial location for squadrons forming up. Between October and November 1942, five Grumman Wildcat fighter squadrons (890, 892, 894, 896 and 898) worked up at the Virginia base. In addition, 882 Squadron disembarked from a carrier and re-equipped at the base three times, 898 Squadron twice, and 896 Squadron once. After November 1942 the focus of squadron training shifted to the Northeast. Between November 1942 and September 1945, seventeen Fleet Air Arm Corsair squadrons formed up at Quonset Point and Brunswick (1830, 1831, 1833, 1834, 1835, 1836, 1837, 1838, 1841, 1842, 1843, 1845, 1846, 1848, 1849, 1850 and 1851). Of these, 1835 was disbanded during training, and 1831 was disbanded on arrival in the United Kingdom.

The working up of the Avenger squadrons took place at Squantum, Massachusetts, which had three asphalt runways and a seaplane dock. The station was large, having a complement or 235 officers and 1887 enlisted men. It had auxiliary sites at Beverly and Ayer, and would typically have 60 aircraft on the strength at any one time. Twelve Avenger squadrons (845, 846, 848, 849, 850, 851, 852, 853, 854, 855, 856 and 857) were formed at Squantum between September 1943 and July 1944. In addition, 832, 838 and 840 Squadrons disembarked from carriers and re-equipped with new Avengers. Dive-bomber Squadron 1820, comprising nine Grumman Helldivers, was also formed in May 1944. In July it left for the United Kingdom.[36] Operational training of British squadrons in New England would typically last two months.

As the war spread and intensified, the success of the American aviation and shipbuilding industries under Lend-Lease combined with the productivity of the Towers training scheme to provide numerous small aircraft carriers, 44 per cent of the aircraft used by the Royal Navy, and the trained aircrew to fly them. All of these developments made the United States a prime location for Fleet Air Arm squadron formation. In January 1943, the Admiralty had to ask the American authorities to allow them to increase the number of men and aircraft it had in the United States in order to work up more squadrons. The United States Navy was unwilling to agree to the Admiralty's ambitious plans, but they agreed to accept an increase from 93 aircraft and 675 men to 150 aircraft and 1,000 men. In May 1944 the United States Navy, which had struggled to provide the necessary facilities for squadron working up, agreed to allow the Royal Navy to increase its establishment to 1,175 men. Nevertheless, lack of repair and training facilities and a shortage of stores dogged the programme.[37]

Behind the arrivals and departures of squadrons lay a vast programme of training. Alistair Michie, who had volunteered for service in 1941 and who had been on the 38th pilots course at HMS *St Vincent*, joined 1837 Fighter Squadron at Brunswick, Maine, in September 1943. He spent three months there. In early January 1944 the squadron practised deck landings on the USS *Charger*. After two weeks of practice, his squadron was loaded onto HMS *Begum* and sailed across the North Atlantic. The squadron arrived in Scotland on 1 February 1944.

Clifford Singleton, who was with Michie, provided an excellent overview of the process of working up 1837 Squadron:

ADVANCED, CONVERSION AND OPERATIONAL TRAINING

We moved east towards the coast, to the US Naval Air Station at Brunswick, and this is where the Royal Naval component of our lives returned. The first Corsair squadron had been 1830 and ours was 1837. There were horror tales of the flying accidents in the preceding seven Corsair squadrons, some of the worst being on the small aircraft carriers where our first sea landings were made. 1834 and 1835 Squadrons were still in training, when 1836 and 1837 began simultaneous training at Brunswick [in January 1944].

Corsair squadrons in the process of working up suffered a high accident rate, which many pilots put down to the nature of the aircraft they were flying. Despite having twice the range of the Wildcat, the Corsair enjoyed an unenviable reputation in some respects. Initial tests by the United States Navy in 1942 concluded that the aircraft was not suited to carrier operations due to the weakness of its shock absorbers, the limited field of forward vision when landing, and a tendency for one wing to drop on approach due to torque stall. The United States Navy had refused to clear the aircraft for carrier operations until Vought brought in modifications. Even after these were made, suspicions remained, and it was not until May 1944 that a United States Navy evaluation board concluded that the F4 Corsair was a better aircraft than the F6 Hellcat. Clifford Singleton later grumbled that

> the machine was not as safe as it should have been, requiring significant adjustments to the landing gear . . . [It had] a wing-based tendency to drop the port wing on landing, also the cockpit hood was low and obscured by reinforcements, which rendered the long nose of the aircraft even more difficult to cope with. The Corsair was a big brute of an aircraft. It gained a reputation for being dangerous and this doubtless, inhibited some of the less skilled.[38]

The working up of 1837 Squadron saw one particularly distressing incident in which their commanding officer, Jackie Sewell, lost his life. Singleton witnessed the entire incident:

> We had been practising turns in squadron formation, whereby one line of aircraft slid underneath the central line, changing rank as it were. This we had been doing on a sunny-cloudy day above the beautiful state of Maine, when Sewell said something like 'I'm going down', and peeled off the formation downwards and left. Watson

was leading the left-hand line of aircraft, and he assumed that
another turning manoeuvre was being ordered, so the two planes
collided in mid-air and fell in pieces 5000 feet or so. We young and
tender pilots were totally shocked. No one took command of the
squadron. Some followed the broken aircraft down to the ground in
the vain hope that the bodies might have been alive.[39]

It was a miracle that the death of Sewell did not lead to a further series of collisions as young pilots followed the wreckage to earth.

Lieutenant Norman Hanson took temporary charge of the squadron before handing over to Lieutenant-Commander Richard Pridham-Whipple. His number two at 1837 Squadron was Lieutenant R.D.B. Hopkins, who went on to command 1834 Squadron. Together they faced the difficult task of rebuilding a squadron shattered by a training accident. Pridham-Whipple had to undergo conversion to the Corsair and then lead the squadron in simulated carrier landings on aerodromes. To improve the pilots' understanding of their aircraft, they were taken on a tour of the Chance-Vought factory in Bridgeport, Connecticut. Pridham-Whipple also learned to act as a batsman to guide his pilots onto the flight deck of a carrier. On 13 January, when 1837 Squadron eventually began carrier landing practice on the USS *Charger*, Pridham-Whipple acted as batsman while his pilots each undertook four deck landings. The day passed without serious incident, but the nerves of some pilots were so stretched by the experience that they never landed on a carrier again.

Fate could indeed be cruel. Having survived primary, intermediate, advanced, conversion and operational training, pilots continued to lose their lives while 'working up'.

A youngster called Harris from 1830 Squadron was flying high –
about 23,000 feet – over Brunswick town at noon. He was tearing
along at high speed with full supercharger going ... Quite suddenly
the engine packed in through failure of the ignition system ...
Harris glided down to around 16,000 feet, a height at which the
magnetos decided to recommence operating, and the engine cut in
again. The boy had already committed himself to a searing and
explosive death. At this moment, he had seconds left to live. When
the engine cut out, he had obviously forgotten to withdraw the
supercharger. Now, as the engine from inertia burst into life again at
a high throttle setting, the thrust exerted on the bearings of the
supercharger was too much. The rear of the power unit completely

destroyed itself, with hardened steel tearing through fuselage, cockpit, wings – and Harris.[40]

The wreckage fell on the town of Brunswick, almost killing a policeman at a school crossing. The strain of continued training and squadron working-up is evident in the story of Morley Wheeler, an Avenger pilot. On 6 April 1943 he had joined 846 Squadron at Quonset Point. Lord Halifax, the British Ambassador to the United States, inspected the squadron in early June before it prepared to embark on the escort carrier HMS *Ravager*. She and more than twenty other escort carriers had been built for Britain in American shipyards under the Lend-Lease agreement. Morley Wheeler and the rest of his squadron were to land their aircraft on her as she steamed along Chesapeake Bay.

Embarkation day and the days which followed, were to be amongst the most awful in Morley Wheeler's life. On 2 July he landed on HMS *Ravager*. The landing did not go smoothly, as he misread the batsman's signals, stalled the aircraft, and ran-off the port side of the deck. The Avenger plunged into the sea, but fortunately it stayed afloat long enough for Wheeler and his crew to escape. The following day Wheeler again ended up in the sea as his aircraft's engine cut out on take-off. Slightly injured, he was forced to sit out operations the next day, but had the tragic experience of watching one of his old Fort Lauderdale classmates also come down in the sea.[41] This time, however, there were to be no survivors, and Morley Wheeler's friend was buried in the Portsmouth Evergreen Memorial Park, Virginia.

On 12 July HMS *Ravager* sailed in convoy for the United Kingdom. Wheeler's experiences exemplify the immense emotional, physical, and mental strains placed on aircrew and ships' crews by the process of training. Preparing to fight could be almost as dangerous as actual combat. To take to the air after two crashes and the death of a classmate required the kind of uncelebrated courage that was demanded of allied aircrew, day-in and day-out, during training as well as on operations against the enemy.

Of course, there was also a humorous side to training, and there were always other attractions. When he arrived at USNAS Squantum as senior pilot for the new 856 Avenger Squadron, David Foster was delighted to find that he could live off base. He quickly picked up a second-hand Packard sedan for two hundred dollars. On one excursion into a suburb south of Boston, the car suffered a blow out, and they returned to the base by taxi. Unfortunately, the next morning they could not remember the car's precise location. Undaunted, Foster organised the flying schedule of 856 Squadron to make his car the object of a search exercise. The vehicle was duly found, repaired, and later sold to someone from another squadron which was forming up at Squantum. The training of 856 Squadron also featured navigational exercises, anti-submarine attacks, glide bombing and, on one occasion, testing the blackout of Boston.

In April 1944 the USS *Charger* was again used for the real deck landings, which had been practised a hundred times before. Again, the process passed off without serious incident, but flying back to Squantum from USNAS Cape May, New Jersey, the squadron received a report that heavy weather was blanketing New England. Rather than return to Cape May, the squadron chose to put down at a small airfield that they had noticed as they had flown over Atlantic City. On arrival, the crews of the six aircraft were greeted by police cars and the mayor, who explained that the field had been closed for some time as it was considered too small for normal use.[42] Normal use, however, did not cover a squadron trained to land on the deck of an aircraft carrier. Given the hospitality of the city, 856 Squadron returned to Squantum and, after further training, they embarked on the Brooklyn-built escort carrier HMS *Smiter* on 1 June 1944.

An important part of the process of squadron formation involved getting to know and work with other members of the squadron and, in the case of Avengers, other members of the crew of the aircraft. The commanding officer of 857 Avenger Squadron, formed at Squantum in early 1944, was Lieutenant-Commander W. 'Doc' Stuart. He insisted on personally checking the flying abilities of his pilots, such as Frank Stovin-Bradford. Meanwhile, Stovin-Bradford had to establish an effective working relationship with his observer, Sub-Lieutenant Clem Spearman, and TAG, Leading Airman Peter Slight.[43] On that relationship, and luck, would hinge the fate of all three. Working up time in the United States was invaluable for this kind of team-building.

Exceptional Visits to the United States

In addition to the formation or re-equipment of Fleet Air Arm squadrons, the facilities which had been developed in the United States for operating the Towers scheme also had to support unanticipated events. In late 1941 the aircraft carrier HMS *Indomitable* ran aground in the West Indies. Originally scheduled to form, with HMS *Prince of Wales* and HMS *Repulse*, part of the ill-fated Force Z based on Singapore, the *Indomitable*, was forced to head for Norfolk, Virginia, for extensive repairs in an American yard under the Lend-Lease scheme. Her aircraft flew off to the Naval Air Station at Norfolk to join the fledgling Fleet Air Arm establishment at that base. The cultural differences to which the Americans and the British aviation cadets in training had to adjust were one thing: those encountered between operational Fleet Air Arm aircrew and their Virginian hosts in a United States still at peace were quite another. Although the sojourn of HMS *Indomitable's* squadrons lasted less than two weeks, the visit invariably loomed large in the memories of the aircrew involved. Hector Mackenzie, an observer from 827 Squadron, who had just finished training in the West Indies, devotes an entire chapter of his memoirs to his short stay at Norfolk.[44]

As the *Indomitable* steamed towards the coast of Virginia, aircrew and sailors were briefed to behave with appropriate discipline and respect. On shore, Mackenzie found that Southern hospitality was limitless. He and his colleagues entered one diner in search of a cup of tea and were served by a young woman:

> 'Good afternoon, gennelmen. What would you all require?' Taken aback, we asked limply whether they had afternoon tea. 'Just a minute, gennelmen, I'll enquier for you all.' Few minutes later, back she came and intoned: 'I'm sorry gennelmen, we have India tea, we have China tea, but we jus'don't have affernoon tea', so we asked what could we get for a dollar? 'Well, seeing as yo'all are visitors an' we can't do your affernoon tea, we will serve any choice you'all care to make off the card.'[45]

Mackenzie found the United States Navy similarly accommodating to the needs of the crews of HMS *Indomitable* and HMS *Formidable*, another British aircraft carrier undergoing repair in a Chesapeake Bay yard after sustaining battle damage in the Mediterranean. The crews of the two aircraft carriers put on an exhibition of rugby in Hampton at the behest of the American Legion. The appreciative audience, more used to the heavily padded players and frequent interruptions to play in gridiron football, were astonished by the frenetic, non-stop and body-armour-free world of rugby.

However, for the aircrew of HMS *Indomitable*, memories of life in Virginia were not all pleasant. Hector Mackenzie found the attitude of white Americans towards African-Americans very disturbing:

The dreadful shock ashore was Negro segregation; buses, seats in the park, even on the cross-harbour ferry, they were not allowed where the whites went. They were treated like dirt all round, and slunk around the streets as though trying not to be there. By the time we had enough of America (about the second day!) we took to crossing the harbour in the Negro compound on the stern of the ferry, but it does not do to protest in other people's countries. The Negroes crouched away from us, embarrassed; the whites shouted out, 'That's where the Limey Officers belong!'[46]

Some Virginians taunted the British sailors about the success of the Germans or about the fact that some Fleet Air Arm aircraft, like the Fairey Albacore bi-plane torpedo bomber in which Mackenzie flew, appeared quaint by comparison with modern American types. In the bars, fights were plentiful to the point where ordinary ratings were under instruction not to go out in groups of less than six. According to one report, it culminated with the arrest of one British sailor for murder.

Even with the United States Navy, Fleet Air Arm aircrew from the *Indomitable* experienced a number of difficulties created by cultural differences between the two services. On the first time of landing in the USA, *Indomitable*'s pilots reacted with glee to the sight of the long, concrete runways at USNAS Norfolk, instead of the narrow strip of heaving metal deck to which they were accustomed. The aircraft landed in formation and so close together that it seemed as if there 'were eight and ten aircraft on the duty runway at the same time'.[47] Circuit discipline, on which the United States Navy insisted for safety reasons, disintegrated entirely to the astonishment of the American personnel in the control tower.

The facilities enjoyed by the British pilots consisted of some fairly basic Nissen huts, but the US Navy went out of its way to be hospitable. This did not stop some unfortunate incidents. One American-piloted Wildcat ran into a line of Fairey Fulmars causing much damage, and one of the fighter pilots of 880 Squadron was carpeted over his unorthodox approach to radio procedure. On landing, the offending pilot received a telephone call:

'Commander were you in the air just now?'
'I was, yes, why?'
'Were you using obscene language over the Radio Telephone? . . .'
'I may have had to swear at my bloody-fool pilots once or twice, why, were you listening?'

'I wasn't . . . but the wives and families of half the fliers on the station were listening. It is their practice to tune in to the various squadron channels on short wave.'
'Well what do they expect. This is a fighter-squadron, not a girls' school.'
'But commander, you don't understand. Language like yours has never been heard over the RT before. They were horrified. My telephone hasn't stopped ringing in half an hour.'
'Tell 'em not to listen.'[48]

While those aircrew who had undergone their flight training under the Towers scheme were perfectly well aware of the differences between British and American culture by the time they began operational training, some of the senior British-trained pilots who would lead the new squadrons found America a strange and wondrous land. Fleet Air Arm sailors who found themselves in the United States for a matter of days or weeks were less willing to fit in with the local customs than the Towers trainees, who could expect to remain in the USA for months.

In one of the truisms of the Cold War, for the United States after 1945 Britain represented an unsinkable aircraft carrier off the shores of Europe. In Britain's global strategy from 1941 to 1945, the United States filled a role as one of the principal bases of the Royal Navy – a foreign and, in some respects, more important version of Plymouth or Portsmouth. Training and working-up of ships and aircraft took place there; re-supply, re-fitting, recreational and recuperation facilities were available; and, for the Fleet Air Arm and the RAF's Coastal Command, the Towers scheme meant a steadily growing pool of trained airmen. By the time advanced training and squadron working up were completed, pilots and other aircrew were ready to be deployed in theatres of operation from the Atlantic to the Pacific, and from the Arctic to the Mediterranean. How they would eventually perform in combat was the crucial test of the American production lines turning out aircrew, aircraft and ships.

8

WAR SERVICE AND POST-WAR LIFE

After successful completion of their flight training, many RAF pilots found that actually getting into combat could be a discouragingly slow process. For the majority, the general reconnaissance course at Prince Edward Island in Canada still had to be completed. Typically, this would be followed by a lengthy voyage home, a posting to an operational conversion unit and then, finally, a posting to a front-line squadron. At every stage, Towers-trained RAF pilots found a degree of prejudice against aircrew who had been trained by the navy of a foreign power. Yet most of the airmen who had experienced it would have agreed with Royal Air Force student Trevor Ford's verdict that, overall, the training had been 'meticulous'. Nevertheless, Ford was one of the many Towers-trained cadets to discover, on his return to the United Kingdom, that the Royal Air Force 'top brass . . . preferred RAF-trained (or Commonwealth-trained) pilots'. As he had done multi-engine training on flying boats, it was suspected that Ford might lack the necessary skill and experience to handle land-based twin-engine aircraft. When he reported for duty at No. 79 Operational Training Unit the authorities there refused to accept him for training on Blenheims and Beaufighters.

Simply getting home was itself often a struggle. David Banton's experience was typical. He was in the third RAF class at Grosse Ile and Pensacola from September 1941. After completing training in March 1942, he was 'posted to No. 31 General Reconnaissance School, Charlottetown, Prince Edward Island, Canada, for 47 hours of navigation training on Anson aircraft during July and August 1942.' After that, he embarked at Halifax aboard the *Athlone Castle*, bound for Liverpool. J. H. Ashley, of the tenth RAF class at Grosse Ile and Pensacola, had a similar experience after completing flight training in January 1943:

> After . . . spending a few days leave in New Orleans, we travelled by train to No. 1 Manning Depot, Toronto, for kitting out in officers' uniforms, and a couple of days leave in that city. We then spent nearly a month waiting in 31 Personnel Depot, Moncton, for a posting. On 27 February we went to No. 31 G.R.S., Charlottetown, Prince Edward Island, for a two-month advanced navigation course on Avro Anson twin-engine land planes. We flew some 40 hours on complicated navigational trips out into the Atlantic. It was a very thorough and interesting course intended for aircrews destined to serve in Coastal Command, where long flights over the sea were their usual occupation. After yet another month in Moncton, we sailed home in the *Pasteur*, arriving at the Harrogate Reception Centre on 4 June 1943.

The journey home for many of the Catalina pilots was more exciting. The route home lay through Elizabeth City, North Carolina. Elizabeth City, on the Atlantic coast, was a modification centre for flying boats bound for British and Russian service. It was conveniently located for landing areas in Bermuda and the Bahamas, and it was approximately half way between Montreal and Miami. Frank Robinson, a member of the first Towers cohort in July 1941, completed flying training at Pensacola in March 1942 and began the long return journey to the United Kingdom:

> Via a wild and memorable weekend in New York, I was sent . . . to Elizabeth City, North Carolina on 3 April to join Captain R.M. Lloyd's ferry crew . . . We picked up a PBY-5 and flew it to Bermuda on 5 April. Extra tankage was fitted in the fuselage, and I flew an air test with Captain Hunt, RAF Ferry Command, on 7 April. After further air tests and fuel consumption test flights, we set off on 13th April for the Atlantic Crossing, alighting at Greenock, Scotland, after 22½ hours of uneventful flying.

Kenneth R. Blevins, of the third Towers cohort, was to return home by the slower surface route:

> At Dorval Airport, we were told that we would have to hang around for several weeks, as we would be flying back as crew members on a

Trans-Atlantic Ferry aircraft (Catalina). In the event, it didn't work out, so we came back by sea (in my case on the newish and fast cruise liner, the *Dominion Monarch*), but not before having a fantastic time in Montreal. We were still poor; our issue flying kit was mostly in hock at 'Uncle's' opposite the CNR railway station!

John R. Revill, who graduated in 1942, spent more time than most on the Catalina run out of Elizabeth City. He became a North Atlantic ferry pilot with 45 Group and, during the course of the war, he would ferry Catalinas, Dakotas and Liberators across the Atlantic. His first flight to Britain was by the northern route from North Carolina via Dorval Airport, Montreal, to Gander, Newfoundland, a refuelling stop at Lough Erne, Northern Ireland, then direct to Largs Bay, Prestwick, Scotland:

I probably spent longer than any of my contemporaries in North America/Canada – well over 2 years... Those years really set me up for a career in aviation, which I still lecture on to various local bodies. My clearest memories are the time we spent in the Hotel Virginia Dare in Elizabeth City and my trip with American friends on a 'pilgrimage' to Kitty Hawk – the Wright Brothers Memorial. I remember also a less happy event when, as a [sergeant] co-pilot staying with two other NCO aircrew, all sharing one room in a hotel on the Main Street (near the War Memorial), a New Zealand lad was shot in the leg (by accident), the bullet missing me asleep by inches.

Elizabeth City was the USN base where we 'staged' from before ferrying the 'Cats' anywhere. It was also where we met the Russian crews. USN instructors gave the Ruskies their initial training & check flights before we arrived. None were very impressed, we soon learned. The northern or summer route to Russia was Elizabeth City to Gander Lake, Newfoundland, Keflavik, Iceland, [and] Murmansk, and took some 23 hours airborne. The winter route to the Soviet Union was Elizabeth City to Puerto Rico, Belem (Brazil), Bathurst (Gambia, then British West Africa), Port Lyautey (Morocco), Sicily, Great Bitter Lakes (ex-British Imperial Airways boat base, Egypt), Habbaniyah (RAF base, Iraq, near Baghdad) and Baku on the Caspian Sea.

Bermuda was used as a permanent wartime RAF Ferry Staging base for, I believe, Catalinas only on Darrel's Island. We used to stage there from Elizabeth City to the UK in winter. The most beautiful place on earth, I think. I was there when my commission to Pilot Officer came through on my first command – some party – September 1943. The Russians never went there, and it was not an OTU – nothing but 'Cats' – they were building the runway on the eastern side then, I think.

Working with the Russians was a particularly hazardous aspect of life as a ferry pilot out of Elizabeth City. Royal Canadian Air Force pilot, and later famous entertainer, Hughie Green was another who regularly worked alongside the Russians on the Catalina run:

> On one occasion I allowed a Russian captain flying with me to land a Catalina in the vast area of water available at the US Navy base at Argentia, Newfoundland. He followed his senior officer, [who was] in the flying boat in front of us, into the roughest bit of water in the bay, in an attempt to land exactly where his superior had put his plane down. Not crediting what I was about to see, I watched with amazement. My pilot bounced his aeroplane, hit a wave, making the giant plane – after I quickly applied full power – bounce over the top of the one in front already in the water. Finally moored up, I staggered ashore, a somewhat shattered man, and took a bearing on the nearest US Navy bar and the largest Scotch in the house. I was intercepted half way by an American admiral. He grabbed me, shook my hand solemnly and said, 'Son, I've been flying and watching flying boats all my life – but that's the first time I've ever seen one of them play leap-frog.'[1]

Just like the pilots, Towers-trained WOp/AGs and navigators also experienced frustrating problems and delays in getting home and being posted to an operational squadron. Robert Kirkpatrick, who had passed the WOp/AG course at Jacksonville before going on to Pensacola in mid-1942 for the operational gunnery course on Catalinas, arrived back in Britain on 22 August. On arrival in Liverpool, he received fourteen days home leave before going to RAF Cranwell on 20 September for a Marconi radio course. Leaving there on 4 November 1942, he went to the No. 1 Air Gunnery School at Pembrey in South Wales. That course lasted from 22 November to 29 December. He was then sent on to the Victoria and Albert Museum in London for a radar course, which lasted a further three weeks. After some home leave and further courses, it was not until 2 November 1943 that he finally joined 203 Squadron flying Wellingtons in India. He would complete 565 flying hours (207 on operations) with 203

Squadron before the end of the war, but the wait to join a front line squadron had seemed interminable.

Robert Farrow, who had trained as a WOp/AG at Jacksonville and Pensacola before returning home in early 1943, faced similar delays before he reached an operational squadron. In the United Kingdom, he was first posted to No. 11 Radio School at RAF Hooton Park for operational radar training on Botha aircraft. In May 1943 he was sent to No. 10 Radio School at RAF Carew Cheriton for airborne radio operational training in Oxford aircraft. On completion of these courses and preparation for posting to an operational crew, he reported in July 1943 to RAF Thornaby, Yorkshire, for Coastal Command training on Halifax aircraft.

There he became a member of Flying Officer Dick Collishaw's crew, and in September 1943 they joined 58 Squadron, one of only two Halifax squadrons in Coastal Command at that time. From bases at RAF Holmesley South, near Bournemouth, and RAF St. David's, South Wales, 58 Squadron carried out anti-U-boat patrols and shipping strikes in the Bay of Biscay and along other areas of the French coast from Dieppe to Spain. Their aircraft were equipped with sonar to detect submerged U-boats, and they were armed with magnetic depth charges, which the crew called 'Creeping Jesus'.

Some RAF men who had trained under the Towers scheme were to find getting any kind of job as a pilot unexpectedly difficult. With the service starting to enjoy a surplus of pilots by 1944, the Royal Air Force could afford to be choosy over whom it allowed to fly its aircraft. When James Kerr left Pensacola in February 1944, having trained on flying boats, he fully expected to serve with Coastal Command. Instead, he found himself assigned as a glider pilot to the British Airborne Division operating in Burma. Kerr was not the only Towers graduate to suffer the indignity of training to fly powered aircraft, only to serve with the Glider Pilot Regiment.

Mark Gordon, who left Pensacola in September 1944, recalled what happened on his return to the United Kingdom:

> Along with about 150 other pilots, we were given a pep talk at Harrogate, where we were reminded that the Glider Pilot Regiment had been decimated at Arnhem, and that with basic military training, our flying experience would enable us to fill the gap. Needless to say, we had considerable reservations on the prospect, but at least it was something new and the alternative would in all probability have been redundancy as aircrew.

We stayed in the RAF, but were drafted to Glider Pilot Squadrons where we wore khaki with RAF insignia and pay! Before joining an operational squadron, I spent January 1945 at No. 21 Heavy Glider Conversion Unit at RAF Brize Norton, Oxfordshire, where I was introduced to Horsa and Hadrian gliders and accumulated 25 minutes day flying time on the Horsa and 20 minutes night flying plus 15 minutes day flying time on the Hadrian (all as second pilot).

There was no flying in February, and we moved on to an ORTU (which I can only guess was an Operational Refresher Training Unit) early in March, where I flew a Horsa (again as second pilot) for a further 30 minutes. In the middle of March I was posted to 'G' squadron of the Glider Pilot Regiment at Marching Green, near Dunmow, Essex. I linked up with one Staff Sergeant Miller, who had done Sicily, D-Day, and Arnhem, and became his second pilot. We were briefed for the Rhine Crossing (Operation Varsity) and, after 4 hours in the air on the morning of 24 March 1945, we landed our Horsa (complete with 25 members of the 12th Devonshire Regiment – infantry who had never been in the air before!) just outside Hamminkeln, NE of Wesel. We did hear some shots fired in anger, but there were no heroics – we believe American paratroopers had earlier been mistakenly dropped in our dropping zone, so things were probably a lot quieter than they might have been.

By the end of the war, Gordon had accumulated 225 hours on powered aircraft to become a fully-fledged pilot, plus a further 14.5 hours training to fly gliders, in order to spend 4 hours in the air on operations. That made 239.5 hours training in the air for 4 hours of actual combat flying.

Among the Towers-trained aircrew to see the most operational flying were the flying boat crews. *Winged Squadrons*, a wartime propaganda publication, gave an insight into their world and the pressures under which they operated:

> The Coastal Command pilots must keep constant watch on shipping and exercise enormous patience, for though the weather may cause them anxiety they seldom encounter much activity on their flights, and often it is difficult to make time pass. The pilots try to do so by eating a large number of sweets . . . Nearly all the flying is at a low level over the waves . . . Often in slow cumbersome land-craft, they go out over the Atlantic as far as their petrol can carry them, five or

six hundred miles at sea. Their missions take them over a flying area that includes the far-flung places of the globe. Since the beginning of the war these men have flown thirty-five million miles, twice the distance to the moon, over half way to the sun. If forced down they have little chance of survival . . . Night after night, day after day, these men have been responsible for tracking down, sinking, or even capturing submarines.[2]

The value of the flying boat missions was not limited to the sinking of enemy submarines. Continual harassment from the air limited the operational effectiveness of the U-boats, even when it did not lead to actual sinkings. The flying boat's capability for saving lives was also put to practical use from time to time. In May 1943 Frank Robinson, flying a Catalina out of Jui Creek, Sierra Leone, located two shipwrecked mariners over 700 miles from the coast and guided a vessel to their rescue. Days later, he landed on the sea to take on board eleven survivors from a ship which had been torpedoed by a U-boat. He would receive the Distinguished Flying Medal for his actions and finish his RAF career with 2,630 hours in his logbook.

Most Towers graduates in the Royal Air Force saw less operational flying than Robinson, and many would undoubtedly have sympathised with the story of J.C. Winandy, who graduated from Pensacola in June 1944. From 13 August he attended course after course while awaiting a posting to an operational training unit. Fearing that he would miss the war altogether, he volunteered for the Fleet Air Arm which, with the war in the Pacific still raging, seemed to offer better prospects for getting into combat. His transfer was completed in August 1945, only for the atom bombs on Hiroshima and Nagasaki to bring about the Japanese surrender. Like many other Towers graduates, he would continue flying after the war, first with the Fleet Air Arm and later with the Royal Air Force Volunteer Reserve. His post-war career lay as a cartographer with the Ordnance Survey. Looking back, he reflected that he would not have missed his time in the United States for the world. 'It taught me a lot about myself, since it was the toughest pilots course one could undertake. It gave me a great sense of achievement.'

As Winandy had suspected, Towers-trained Fleet Air Arm pilots tended to see action rather faster than their RAF counterparts, after being posted singly or in groups to ground stations or carrier squadrons. The Fleet Air Arm pilot cut a romantic but quirky figure. Cecil Beaton's *Winged Squadrons* provided a pen portrait for its readers:

There is a certain type of man who is equally attracted to the sea as to the air. He is to be found in the Fleet Air Arm. The flying sailors are disparagingly known as the 'Web Feet,' but their work has brought in more dividends of success with the passage of each month so that recently they have been sinking enemy ships at the rate of one a day. Their 'home station' is an aircraft carrier – their CO is the Captain. Their aircraft are naval aircraft, their uniforms a navy blue, the operations they perform are naval operations. At first these men may have been disappointed that their aircraft were slower than some types used in the RAF, but soon they realized that they are the most suitable for their particular and specialized job. These pilots must be proficient by day and by night in taking off on their reconnaissance duties, flying for hundreds of miles on an accurate course at a given speed, in order to land safely on the aircraft carrier. Their work consists of dropping depth charges, spotting and attacking submarines, shadowing the enemy without being seen themselves.[3]

In 1944 and 1945 the strength of the Fleet Air Arm, which America had done so much to build up through the Towers scheme and Lend-Lease, was demonstrated by major aircraft carrier actions. Operation Tungsten, on 3 April 1944, resulted in severe damage to the German battleship *Tirpitz*, which lay in Kaa fjord. The operation had begun as an idea in late 1943, after the *Tirpitz* had been subjected to an attack by midget submarines.

The Admiralty was aware that urgent repairs were being carried out on the huge battleship, which had been badly damaged in that attack. Sooner or later she would be seaworthy and ready to threaten the important allied convoys heading for north Russian ports. The Commander-in-Chief Home Fleet received a signal from the Admiralty in late January 1944: 'In view of the great importance of putting *Tirpitz* out of action, it is requested that you will plan to attack *Tirpitz* . . . with naval aircraft during the period of 7-16 March.'[4] The operation was later put back to early April. During March, Fleet Air Arm crews practised at Loch Eriboll, in Scotland, where a full-scale mock-up of the Norwegian fjord, including simulated anti-aircraft defences, was constructed. There they were able to rehearse their attack on the German battleship. The delay meant that two extra Corsair squadrons, 1834 and 1836, which joined HMS *Victorious* in February and early March, would also be available. In total, three different types of aircraft carrier and five different kinds of aircraft would be used in the attack.

The official report concluded that the operation was 'carried out according to plan'. Two bombing strikes were launched against the *Tirpitz*, while fighters strafed ground targets and protected the strike force against enemy aircraft. 'The number of hits was considerably greater than had been expected [and the losses] remarkably small.' In total, 40 Barracudas (827, 829, 830, 831 Squadrons) and 81 fighters, mostly Corsairs (1834 and 1836 Squadrons) and Hellcats (800 and 804 Squadrons), took part in the operation. Wildcats from 882 and 898 Squadrons supported the attack, and a combat air patrol over the fleet was provided by Seafires (801 and 880 Squadrons), Wildcats and 12 Swordfish from 842 Squadron.[5] The outcome of the operation was 14 confirmed hits on the *Tirpitz*, which was damaged but not disabled.

That was scarcely the fault of the Fleet Air Arm crews, who had pressed home their attacks with great skill and daring. Carrier aircraft could not launch really heavy bombs against their targets. The largest bomb dropped on the *Tirpitz* was only 1,600 lbs in weight. The damage done may not have been exceptionally heavy, but it was sufficient to keep her out of operations until 12 November 1944, when Lancaster four-engine bombers from 617 and 9 Squadrons of the RAF sent her to the bottom with five-ton bombs. Operation Tungsten, in keeping the *Tirpitz* quiet for a further six months, had an importance that few could guess at in April 1944. Perhaps more significantly, the operation showed that, thanks in part to American-built aircraft and American-trained pilots, the Fleet Air Arm was becoming a major force in naval warfare. It was now strong enough to contemplate the kind of large-scale carrier operations that had become an important feature of the war in the Pacific.

The Fleet Air Arm enjoyed a significantly enhanced status after Operation Tungsten. The ugly, flat-topped ships of the carrier force had not, hitherto, commanded the kind of public esteem which the carriers of the United States Navy enjoyed among the American public. The effectiveness of the carriers against the Tirpitz in 1944 produced something of a change. The dispatch of a Reuter's correspondent, who witnessed Operation Tungsten from HMS *Victorious*, caught the mood of the moment with his description of the homecoming of the force:

> The flagship and other ships of the Home Fleet cleared the lower decks, and gave three rousing cheers as the fleet carrier force that smashed the *Tirpitz* steamed line ahead into port. The carriers were

welcomed home with full honours. As we passed each ship, the officers and ratings lining the quarter decks, took off their caps and cheered, the sound reverberating across the blue waters. It was an inspiring sight, and, standing on the Admiral's bridge of the carrier, I felt very proud of being in such a ship. The sleek, green Barracudas that had done the job were lined up astern on the flight deck and up forward, and the blue-uniformed pilots, observers and gunners stood in line. The Fleet Air Arm boys are happy tonight, and they deserve to be.[6]

Now able to operate together as a separate striking force, rather than as single units providing an air umbrella for a combat group of surface ships, the carriers had come into their own. The Far East would be the venue for the next demonstration of the Fleet Air Arm's effectiveness, for which the Americans had paved the way with their Task Force system. The US Navy had elevated aircraft carriers to premier status, a role in which they had displaced the once omnipotent battleships.

Only sixteen days after the British Home Fleet's attack on the *Tirpitz*, the Eastern Fleet, based on Ceylon, also launched a carrier-borne air offensive. Aircraft from HMS *Illustrious* and the USS *Saratoga* attacked oil storage tanks, shipping and airfields at Sabang in northern Sumatra. It was the first operation in an offensive which grew rapidly in both scope and confidence.

The same carriers sailed in May from Exmouth Gulf, Western Australia, to destroy the oil refinery and former Dutch naval base at Soerabaya, east of Java. The subsequent departure of the *Saratoga* for the United States was offset by the arrival of the British aircraft carriers *Indomitable* and *Formidable*, allowing the Eastern Fleet to launch attacks on targets in the Andaman and Nicobar islands, and to make a second raid on the Japanese in Sabang. The fleet continued to operate aggressively until the end of the year.

Determined that the Royal Navy should play a part in the naval war in the Pacific Ocean, Churchill gave orders that most of the major warships of the Eastern Fleet should be transferred eastwards, via Australia, to form a British Pacific Fleet. Before leaving the Indian Ocean, however, they still had time to deliver further strikes on Japanese oil installations in the East Indies.

On 1 January 1945 the embryo British Pacific Fleet, including the carriers HMS *Illustrious* and HMS *Indomitable*, under Rear-Admiral Sir Philip Vian's command, sailed from Trincomalee, Ceylon, for operations off Sumatra. Operation Lentil was launched three days later. It was designed to interrupt fuel supplies to Japanese forces in the Pacific by attacking the oil refinery and installations at Pankalan Brandan, in northern Sumatra. The operation would involve flying long distances over water, jungle and a mountain range, testing crews and aircraft to the limit. Large numbers of enemy fighters could be expected. Thirty-two Avengers, each carrying four 500-pound bombs, and 16 Fairey Fireflies, armed with rockets, would carry the bulk of the offensive firepower. Twenty-four Hellcats and 24 Corsairs provided fighter cover for the fleet and support for the bomber force. The attack was pronounced a moderate success, and follow-up attacks on Japanese oil production in Sumatra were launched, code-named Operation Meridian One and Two.

This time, the *Indomitable* and *Illustrious* were joined by HMS *Indefatigable* and HMS *Victorious*, creating a British Task Force with four fleet carriers and 238 aircraft. On 24 January, in Operation Meridian One, the British force attacked the refinery at Pladjoe, and on 29 January, in Meridian Two, they struck the facility at Soengi Gerong. The latter attack involved 124 aircraft made up of:

12 Avengers from 857 Squadron,
12 Avengers from 849 Squadron,
12 Avengers from 854 Squadron,
12 Avengers from 820 Squadron,
24 Corsairs from 1830 and 1833 Squadrons,
24 Corsairs from 1834 and 1826 Squadrons,
16 Hellcats from 1839 and 1844 Squadrons,
12 Fireflies from 1770 Squadron.[7]

These operations in January 1945 were a testament to the Anglo-American co-operation embodied in the Towers scheme: American aircraft, American-trained pilots, and squadrons which had worked up in America predominated. The Fleet Air Arm component of the British fleet owed most of its strength to the productivity of American factories and the productivity of the Towers training scheme.

Sub-Lieutenant Frank Stovin-Bradford was one of the Towers-trained Avenger pilots who took part in Meridian Two. In December 1943 he had arrived at Fort Lauderdale to train on Avengers. He had joined 857 Squadron on HMS *Rajah* in April 1944, and the squadron embarked on HMS *Indomitable* in October. After take-off on 29 January, Stovin-Bradford's aircraft was attacked by enemy fighters and was also subjected to heavy anti-aircraft fire. He dropped his bombs at 3,000 feet over the target, before heading for the fleet. By this stage, his aircraft was a flying wreck. The airframe was holed in several places, the throttle was jammed, aileron control was irregular. The port wheel had been removed by an anti-aircraft shell, leaving a hole in the wing and the port oleo leg dangling uselessly below the aircraft. By a remarkable feat of flying, he was able to get back to the fleet. While slowly losing height, Stovin-Bradford used the controls that did work to compensate for those that did not, before successfully ditching in the sea. He and the other members of his crew were rescued by HMS *Wessex*. As Stovin-Bradford later reflected, during his desperate flight back to the fleet 'the early training . . . came into its own. We were still alive, and staggered along wobbly-mannered until the sea appeared beneath us, and we stayed on that course.'[8]

The results of Meridian One and Two were impressive. The output of the first refinery attacked was halved, and the output of the second refinery, the one that Stovin-Bradford had attacked, was halted completely. During a total of four strikes against the Japanese-controlled refineries, the Fleet Air Arm lost 41 aircraft. The Japanese captured at least nine of the shot-down airmen on or near Sumatra. Taken to prisons located in Singapore and in China, these Fleet Air Arm prisoners of war were executed by the Japanese in August 1945.

The departure of the large fleet carriers to the Pacific did not mark the end of the Fleet Air Arm's role in the Indian Ocean. The existing force of three small escort carriers, which remained in the Indian Ocean, had tripled by May 1945. They formed the 21st Aircraft Carrier Squadron, with nine escort carriers, all built in the United States. Their crews operated a mixture of British Seafire fighters with American Avengers and Hellcats. In addition to general reconnaissance and providing air cover for the Eastern Fleet, they also participated in a series of offensive operations in support of the army in Burma. They provided air cover for landings on Ramree and Cheduba Islands and the eventual reoccupation of Rangoon. They attacked Japanese positions in northern Sumatra and in the Andaman and Nicobar Islands. Finally, in preparation for the seaborne invasion of Malaya, which was being planned by South East Asia Command, special photographic reconnaissance Hellcats of 888 Squadron carried out a complete survey of the Kra Isthmus, Penang, and the whole length of the Malacca Straits as far south as Singapore.

Meanwhile, the large fleet aircraft carriers had arrived in the Pacific, where the British Fleet was based on Manus. It operated as a task force under the orders if the American commander-in-chief. In April and May

1945 the aircraft carriers attacked Japanese airfields in the Sakishima Gunto, southwest of Okinawa, and in northern Formosa. During these operations the Fleet Air Arm flew more than 5,000 sorties and lost over 150 aircraft. In June attacks were made on the Japanese base at Truk, in the Caroline Islands, and by July the British aircraft carriers were mounting air strikes on the Japanese mainland.

While serving in the Pacific, the British aircraft carriers *Indefatigable*, *Formidable*, *Victorious* and *Indomitable* were all hit by Japanese kamikaze aircraft, but their armoured flight decks proved very effective in limiting the extent of the damage, and they were all able to continue operating.

In August, as the British carrier aircraft were attacking targets on the Japanese island of Honshu, the war ended with dramatic suddenness, when the enemy surrender was precipitated by the terrible destruction of the atomic bomb attacks on Hiroshima and Nagasaki. When the formal surrender was signed on board the USS *Missouri* in Tokyo Bay on 2 September, the presence of the British aircraft carrier *Indefatigable* was a poignant symbol of the contribution which British naval aviation had made to final victory. It was in the Tokyo area, on 15 August, that aircraft from the *Indefatigable* had scored the final air victory of the war by shooting down nine Japanese fighters for the loss of one Seafire and one Avenger.

With the end of the war, surviving aircrew who had trained under the Towers scheme came to a crossroads in their careers. While the majority would return to civilian life, many would remain in the services. In the 1980s, when Frank Robinson decided to compile a log of the British flight battalion at Pensacola from 1941 to 1945, he amassed a large amount of information from surviving Towers cadets. Using his personal experiences and the historical treasure trove which he had gathered, he attempted to draw some conclusions about the wartime and post-war careers of as many British Pensacola veterans as possible:

> A number of the contributors to this record became dedicated to careers in aviation and continued to fly after the war: 10% remained in the services, 10% went on to civil aviation and 5% did both. Thus, 25% made it a lifelong career and contributed in no small measure to the amazing series of revolutionary post-war developments in aviation. Even when their active flying careers ended, 25% retained their service connections for very many years in such fields as Air Traffic Control, the Air Training Corps, and the Trinity House service. Of the Fleet Air Arm pilots, 66% flew fighter planes; the remainder flew a variety of bomber, torpedo-bomber or

dive-bomber aircraft. Of the RAF pilots, 70% flew at least one flying boat operational tour in Coastal Command, or in Bomber Command, Ferry Command, Air Transport Command, or in research. The numbers of Towers scheme pilots trained for Royal Air Force service were twice as great as those trained for the Royal Navy's Fleet Air Arm. Collectively, the pilots of the two air services acquitted themselves with distinction, and 15% of the contributors were decorated for outstanding achievements . . . The number of pilots killed in action is difficult to determine, but it appears to me to have been not less than 7%.[9]

Robinson was undoubtedly wise to draw only the most tentative of conclusions about his findings. His sample was far from complete, being biased towards survivors, rather than casualties, and towards those who had maintained close links with their fellow trainees. However, it does afford some kind of overview of the post-training careers and lives of the men who trained under the Towers scheme. The scheme had given hundreds of men the necessary skills of pilots, navigators and gunners. It had also given them a love of flying that many would continue to indulge long after 1945. It had also given them a profound respect for the United States, and some would eventually settle over there. Several would marry American women. Commander Suthers, Senior British Naval Officer at NAS Bunker Hill, Indiana, would later explain: 'Marriage was not permitted. Any hint of such taking place meant termination of flight training and return to the UK. However, when training lessened at the end of the war, and just before my return to the UK, I discovered that three students had secretly married! Good luck to them!'

9

CONCLUSIONS

Naval aviation is a term which is often applied very narrowly to those aviation activities which are based on board ships or to land-based activities which are manned and controlled by a country's navy. A rather wider application would use the term to cover all aspects of aviation which make a contribution to winning command of the sea. That has been the strategic objective of navies for centuries and, in the 20th century, aircraft came to be seen as an inescapable element of sea power, irrespective of the service to which the men flying those aircraft belonged.

As early as 1919 an Admiralty committee set up to examine the lessons of the First World War heard evidence from a naval officer, Captain the Hon. A. Stopford, who speculated that a time would come when surface warships would be unable to operate in seas where an enemy could deploy large numbers of aircraft. He also expressed the view that a large part of the navy's functions might, at some future date, be exercised by aircraft of the Royal Air Force.[1] Other witnesses, such as Rear-Admiral Sir Walter Cowan and Lieutenant-Commander R.B. Davies VC, also spoke of the increasing significance of aviation, but in more measured terms. Stopford's views were not, at that time, shared by many experienced naval officers, but the debate about the future importance of aviation in relation to sea power was to rumble on until the Second World War. The debate was conducted at several different levels: within the Royal Navy, between seamen and airmen, inside the Committee for Imperial Defence, in the Press, and on the floor of the House of Commons, where there was no shortage of retired naval officers who could speak with some authority.

In 1936 one of those naval Members of Parliament, Admiral of the Fleet Sir Roger Keyes, wrote a foreword recommending a new book to 'all naval officers, who are striving to carry on the great traditions which our forefathers have handed down to us, and to the general public, whose very

CONCLUSIONS   149

existence depends upon the security of Great Britain's sea communications.'² The book's author, Commander John Cresswell (a well respected thinker on naval strategy), tried to reach a considered verdict on the unresolved aviation debate:

> If it could be shown that a fleet of aircraft can render a vital area of sea untenable by battleships and can at the same time exercise continuous control of all merchant shipping passing through that area . . . then it might well be that the battleship is doomed. At present (1936) there are so many unknown factors in this problem that one could discuss hypothetical cases *ad infinitum*. But when one bears in mind some of the factors that are known, the case for the aircraft becomes less attractive than at first sight. [After discussion of such questions as the limited endurance of aircraft, their inaccurate navigation, their relatively short radius of action, weather conditions and costs, he concluded:] When one takes all these matters into consideration, there seem strong grounds for believing that a fleet of battleships is a more effective basis for the control of sea communications than a force of aircraft embodying a similar or even a substantially greater proportion of national effort.³

A quarter of a century later, looking back to those pre-war days, Captain Stephen Roskill wrote: 'It now seems clear . . . that too much faith continued to be placed in the big gun as the principal arbiter of defeat or victory at sea, and too little imagination had been shown towards the potentialities of sea-borne aircraft.'⁴ For those errors of judgement Roskill suggested various explanations, including the 'prejudices' and 'conservatism' of the older school of naval officers, but he also criticised 'the excessive claims of the extreme enthusiasts for airborne weapons'. But when Roskill wrote 'It NOW seems clear . . .' he was emphasising that what had become clear by 1962 had been by no means clear in the mid-1930s.

The admirals who were in command of the Royal Navy at that time ought not to be pilloried as obscurantist, gold-braided, nautical Luddites, determined to cling on to their 'useless' old battleships under the pathetic delusion that they represented the final word in striking power at sea. They had no crystal ball enabling them to see into the future. They had to make their decisions on the evidence which existed in the 1930s. They were well aware of the proven worth of the big naval gun, mounted on ships already paid for and available for action whenever a new war might break out. Against that, they had to weigh the, as yet unproven, estimate of what air power would be able to achieve at some unspecified future date when aircraft and their weapons systems would have been transformed by advances in technology whose precise nature and timing were by no means certain. The admirals can hardly be blamed for being cautious. They would have been foolhardy if, in a period of mounting international tension, they had set about scrapping the battleships they had, in favour of an aviation-based policy which might not turn out to carry the same 'punch' for some years and might, in any case, be too expensive for the politicians and electorate to accept.

Even if the admirals of the 1930s had enjoyed access to a crystal ball, enabling them to see what lay in store over the next ten years, they would still have had to plan within the constraints imposed by the finances of a country impoverished by the costs of the First World War and the world economic crisis; they would still have been controlled by politicians who were hoping to avoid another war, either through the collective security of the League of Nations or by negotiating an accommodation with potential enemies; and they would still have been serving a democratic country whose voters showed no enthusiasm for expenditure on armaments until the aggressive intentions of the European dictators had become undeniable.

Critics may point to the fact that the aircraft carriers of the Royal Navy at that time were, in some respects, a rather elderly collection of adaptations and improvisations. The *Courageous, Glorious* and *Furious* had all been started as heavy cruisers in the middle of the First World War, and had been hastily converted into aircraft carriers. Even after expensive redesign and refitting in the 1920s, they would never amount to purpose-built aircraft carriers. The *Eagle* was another conversion. She had begun building as a battleship for the Chilean Navy in 1913, but the hull had been taken over by the Admiralty in 1917 and converted into an aircraft carrier, with further alterations in the 1920s. The *Argus* was basically a flight deck constructed on top of a hull originally intended to become the Italian passenger liner *Conte Rosso*. Only HMS *Hermes* could claim to have been purposely designed and built as an aircraft carrier. Begun in 1918, she had not been completed until 1923.[5]

If, with hindsight, those aircraft carriers might be judged as inadequate for the war which, in 1936, lay just three years ahead, it is instructive to look at the aircraft carrier strength of the other European naval powers. France had just one, the *Béarn* (another converted battleship hull of World War I vintage), while Germany and Italy, the most likely potential enemies, possessed no aircraft carriers at all. Further afield, the Japanese had four aircraft carriers in service and the United States Navy had five. Those figures do not support the charge that the Royal Navy had been uniquely neglectful in failing to build a more impressive fleet of carriers.

When British politicians at last found the money and the will to reinforce the fleet, in anticipation of a future war, the Royal Navy was able to begin building, in 1937, the five new battleships of the *King George V* class, armed with 14-inch guns. Their building should not be taken, however, as an indication that the Admiralty was oblivious of the importance of naval aviation. Having at last managed to regain control of its own aircraft and aircrew from the Air Ministry, the Royal Navy was fully prepared to invest in the Fleet Air Arm. In 1938 the new aircraft carrier *Ark Royal* was completed, and by then the building of four aircraft carriers of the *Illustrious* class had already begun. Two more – *Implacable* and *Indefatigable* – were started before war broke out in September 1939. In that same period, Germany, France, Japan and the United States were similarly building, or planning to build, both battleships and aircraft carriers.[6] Like their British contemporaries, the admirals of these other maritime powers were also unable to decide which type of vessel might play the decisive role in the conflict that was beginning to seem inevitable.

Even though the Royal Air Force was no longer responsible for the navy's fliers after 1937, in the last years of peace the RAF was still preparing to make an important contribution to naval aviation in the widest sense. Coastal Command had been set up in 1936. Its mainly land-based aircraft and flying boats were intended to support the work of the Royal Navy in the application of sea power. The contribution of Coastal Command was expected to lie mainly in reconnaissance and the protection of convoys in home waters, but it was always intended to develop an offensive capability against enemy vessels as soon as suitable aircraft, aircrew and weapons became available. The great handicap of Coastal Command, in those early days, lay in its inability to match the influence of Bomber Command and Fighter Command when decisions were made about priorities in developing and acquiring new types of aircraft.

At the outbreak of war, Coastal Command could muster only 17 squadrons. Four of them were flying such outdated aircraft as the 10-year-old Vildebeest torpedo-bomber or elderly flying boats such as the London and Stranraer. Ten squadrons were equipped with the Avro Anson, an aircraft of low speed, inadequately armed for its own defence, incapable of carrying bombs of more than 100 pounds, and with a range barely capable of spanning the North Sea. The only truly modern aircraft were two squadrons of British, four-engine Sunderland flying boats and a solitary squadron of Lockheed Hudsons, recently bought in the United States.[7]

Even before the outbreak of war, the Royal Air Force had shown interest in buying American aircraft. Coastal Command recognised that aircraft such as the Hudson, Catalina and Liberator could offer the longer endurance which was essential to operating far out over the sea. After the strategic reverses of 1940, when Germany's acquisition of submarine bases in western France enabled their U-boats to attack convoys in mid-Atlantic, Coastal Command's need for long-range aircraft and the men to fly them became acute. Hence the sense of relief and gratitude when the Lend-Lease programme allowed the RAF to tap into the enormous know how and productive capacity of the US aircraft industry. The eagerness of the British armed services to accept the United States Navy's offer to train aircrew under the Towers scheme was, however, far from being wholehearted or unanimous.

Throughout the war, the RAF fully recognised the value of American aircraft such as the Catalina and Liberator, especially when it came to providing air cover for convoys far out in the Atlantic Ocean, but there were serious reservations about the value of aircrew trained in America.

> The US Navy scheme of pilot training is akin to the mass production assembly line of manufacturers. There is no question of an all round training all the way through: each of the stages . . . is in turn divided into stages and the pupil learns and perfects one thing at a time. One disadvantage of the scheme is that, strangely, it makes for delays and not for speed. A cadet cannot be passed on to the next stage until he has completed the present one entirely, or he would be passing on with a serious deficiency in his training. For instance, four hours of night flying are done in the primary stage. They are the last four hours of the course. Bad weather at the end of the course delays the cadet for as long as it lasts, because four hours deficiency would mean total deficiency of night flying. Cadets have sometimes waited three weeks or more at Pensacola to put in the last one-hour's flying.[8]

As expressed by the Royal Air Force Delegation, Washington, in its 1943 paper on training under the Towers scheme, Anglo-American differences of approach remained acute, even in such comparatively new fields of human endeavour as aviation. The early models of the British Spitfire fighter, that saw service in the Battle of Britain, may have been mass-produced, but important parts of the aircraft were still hand-made and hand-finished. The Royal Air Force favoured craftsmanship over volume of production. Even after the demands of war forced an emphasis on the latter, a prejudice in favour of the former remained. The RAF's desire for craftsmanship over volume was also apparent in pilot training. In the First World War, the Americans observed British and French air training systems, and learned much from them. By 1940 the underlying principles of industrial mass production had been adapted and applied to the training of American aircrew.

There was nothing wrong with that, when serious shortages of pilots, instructors and aircraft had to be overcome. The urgent demands of war forced the Royal Air Force to make use of the training facilities generously offered by the President of the United States – and American training methods were an inescapable part of that 'package deal'. Nevertheless, the training of RAF aircrew in such an alien culture excited the passions and stirred up resentments within the Air Ministry and the RAF Delegation in Washington.

At the end of the First World War and in the years which followed, the Royal Air Force had fought a difficult political battle to become, and remain, a separate service. Being reduced to having its pilots trained by the United States Army Air Force and United States Navy touched long-standing sensitivities that were both military and political in origin. As a result, between 1941 and 1945 the Royal Air Force sometimes appeared ungrateful for the training facilities which were extended to it, particularly by the United States Navy. The emphasis on the strategic bomber offensive, which saw trained flying boat pilots, intended for service with Coastal Command, put to work on general reconnaissance duties in light bombers, added a further complicating factor to the RAF's estimation of the value of the scheme. In effect, the United States Navy trained pilots for one purpose, only to find a significant proportion of them forced into other roles. The Royal Air Force then saw fit to question, at least internally, the value of the training which those pilots had received.

Within the Admiralty, there was a great deal of disquiet about the fact that Towers-trained flying boat pilots were being diverted to other flying duties in this way. There was also resentment that Bomber Command received priority in terms of resources. On relinquishing his temporary appointment as Chief of Naval Air Services on 13 January 1943, Admiral Sir Fredric Dreyer reflected sombrely on his term of office since 11 July 1942:

> During my 6 months tenure of the post of Chief of Naval Air Services I have become more and more convinced that too much of our air effort is being expended in bombing Germany at the expense of the provision of air protection for convoys. While I fully agree with the War Cabinet's policy of bombing Germany, what I hold is that we should not also bomb Germany with the blood of the Merchant Navy.

The diversion of Towers-trained pilots from Coastal Command work was a symptom of a wider malaise in the Allied air effort, which Dreyer wished to highlight. Unfortunately, it was to little effect. With Churchill's backing, the policy of giving priority to Bomber Command would continue.

Despite the predations of Bomber Command, the Towers training scheme did eventually help RAF Coastal Command to develop into a potent striking force. 'It had been one of the ambitions of the Command to possess a striking force of torpedo bombers with which to attack German naval and merchant vessels. But every time that goal seemed to be within its reach . . . overseas demands [for Africa and the Far East] deferred the time when it would be able to exercise a decisive influence in this part of the war.'[9] By 1943 Coastal Command was in a position to fulfil its hopes of an onslaught against German merchant shipping from the air. That offensive, which increased steadily in intensity, has largely been forgotten. In all, some 365 'German or German-controlled vessels' were sunk by Coastal Command during the war.[10] These losses also meant lost cargoes and the diversion of some of the German navy's resources to the protection of their merchant shipping.

Sir Arthur Harris, Commander-in-Chief of Bomber Command from 1942, regarded the navy as an irrelevance, not deserving the share of human and industrial resources that it claimed to require. He considered that both the navy and the army were reactionary and hide-bound: 'The navy with its battleships – the most expensive and the most utterly useless weapons employed in the whole of the last war – provide the outstanding example of that parochial spirit which springs from the existence of separate services.'[11] The views of Harris and other senior RAF officers were coloured by the political realities of the inter-war period. Then the RAF's very existence often seemed in doubt, because the navy and the army were, for some years, favoured over the air force. Harris considered that, but for one or two determined defenders of Britain's military interests in the inter-war period, Britain would have been faced with an even bigger disaster in 1940:

If they [the reactionary and hide-bound forces in the navy and army] had succeeded, they would have abolished our air power as they succeeded in abolishing our tank power, while retaining the Camberley drag hunt, and as the pinnacle of our sea power, those scarcely more useful battleships whose bones now lie where air power so easily consigned them, littering the floors of the ocean or obstructing the harbours of the world.[12]

It was not surprising that Harris resisted and resented any diversion of effort from the bombing offensive against Germany, no matter how loudly the Admiralty pleaded or protested. Indeed, it would also be manifestly unfair to ignore the fact that Bomber Command was making its own contribution to ensure that the Allies retained command of the sea. The intense bombing campaign which eventually made Brest untenable as a base by the German battle-cruisers *Scharnhorst* and *Gneisenau*, the use of bombers to mine German waters and the U-boat training areas in the Baltic; and attacks on U-boat bases and building yards were directly concerned with the application of air power to sea power. The strategic bombing of Germany's oil installations, transport infrastructure and industrial centres was bound to have exerted an adverse effect on German shipbuilding and the flow of equipment and spare parts, even if only indirectly.

Like any armed service in any country in the world, Britain's Fleet Air Arm would have wished to go to war more generously supplied, better equipped, more numerous, faster, more destructive and with stronger reserves. Nevertheless, in the early stages of the war the Fleet Air Arm gave ample proof of its professional skill, courage and striking power. In the dark days of 1940, the sinking of the German cruiser *Königsberg* in Bergen harbour and the sinking of three Italian battleships in Taranto harbour provided convincing evidence of the Fleet Air Arm's offensive capability. In 1941 and 1942 the aircraft carriers proved their value in surface operations by ferrying fighter aircraft to Malta and helping to fight vital convoys through to that beleaguered island, even in the face of enemy air superiority in the central Mediterranean narrows.

On 28 March 1941 Fleet Air Arm aircraft from HMS *Formidable* were ordered to attack an Italian fleet withdrawing to the westward after a sortie towards Crete. They damaged the battleship *Vittorio Veneto* and stopped the heavy cruiser *Pola*. Those successes were the prelude to a night action known as the Battle of Matapan, in which the 15-inch guns of the pursuing British battleships *Warspite*, *Barham* and *Valiant* took only a few salvoes to reduce the Italian heavy cruisers *Zara* and *Fiume* to useless hulks. The attendant British destroyers were then able to sink both, plus their damaged sister ship *Pola* and two destroyers. At Matapan naval aircraft had filled one of the major roles envisaged by pre-war tacticians – slowing a fleeing enemy to enable the big ships to get into action.

Two months later, naval aviation played much the same role in helping to thwart the German battleship *Bismarck's* foray into the Atlantic. Located by a Catalina of Coastal Command, then damaged and slowed down by torpedoes from Swordfish aircraft flown from the carriers *Victorious* and *Ark Royal*, the tremendously powerful enemy battleship was finally battered to destruction by the big calibre guns of HM Ships *Rodney* and *King George V*. Perhaps more than any other naval engagements, the Battle of Matapan and the pursuit of the *Bismarck* showed the futility of the pre-war debate between the passionate advocates of air power and the equally passionate advocates of the traditional capital ship. Both were still needed for the effective exercise of sea power in the early 1940s.

The Fleet Air Arm's successes could not disguise the need for more aircraft carriers, more high-performance aircraft and more men trained in the very special skills required to fly them from the rolling and pitching decks of aircraft carriers in unpredictable weather conditions. The generous American Lend-Lease programme would, in time, provide the rugged, high performance aircraft. The United States Navy's Towers scheme would provide many of the trained pilots and other aircrew. Compared with the impressive numbers trained under the Commonwealth Air Training Plan, the Towers scheme provided only a small fraction of Britain's total aircrew requirements, but it made a particularly important contribution in the specialised field of naval aviation.

In many respects, the American training of Fleet Air Arm pilots was a double blessing: not only were they trained well, but their training overseas also removed a further potential bone of contention between the Royal Air Force and Royal Navy. While the RAF had concerns about the quality of pilots trained under the Towers scheme, the Fleet Air Arm had few qualms about the quality of the training that its pilots received at the hands of the United States Navy. In part this reflected the fact that, prior to the Towers scheme, Fleet Air Arm pilots had been trained outside the Royal Navy by the RAF. Thus, having the United States Navy, instead of the RAF, train its pilots did not upset the professional sensibilities of the Fleet Air Arm. Their satisfaction with the training provided by the United States Navy also reflected the fact that training for carrier-based warfare was the primary purpose of the USN's air training establishment. In many respects it was better to have Fleet Air Arm pilots trained by carrier specialists, especially where those specialists had recent combat experience of the war in the Pacific.

A good American carrier pilot was likely to make a better instructor for a future Fleet Air Arm carrier pilot than would an RAF instructor, used to flying land-based aircraft under European combat conditions. This was especially true as the Royal Navy increased its deployment in the Indian Ocean and Pacific in 1944-5 and as the various types of American aircraft, such as the Avenger and Corsair, in British service continued to grow. The Fleet Air Arm recognised that the United States Navy turned out good pilots, experienced in handling American aircraft. The wartime exploits of some Towers-trained pilots and the continuing involvement of many of them in aviation after the war should remove any lingering doubts about the effectiveness of the training.

Despite the impressive success of the Towers scheme, it could sometimes make mistakes in its over-hasty assessment of individual student pilots. Take, for example, the case of Fleet Air Arm pilot Douglas Williams. He eventually qualified in 1942 at Kingston, Ontario, as an 'above average' pilot. During 1942 and 1943 he gained experience on an unusually large number of aircraft types, including Swordfish, Helldiver, Roc, Skua – even Lancasters, courtesy of some unofficial hours flying with 100 Squadron RAF. In April 1944 he joined 828 Squadron flying Fireflies in their role as night fighters. Considerable ability and a wide diversity of experience were the hallmarks of his wartime career. And yet, this was a man who had washed out of the first Towers draft in 1941. A little bad luck and the rigidity of a system by which trainees were allowed only a set number of hours to master the different elements of training were his undoing. As a result, he had found himself dismissed from the course and dispatched to the 'legion of the lost' at Moncton to await a fate which might have seen his flying career permanently terminated. Training pilots by methods of mass production was perhaps inevitable in the circumstances of war, but the Towers system – just like every other wartime system – was not particularly efficient in making allowances for individual differences between students. On 24 August 1944, flying Barracuda MD675, Douglas Williams took part in Operation Tungsten against the *Tirpitz*.

For the United States Navy, the Towers scheme turned out to be a considerable burden. The rapid expansion of the US Navy's air training establishment had been as uneasy as it was rapid. The passing of the Naval Aviation Cadet Act in 1935, as part of the New Deal, began the process of developing the training base of the United States Navy. Prior to the Act, to train as a naval aviator meant first passing through the Naval Academy at Annapolis and then serving two years at sea. Under the Naval Aviation Cadet Act trainee pilots were given 800 hours of ground and flight school before graduating.[13] They would then serve two years at sea before being commissioned as ensigns.

With the approach of war the training programme was speeded up, reducing the training period from twelve to six months under the 1938 Naval Aviation Cadet Act. In that same year the Hepburn Board recommended that Pensacola's training facilities should be supplemented by the development of new Naval Air Stations to handle the expected demand for trained naval aircrew. The opening of new facilities at Jacksonville in December 1940 and Corpus Christi in March 1941 followed.[14] With the outbreak of war, and the gradual slide by the United States from strict neutrality to pro-British non-belligerency, the programme continued to evolve, and the Towers scheme became part of it. After Pearl Harbour the programme was put under intense strain to meet the United States Navy's requirements for pilots. In a paper on naval aviation training, prepared in 1945 by the US Navy's Historical Unit, there was a great deal of satisfaction about what had been achieved: 'It may be conservatively stated that, in the 5-year period just completed, the expansion of naval aviation has been equal to or greater than that of the previous 15-year period . . . During the current year we have embarked on an expansion program undreamed of even at the beginning of the year.'[15]

In 1942 the US Navy was forced into a complete reorganisation of its training establishments. Primary training was transferred to the Naval Reserve aviation bases, while Pensacola and Corpus Christi becoming centres for intermediate training. On 30 October 1942 the Air Operational Training Command was established to oversee the expanding network of bases and schools. It would have to find solutions, albeit imperfect ones, to shortages of instructors and aircraft and, after 1941, the navy's inability to guarantee adequate time at sea for trainee aircrew. The best student pilots were retained to act as instructors, and aviation cadets were rarely taught by the same instructor. Instructors were rotated to ensure that all cadets received an equivalent standard of instruction through a mix of the teachers of all abilities. Many British trainees were unhappy with the system but, in the circumstances, it represented a sensible solution to the fundamental problem of variations in the quality of the instructors who could be provided. The Bureau of Aeronautics pioneered new methods of teaching and learning to raise standards in training. After 1941 heavy use was made of visual teaching materials. Films and slide shows would be accompanied by student discussions prompted by a 'set of questions . . . furnished for the use of the instructor'.[16]

While there was a pressing need to ensure that pilots were exposed to the most up-to-date aircraft available, obsolescent types were retained in training long after reliability problems should have meant their withdrawal. The Great Depression, which had followed on the heels of the Wall Street Crash of 1929, meant that in 1940 American industry, including its aviation sector, had a hard job keeping pace with the increased demands of wartime. With production for front-line units very properly given priority, the US Navy had to fight hard to modernise its fleet of training aircraft. Before 7 December 1941 it also faced the added difficulty that British Flying Training Schools in the United States received priority in the allocation of new aircraft. An internal memorandum of 1941 complained: 'The British have the most modern ships in their schools. The Army provides their schools with new airplanes; this is true even in the civilian schools which are training army mechanics.'[17] The United States Navy and Army Air Corps suffered to support the expansion of British pilot training in the USA, and to provide them with the necessary combat aircraft.

At times the shortage of aircraft for training and combat threatened to sour relations between the British and American navies, if not their governments. The demand for Catalina flying boats constantly outstripped supply, and in October 1941 the United States Navy was outraged when the British asked that their allocation of F4 Corsair fighters should be increased from 147 to 260, out of a total production run of only 443 up to 30 June 1942. The United States Navy objected to the British request because, as was explained in a memo of 10 October 1941, 'their own carriers do not have sufficient complement of fighting craft now, whereas they feel that the British may be trying to build up a reserve'.[18] Desperate politicking over the provision of combat aircraft meant that sometimes there were few to spare for the training programme.

The struggle to give Britain the aircraft it needed for training and combat was about production just as much as it was about politics. The price of providing Britain with what it needed in terms of aircrew and aircraft was considerable, and it involved an enormous effort on the part of the Roosevelt administration. In May 1942 statistician Isador Lubin wrote to Harry Hopkins, federal administrator and President Roosevelt's right hand man on Lend-Lease, to express his exasperation at the slow expansion of aircraft production:

Approximately six months ago Lord Halifax dedicated the first 'Vengeance' dive-bomber for the British. The second is still to be delivered. It is beside the point whether shortages of material, lack of skilled workers, lack of equipment or improperly designed parts have caused the delays. The important thing is that when a veritable swarm of dive-bombers are needed in a dozen different areas we find a huge, well-equipped plant and some 4,000 workers contributing practically nothing to the war effort.[19]

Situations like that at the Vultee plant in Nashville, Tennessee, called for speedy action on the part of administrators like Hopkins. There were few better at finding solutions to problems, however, than the members of an administration who had spent most of the previous decade improvising answers to the depression. The American aviation industry was able to expand massively during the war. Aided by increased production, the United States Navy slowly won its battle to get newer aircraft into the training programme.

The impressive ability of American industry to respond to the urgent demands of war was also shown in the speedy building of small, cheap, escort carriers. From 1939 the Royal Navy had been steadily losing aircraft carriers to enemy action. The *Courageous* had been torpedoed when the war was only a fortnight old, and the *Glorious* was sunk by enemy surface action in 1940. The *Ark Royal* was torpedoed near Gibraltar in 1941, and in 1942 the *Eagle* was also torpedoed in the Mediterranean. The *Hermes* was sunk by Japanese aircraft in 1942. As the new carriers of the *Illustrious* class, ordered before the outbreak of war, came into service in 1940 and 1941, they merely represented the replacement of losses, rather than a significant increase in numbers. Yet the drastically changed strategic situation called for naval aviation to be available in more and more far-flung locations.

Germany's control of the European coastline from the North Cape in Norway to the Franco-Spanish frontier on the Bay of Biscay posed a threat from the air to British shipping over a wide arc of the Atlantic. Britain was driven to adopt the desperate expedient of mounting aircraft catapults on the bows of merchant ships to enable a single fighter to be launched in defence of a convoy. Except in rare instances of land being close by, the launch involved a strictly one-way trip, which would end with the loss of the aircraft, while the pilot could do no more than hope to be rescued after either 'ditching' his aircraft or parachuting into the sea. For both the Admiralty and the pilots there was much to be said in favour of improvising small aircraft carriers by constructing flight decks on basic merchant ship hulls. The handful which were built in Britain showed promise in the dual role of providing some fighter protection for convoys and flying standing patrols to compel shadowing U-boats to submerge and lose their speed advantage over the slow-moving merchantmen.

British shipyards were already fully occupied in building other types of vessel, including a new generation of seven light fleet aircraft carriers of the *Colossus* class. There was no possibility that they could find the spare capacity to build escort carriers in the numbers required, but shipyards in the United States could supply them very quickly under the Lend-Lease scheme. In combination with very long range aircraft of Coastal Command, the escort carriers ensured that, in the closing stages of the war, no U-boat could feel safe from aerial attack whenever it approached a convoy, even in mid-ocean. The importance of providing air cover for convoys may be illustrated by the casualties inflicted on German U-boats attempting to attack convoys to north Russian ports. Between 1942 and the end of the war in Europe, thirty-one U-boats were sunk in those circumstances. Nine of them were sunk by aircraft flying from escort carriers, a further six were sunk by a combination of surface escorts and carrier-borne aircraft, and three were sunk by Catalina aircraft of Coastal Command's 210 Squadron.[20]

The same story was repeated across the whole Battle of the Atlantic, following the critical convoy battles of March 1943. The balance had shifted dramatically against the U-boats. The German Naval High Command was driven by the mounting toll of U-boat losses to analyse the problems facing them out in the Atlantic. In such a complex, protracted and wide-ranging battle, no single explanation could be identified. More allied escort vessels, improved detection systems and new anti-submarine weapons all put the U-boats at a disadvantage, but the writers of the report had no hesitation in identifying the major problem: 'The enemy's air force can now provide air-cover for convoys over almost the whole area of the North Atlantic, and we must expect that before long the remaining gaps will be closed by land-based aircraft or by the use of auxiliary aircraft carriers.'[21]

By the summer of 1943 the German submarine offensive was in a state of collapse. The German Naval High Command needed to regroup and re-equip its forces. That would take two directions, with the imperative being to minimise the aerial threat to U-boats by ensuring that they could remain submerged for longer. Grand Admiral Dönitz later explained his priorities:

First to produce as quickly as possible a new U-boat with as much manoeuvrability when submerged as U-boats had, up until now, possessed on the surface. Second, until production of these new boats, to make all possible alterations to the existing U-boats so that in spite of the enemy's radar and superior air power they might be as effective as possible.[22]

A new generation of U-boats with high underwater speed would not be ready to enter service until the last days of the war. Developments such as the schnorkel would bring some relief to the hard-pressed crews of traditional U-boats, but there was one salient fact that could not be ignored: Allied maritime power, in its many manifestations, had broken the back of the German submarine offensive, although the struggle would continue until May 1945. A submerged submarine had a very limited capacity to locate allied convoys, shadow them and launch effective attacks. Without the improved security of the convoy routes, the build-up of men and material in preparation for the invasion of Europe would have entailed appalling losses, and D-Day could not have been launched on 6 June 1944. The training and equipping of British Fleet Air Arm and Coastal Command squadrons was among the many pre-requisites to the liberation of Western Europe. The aircrew turned out under the Towers scheme and the aircraft and escort carriers built by American industry combined to deadly effect, causing the deaths of thousands of German submariners.

The final stages of the war saw significant changes in the Royal Navy's thinking about the role of naval aviation in the application of sea power. During the First World War, the Royal Naval Air Service had been pioneers in the use of aircraft at sea, but the inter-war years brought little in the way of fundamental reappraisal of aviation's role. The blame for that omission has often been placed on the Air Ministry. For example, in 1943 there was a suggestion that the separate air elements of the United States should be combined into a single force. The US Navy countered by producing a report examining the British experience.[23] Claiming that the Fleet Air Arm's problems early in the war had been a direct result of the domination of air policy by the Air Ministry and the RAF, the report argued that the United States Government should not make the same mistake.

In 1939 the Royal Navy expected the aircraft carriers to play a distinctly secondary, and supportive role to the work of the battleships. The Fleet Air Arm was to locate and attack enemy vessels at sea, provide air cover for the battleships, spot for their fall of shot, and support the activities of surface vessels generally. The Fleet Air Arm's spectacular successes and their more humdrum operational exploits were scarcely distinguishable, in fundamental principle, from those of their 1914-18 predecessors in the Heligoland Bight, the Straits of Dover and the Dardanelles. This was hardly surprising, in view of the lack of interest in naval aviation shown by the German and Italian navies. After severe losses off Norway, Dunkirk, Crete and Malta, the Royal Navy was well aware of the destructive power of enemy land-based aircraft, but they tended to see this as a serious problem only in certain restricted waters close to land. Even the sinking of the *Prince of Wales* and *Repulse*, by Japanese land-based aircraft in 1942, could be seen as falling into that category – an unfortunate tragedy which might have been avoided if only they had been accompanied, as originally intended, by an aircraft carrier to provide protective air cover.

After 6 December 1941, however, the war in the Pacific showed that naval aviation could be applied in new ways. The aircraft carrier was no longer simply a useful element in a balanced surface fleet. At Pearl Harbour, the Coral Sea and Midway aircraft carriers supplied the main strike weapon, effective over hundreds of miles, rather than the 20-mile extreme range of the big calibre guns. Even the most hide-bound, big-gun-obsessed admiral was compelled to recognise that air power had transformed the nature of war at sea and, as the Americans went on the offensive, air power also transformed amphibious operations.

That was why, when the Royal Navy was in a position to take the offensive against the Japanese in the Indian Ocean, aircraft carriers had come to be seen as the key ships in the fleet. They continued in that role as the British Pacific Fleet, operating as a task force under American command, carried the white ensign all the way to Tokyo Bay. Raw figures tell the story of the transformation of the Royal Navy most effectively: 'The end of the war found the Royal Navy with seven large, or fleet, aircraft carriers including the elderly *Furious*, as well as the maintenance carrier *Unicorn*, the elderly *Argus*, five light carriers with more under construction, and forty escort carriers. Half of the naval aircraft and three-quarters of the escort carriers had come from the United States.'[24] Many of the men who flew the aircraft had also been trained in the United States under the Towers scheme. Their training had familiarised them with American aircraft, while their instructors had not merely taught the British students to fly aeroplanes; they had also passed on their own battle experience of carrier operations in the Pacific theatre.

Following hard on the Japanese surrender came the winding up of training programmes, the cancellation of huge contracts for building ships and aeroplanes, the return or scrapping of Lend-Lease equipment, and the whole bewildering gamut of painful adjustments required by the transition from war to peace. Some of the British airmen who trained under the Towers scheme may have felt cheated of the excitement and challenge of the aerial combat for which they had volunteered and in preparation for which they had undergone a very demanding course of training. Many of the men must, however, have been relieved that, instead of having to face an uncertain future risking their lives over the distant islands of the Pacific or over the Japanese home islands, they could return to their families and begin yet another training course for peaceful careers as accountants, architects, schoolmasters, businessmen, civil servants, lawyers or clergymen. A glance down the names of former Towers trainees, listed as having contributed much of the source material used in the writing of this book (see pp. 178-186), gives some indication, even though incomplete and inadequate, of their subsequent operational service. The love of flying, which some of them developed, led on to full-time careers in the Royal Air Force, the Fleet Air Arm or Civil Aviation.

Training overseas had provided them with experiences denied to most men of their generation. The sights and sounds of America changed them, and a lasting affection for the United States was almost universal amongst Towers trainees. A handful married American girls, while many developed lasting friendships with the American people, who had done so much to welcome them. Perhaps America, too, was a little changed by the visitors. The influx of men from Britain, New Zealand and other parts of the British Empire offered a valuable learning opportunity for the Americans who found them in their midst. Perceptions about the British people, about British society, British reticence, and British stuffiness were altered, sometimes profoundly.

Many Americans were surprised to discover that the fliers of the RAF and Fleet Air Arm were not unlike their own young men. They knew how to fool around and have a good time; they could jitterbug, liked jazz, and were not stuffy. Some even liked the spicier food of the American South. Towers trainees were agents for change, but they were also elements for continuity in the developing relationship between Britain and the United States. In 1950 just over a hundred of the Towers trainees came together in a London pub to form the British Pensacola Veterans. For fifty or more years after finishing their training in the United States, airmen trained under the Towers scheme would continue to be numbered, individually and collectively, among the many supporters of the Anglo-American special relationship, especially during the tensions of the Cold War. That special relationship was not just a matter of national self-interest and formal alliances: it existed in the hearts and minds of individuals.

The careers of two distinguished fliers, Richard (Gordon) Wakeford and Roy (Gus) Halliday, may serve as examples of where the Towers training scheme could eventually lead. Training at Pensacola and flying Catalina aircraft on wartime patrols with RAF Coastal Command were the first steps in Wakeford's full-time career in the service. That career saw him employed in such varied appointments as instructing at the RAF College, Cranwell, commanding the Queen's Flight, station commander at RAF Scampton, a Bomber Command staff post, commander of the Northern Maritime Air Region, and ANZUK Force Commander at Singapore. From 1975-78 he served as Deputy Chief of Defence Staff (Intelligence). He eventually retired from the RAF as Air Marshal Sir Richard Wakeford KCB, LVO, OBE, AFC.

Halliday volunteered for the Royal Navy and, after training under the Towers scheme, he was commissioned as a sub-lieutenant in the Royal Naval Volunteer Reserve. He joined 845 Squadron in 1942. There he flew anti-submarine patrols in American-built Avenger aircraft from the American-built escort carrier HMS *Chaser*. The squadron saw further action in the Indian Ocean flying from another American-built escort carrier, HMS *Ameer*, and from the fleet aircraft carrier HMS *Illustrious*.

During 1944 Halliday was posted to 849 Squadron on board HMS *Victorious*, and, still flying Avengers, he took part in the British carrier strikes against Japanese targets in Sumatra. Shot down during the second strike on Palembang oil refinery, he was plucked from the sea by HMS *Whimbrel*, whose first lieutenant was Prince Philip. Halliday saw more action when the *Victorious* took part in the British Pacific Fleet's attacks on the Sakishima Gunto and Formosa.

A permanent commission led to post-war appointments such as work as a test pilot, command of 813 Squadron of the Fleet Air Arm, senior officer of 104 Minesweeping Squadron, and Deputy Director of Naval Air Warfare. As a commodore, he served as Director of Naval Intelligence, and he was also in charge of amphibious warfare for a time. Halliday returned to the United States as commander of the British Naval Staff and Naval Attaché in Washington DC, and from 1978-81 he succeeded Wakeford as Deputy Chief of Defence Staff (Intelligence). The young naval airman who had trained at Pensacola in 1941 eventually retired from the Royal Navy as Vice-Admiral Sir Roy Halliday KBE, DSC, MiD

NOTES

Preface
1 Richard Collier, *The Years of Attrition: 1941 Armageddon*, London, Allison & Busby, 1995, p. 1.

Chapter 1
1 For the precise figures see Stephen Roskill, *Hankey: Man of Secrets*, London, Collins, 1970-4, III, p. 663.
2 *Parliamentary Debates (Commons)*, vol. 270, col. 632; Stanley Baldwin, Lord President of the Council and Conservative party leader, speech winding up House of Commons debate on European disarmament, 10 November 1932.
3 *Daily Mail*, 17 November 1932; article by Winston S. Churchill.
4 *Parliamentary Debates (Commons)*, vol. 281, col. 137; Winston S. Churchill, speech in House of Commons adjournment debate, 7 November 1933.
5 G.H. and R. Bennett, *Hitler's Admirals*, Annapolis, Naval Institute Press, 2004, p. 23-4.
6 *Parliamentary Debates (Commons)*, vol. 285, col. 1198; speech, House of Commons, 7 February 1934.
7 *Ibid.*, vol. 286, col. 2072; speech on the Air Estimates, House of Commons, 8 March 1934.
8 TNA:PRO CID 1147-B.
9 *Parliamentary Debates (Commons)*, vol. 286, col. 2078; speech on the Air Estimates, House of Commons, 8 March 1934.
10 For the precise figures see Stephen Roskill, *Hankey: Man of Secrets*, London, Collins, 1970-4, III, p. 663.
11 John Terraine, *The Right of the Line: The Royal Air Force in the European War 1939-1945*, London, Hodder & Stoughton Sceptre paperback, 1988, p. 23.
12 Geoffrey Till , 'The Fleet Air Arm Controversy and its Implications for British Defence,' *Army Quarterly*, vol. 107, no. 4, October 1977, pp. 406-7.
13 Ludlow-Hewitt to Air Ministry, 10 November 1937, AHB, Box 2, Folder 7, quoted in Terraine, op. cit., p. 82.
14 Ibid.
15 Charles Webster and Noble Frankland, *The Strategic Air Offensive against Germany 1939-45*, London, HMSO, 1961, official history, I, p. 113, note 1.

16 Ludlow-Hewitt memorandum, 25 May 1939, quoted in Terraine, op. cit., p. 87.
17 M. Smith, 'Sir Edgar Ludlow-Hewitt and the Expansion of Bomber Command 1939-40', *RUSI Journal*, March 1981, p. 54, cited in Terraine, op. cit., p. 85.
18 View of MRAF Sir Arthur Harris., *Bomber Offensive*, Barnsley, Pen & Sword paperback, 2005, pp. 34-5.
19 These operations are described in more detail in Terraine, op. cit., pp. 99-105.
20 Terraine, op. cit., pp. 162-3, citing Air Historical Branch narrative.
21 Winston Churchill, *The Second World War: II Their Finest Hour*, London, Reprint Society, 1951, pp. 500-501.
22 Terraine, op. cit., p. 220.
23 AHB/II/116/14, p. 137, quoted in Terraine, op. cit., p. 44.
24 H. Popham, *Sea Flight: A Fleet Air Arm Pilot's Story*, Par, Old Ferry Press, 1994, p. 18. He later completed his pilot training in Canada.
25 Terraine, op. cit., p. 188.
26 Ibid. p. 257.
27 D. Richards and H. St G. Saunders, *The Royal Air Force 1939-1945*, London, HMSO, 1975, III, pp. 371-2.
28 Ibid., p. 372.

Chapter 2

1 Viscount Swinton, *I Remember*, London, Hutchinson, nd, p. 124.
2 MRAF Sir Arthur Harris, *Bomber Offensive*, Barnsley, Pen & Sword paperback, 2005, pp. 27-8.
3 Elizabeth-Anne Wheal et al, *Encyclopaedia of the Second World War*, Edison NJ, Castle, nd but original edition dated 1989, p. 179.
4 Harald Penrose, *British Aviation: The Ominous Skies 1935-1939*, London, HMSO, 1980, p. 210.
5 Hans-Adolf Jacobsen and Arthur L. Smith, *World War II: Policy and Strategy – Selected Documents with Commentary*, California, Clio Books 1979, p. 138.
6 D. Saward, *Bomber Harris*, London, Sphere, 1990, p. 125.
7 G. Guinn, 'British Aircrew Training in the United States 1941-45,' *Journal of Southwest Georgia History* ,VII, 1989-92, pp. 59-80.
8 W.S. Churchill, *The Second World War: III The Grand Alliance*, London, Reprint Society, 1952, p. 595.
9 Churchill papers 20/39, quoted in Martin Gilbert, *Winston S. Churchill: VI Finest Hour 1939-1941*, London, Heinemann, 1983, p. 1087, note 1.
10 Air Commodore Pirie to Admiral Towers, TNA:PRO AIR 42/2.
11 See United States Navy Records, Aer-PL-DS, memorandum, Navy Department, Bureau of Aeronautics, Washington, 15 January 1942. It shows that the Towers scheme received final approval on 21 July 1941.
12 TNA:PRO AIR 42/2, British Air Military Mission, Washington DC, to Air Ministry, 18 June 1941.
13 *War Illustrated*, 2 August 1941, p. 67.
14 US Navy Records, Op-33-2-RRB, serial 4093, Chief of Naval Operations to Superintendent, British Air Training, 3 August 1944.
15 Later marks of the type were called Wildcat.

16 TNA:PRO ADM 1/14106, minute by Director of Air Warfare & Training, Admiralty, 13 October 1943.
17 US Navy Records, OP-33-3-RRB, serial 357833, Chief of Naval Operations to Chief of Naval Air Training, 10 July 1944, Office of US Naval History, Washington DC.
18 TNA:PRO ADM 117/17286, Survey of Royal Navy Training in the United States, May 1945; see also Towers Scheme Training File OP-O5D4, Office of US Naval History, Washington DC.
19 TNA:PRO ADM 1/14106, minute, Director of Air Warfare & Training, Admiralty, 13 October 1943.
20 TNA:PRO ADM 1/13328, Admiralty to British Air Delegation, Washington, 5 March 1943.
21 TNA:PRO ADM 199/1468, see British Air Delegation Report for 1942, p. 122.
22 TNA:PRO ADM 1/15862, Personnel, Administration and Base Accounting Work in the United States.
23 TNA:PRO ADM 177/17286, Survey of Royal Navy Training in the United States, May 1945; also Towers Scheme Training File OP-O5D2, Office of US Naval History, Washington DC.
24 A.R. Buchanan, *The Navy's Air War: A Mission Completed*, New York, Harper and Brothers, 1946, p. 315.
25 Ibid., p. 324.
26 TNA:PRO ADM 1/13328, Towers Training, Royal Air Force Delegation, Washington, March 1943.
27 Chief of Naval Operations to Chief of Naval Air Training, 20 November 1944, USN Bureau of Aeronautics Correspondence, Research Group 72, Box 396, National Archives, Washington DC.
28 United States Navy Records, Op-33-2-RRB, Changes in Foreign Training Programs during December 1944, by Office of the Chief of Naval Operations to Historical Office, 18 February 1945, Office of US Naval History, Washington DC.
29 TNA:PRO ADM 177/17286, Survey of Royal Navy Training in the United States, May 1945; see also Towers Scheme Training File Op-O5D2, Office of US Naval History, Washington DC.

Chapter 3
1 'When a Sailor Learns to Fly', *Fleet Air Arm*, London, HMSO, 1943, p. 23.
2 TNA:PRO AIR 2/7595.
3 Ray Gough to his parents, 1 January 1944.
4 TNA:PRO AIR 29/477.
5 William Warner to his wife, August 1941.
6 William Warner to his wife, August 1941, written on board the *Stratheden*.
7 Ray Gough to parents, undated (circa April-May 1944).
8 William Warner to his wife, 17 August 1941.
9 Ibid.
10 William Warner to his wife, 20 August 1941.
11 William Warner to his wife, 23 August 1941.

Chapter 4

1   William Warner to his wife, 30 August 1941.
2   Alicia Street, *USA at Work and Play*, London, Cassell, 1942, p. 1.
3   *Pensacola News Journal*, 11 April 1942; see also ibid., 31 May 1942, which featured a profile of George Brady, another Dunkirk veteran.
4   TNA:PRO CAB 122/663, undated (circa July 1941) notes for Address to United Kingdom Students Beginning Courses in the United States.
5   Ibid.
6   Ibid.
7   William Warner to his wife, 20 September 1941.
8   Frank Robinson to his fiancée, 7 October 1941.
9   Frank Robinson to his fiancée, 23 August 1941.
10 N. Hanson, *Carrier Pilot*, Cambridge, Patrick Stephens, 1979, p. 57.
11 William Warner to his parents, 25 January 1942.
12 Frank Robinson to his fiancée, 3 November 1941.
13 Frank Robinson to his fiancée, 25 August 1941.
14 Ibid.
15 Father of Frank Robinson to his son, 24 August 1941.
16 William Warner to his parents, 5 July 1942.
17 *Pensacola News Journal*, 27 July 1941.
18 Ibid., 2 and 3 August 1941.
19 Ibid., 4 August 1941.
20 *Detroit Free Press*, 28 August 1941.
21 See, for example, *Pensacola News Journal*, 14 December 1941, for report of Christmas dance attended by local girls and British military personnel.
22 *Pensacola News Journal*, 4 January 1942.
23 Ibid., 14 December 1941.
24 Throughout the war the American press routinely reported the deaths of British airmen in training; see, for example, *Kokomo Tribune*, 13 January 1945, for a report of the death of British aviation cadet E.G. Wagland at USNAS Bunker Hill.
25 *The WAG*, newsletter of RAF Course 5-42 at USNAS Jacksonville, June 1942.
26 *The WAG*, newsletter of RAF Course 9-42 at Jacksonville, October 1942.
27 Ibid.

Chapter 5

1   F. Robinson, *The British Pensacola Battalion: a Flight Log Representing the British Flight Battalion, US Naval Air Station Pensacola, Florida, 1941-1944*, Kansas, Sunflower University Press, 1984, pp. 1-2.
2   History of USNAS Grosse Ile, Records of the United States Navy, NA19/SCH: del/A12, Office of US Naval History, Washington DC.
3   J.J. Collins, 'The Brits who Invaded Grosse Ile', *Michigan History*, May/June 1990, p. 42.
4   William Warner to his wife, 17 September 1941.
5   William Warner to his wife, 20 September 1941.
6   William Warner to his wife, 17 September 1941.
7   Ray Gough to parents, 19 July 1944.

NOTES   171

8   N. Hanson, *Carrier Pilot*, Cambridge, Patrick Stephens, 1979, p. 41.
9   TNA:PRO AIR 2/4981, internal Air Ministry memorandum on arrangements for the allocation of aviation candidates to pilot, observer, or other crew duties, and their selection for command rank, January 1940.
10 Ray Gough to parents, 5 August 1944.
11 Ray Gough to parents, 22 August 1944.
12 Ray Gough to parents, 30 July 1944.
13 M.L. Shettle, *United States Naval Air Stations of World War II, vol. 1 – Eastern States*, Georgia, Schaertel Publishing, 1995, p. 41.
14 Ray Gough to parents, 29 August 1944.
15 Ibid.
16 From History of USNAS Bunker Hill, US Navy Records OP-33-J-G.
17 Ibid.
18 *Gosport*, 17 November 1944.
19 Captain A.C. Read, 'Training the Naval Aviator', *Flying and Popular Aviation*, January 1942, p. 80.
20 *Limey*, no. 8, 8 March 1942.
21 William Warner to his wife, 25 October 1941.
22 *Limey*, no. 8, 8 March 1942.
23 William Warner to his wife, 17 October 1941.

Chapter 6
1   N. Hanson, *Carrier Pilot*, Cambridge, Patrick Stephens, 1979, p. 33.
2   From US Navy Records OP-33-JG, Appendix 1, Library of NAS Bunker Hill, Office of US Naval History, Washington DC.
3   *Toronto Star*, September 1941, with photograph of Air Commodore Critchley and article.
4   G. Guinn, 'British Aircrew Training in the United States, 1941-1945,' *Journal of Southwest Georgia History*, VII, 1989-1992, pp. 59-80.
5   Air Ministry, *Flight Training*, I, Air Historical Branch, London, 1952, p. 144.
6   TNA:PRO AIR 2/4981, Air Commodore D.V. Carnegie, Director of Flying Training, Air Ministry, to Director of Air Warfare and Training, 15 November 1943.
7   Ibid., minute by Lieutenant-Commander G.N. Torry.
8   Ibid., Air Commodore D.V. Carnegie to Director of Air Warfare and Training, 15 November 1943.
9   Ibid., Air Commodore D.V. Carnegie, memorandum on visit to Canada, 21 April 1945.
10 C.G. Jefford, *Observers and Navigators and other Non-Pilot Aircrew in the RFC, RNAS and RAF*, Shrewsbury, Airlife, 2001, p. 176, claims that 662 WOp/AGs were trained for the RAF in the USA under the Towers scheme, with the last class graduating in September 1942.
11 A.A. de Gruyther for Group Captain, Director of United Kingdom Training, Air Ministry, to Royal Air Force Administrative Officer, Pensacola and to Superintendent Aviation Training, Pensacola, 3 February 1942, US Navy Records.

12 G. Guinn, 'British Aircrew Training in the United States, 1941-1945', *Air Power History*, vol. 42, no. 2, 1995, pp. 4-19.
13 H. Mackenzie, *Observations*, Edinburgh, The Pentland Press, 1997, p. 12.
14 Ibid., p. 35.
15 Group Captain Carnegie to Admiral Towers, 6 April 1942, US Navy Records, Office of US Naval History, Washington DC.

Chapter 7

1 A.R. Buchanan, *The Navy's Air War: A Mission Completed*, New York, Harper and Brothers, 1946, p. 312.
2 TNA:PRO AIR 2/8179.
3 Ray Gough to his family, 24 February 1945.
4 Ray Gough to his family, 12 March 1945.
5 Ray Gough to his family, 11 May 1945.
6 M.L. Shettle, *United States Naval Air Stations of World War II, vol. 1 – Eastern States*, Georgia, Schaertel Publishing, 1995, p. 139.
7 N. Hanson, *Carrier Pilot*, Cambridge, Patrick Stephens, 1979, p. 50.
8 www.geocities.com/CapeCanaveral/runway/9601/newzealand.html
9 War Diary, Naval Air Station Fort Lauderdale, United States Navy Records NM29-4/A-12/A 9-4.
10 The two men killed on 2 April 1944 were S/Lt Peter Louis Alen, age 20, son of Louis William and Queenie Alen of West Wickham, Kent, and S/Lt Ronald James Clayton, age 20, son of William James and Dorothy Beaumont Clayton, of Sutton, Surrey. They are buried in Woodlawn Park Cemetery, Miami.
11 TNA:PRO ADM 1/18120, minute by Assistant Chief of Naval Staff, 25 May 1943.
12 A.A. de Gruyther, RAF Delegation, Washington, to Navy Bureau of Aeronautics, 21 March 1942, USN Bureau of Aeronautics Correspondence, Record Group 72, Box 1137, National Archives, Washington DC.
13 G.F. Brogan, commanding officer of USNAS Miami, to Chief of the Bureau of Aeronautics, 9 June 1942, US Navy Records NA30/P11-1 EF 13 T-JAT-er.
14 A. Pearcy, *Lend-Lease Aircraft in World War II*, Shrewsbury, Airlife, 1996, pp. 80-2.
15 TNA:PRO AIR 2/7513, RAF Delegation, Washington, to Air Ministry, 8 May 1942.
16 TNA:PRO AIR 20/1387, Towers training, RAF Delegation, Washington, March 1943.
17 TNA:PRO AIR 2/7513, RAF Delegation, Washington, to Air Ministry, 3 April 1943.
18 Ibid., minute by Air Commodore D.V. Carnegie, Director of Flying Training, Air Ministry, 12 April 1943.
19 Ibid., Air Ministry to RAFDEL, Washington, 11 November 1943.
20 For the Arnold-Towers-Portal agreement see TNA:PRO AIR 19/349 and AIR 8/1360.
21 Dr R. Scheina, 'A History of Coast Guard Aviation', *Commandant's Bulletin*, 10 October 1999, p. 25.

22 J. Dowling, R.A.F. Helicopters: The First Twenty Years, London, HMSO, 1992, p. 4.
23 E. Bishop, The Daily Telegraph Book of Airmen's Obituaries, London, Grubb Street, 2002.
24 www.history.navy.mil/arh-1910/APP31.PDF: United States Naval Aviation 1910-1995, pp. 755-6.
25 TNA:PRO ADM 1/16464, minute by Director of Naval Air Division, 2 September 1942.
26 Ibid., minutes by Director of Personnel Services, 16 September 1942, and Director of Pre-Entry Training, 23 September 1942.
27 Ibid., minute by Director of Naval Air Division, 19 November 1942.
28 Ibid., minute by Director of Air Warfare and Flying Training, 12 February 1943.
29 Ibid., Under-Secretary of State, Air Ministry, to Secretary, Admiralty, 30 March 1943.
30 Ibid., British Admiralty Delegation, Washington, to Admiralty, 9 March 1943.
31 Ibid., RAFDEL, Washington, to Air Ministry/Admiralty, 1 February 1943.
32 M.L. Shettle, United States Naval Air Stations of World War II, vol. I – Eastern States, Georgia, Schaertel Publishing, 1995, p. 187.
33 L. Sayer and V. Ball, TAG on a Stringbag, Dyfed, Aspen Publications, 1994, pp. 226-7.
34 F. Stovin-Bradford, 'Last Off, Last Back', Aeroplane, November 2002, pp. 22-7.
35 M.F. Shettle, op. cit., p. 25.
36 Ibid., p. 207.
37 TNA:PRO ADM 177/17286, Survey of Royal Navy Training in the United States, May 1945; see also Towers Scheme Training File OP-O5D2, Office of US Naval History, Washington DC.
38 J. Cotter, 'Pacific Corsairs', Fly Past, no. 263, June 2003, pp. 44-8.
39 See also N. Hanson, Carrier Pilot, Cambridge, Patrick Stephens, 1979, p. 107.
40 Ibid., pp. 106-7.
41 Three men were killed in the accident: S/Lt Donald Frank Ellwood, age 23, son of Cyril and Florence Ellwood of Great Horkesley, Essex; Lt Edgar Thomas Trotman, age 29, son of Thomas and Amy Trotman, husband of Ivy Trotman of Rainham, Essex; Ldg/Airman Dennis Ritchie, age 20, son of George and Eleanor Ritchie of Gateshead, County Durham.
42 D. Foster, Wings over the Sea, Harrop, Canterbury, 1990, pp. 155-6.
43 F. Stovin-Bradford, 'Last Off, Last Back', Aeroplane, November 2002, pp. 22-7.
44 H. Mackenzie, Observations, Edinburgh, The Pentland Press, 1997, pp. 73-7.
45 Ibid., p. 74.
46 Ibid.
47 H. Popham, Sea Flight: A Fleet Air Arm Pilot's Story, Par, Old Ferry Press, 1994, p. 76.
48 Ibid., p. 78.

Chapter 8

1. H. Green, 'Flying Boat Captain' in M. Fopp, *High Flyers*, London, Greenhill Books, 1993, pp. 92-8.
2. Cecil Beaton, *Winged Squadrons*, London, Hutchinson, nd, p. 26.
3. Ibid., p. 28.
4. John Sweetman, *Tirpitz: Hunting the Beast: Air Attacks on the German Battleship 1940-44*, Stroud, Sutton, 2000, p. 57.
5. TNA:PRO ADM 116/5468, report on Operation Tungsten by Office of the Vice-Admiral, Second-in-Command, Home Fleet, 10 April 1944.
6. Lieutenant-Commander M. Apps, *Send Her Victorious*, Purnell, London, 1971, pp. 139-40.
7. F. Stovin-Bradford, 'Last Off, Last Back', *Aeroplane*, December 2002, p. 44.
8. Ibid., p. 45.
9. F. Robinson, *The British Pensacola Battalion: A Flight Log Representing the British Flight Battalion, US Naval Air Station, Pensacola, Florida, 1941-1944*, Kansas, Sunflower University Press, 1984, p. 4.

Chapter 9

1. Geoffrey Till, 'Air Power and the battleship,' in Bryan Ranft (ed.), *Technical Change and British Naval Policy 1860-1939*, London, Hodder & Stoughton, 1977, pp. 110-11.
2. Admiral of the Fleet Sir Roger Keyes, 'Foreword', in Commander John Creswell, *Naval Warfare*, London, Sampson Lowe, Marston & Co., 1936, p. viii.
3. Commander John Creswell, ibid., pp. 42-3.
4. Captain S.W. Roskill, *The Strategy of Sea Power: Its Development and Application*, London, Collins, 1962, p. 238.
5. *Janes Fighting Ships of World War II*, London, Random House, 2001, pp. 33-7.
6. Ibid., passim.
7. AHB/II/117/3(A), *The RAF in Maritime War*, Appendix V, quoted in John Terraine, *The Right of the Line*, London, Sceptre paperback, 1988, note 2, p. 713.
8. TNA:PRO AIR 20/1387, Towers Training, March 1943.
9. ACM Sir P. Joubert de la Ferté, *The Third Service: The Story Behind the Royal Air Force*, London, Thames and Hudson, 1955, p. 175.
10. C.J.M. Goulter, *A Forgotten Offensive: Royal Air Force Coastal Command's Anti-Shipping Campaign 1940-1945*, London, Frank Cass, 1995, p. 274.
11. MRAF Sir Arthur Harris, *Bomber Offensive*, Barnsley, Pen & Sword paperback, 2005, p. 276.
12. Ibid., p. 277.
13. R. Hargis, *US Naval Aviator 1941-45*, Oxford, Osprey Books, 2002, pp. 9-10.
14. J.B. Lundstrom, *The First Team: Pacific Naval Air Combat from Pearl Harbour to Midway*, Annapolis, Naval Institute Press, 1990, p. 452.
15. Deputy Chief of Naval Operations (Air), volume XIV, Aviation Training 1940-1945, p. 8, US Navy Historical Unit, Washington, 1945.
16. Ibid.

17 Ibid., p. 97, Lieutenant-Commander Brimm to Capt A.W. Radford, 29 November 1941.
18 Phil Young, Office for Emergency Management, Defence Aid Division, to E.R. Stettinius jr., 10 October 1941, Harry Hopkins Papers 24, Box 125.
19 Isador Lubin to Harry Hopkins, 14 May 1942, Harry Hopkins Papers 24, Box 125. In fact Lubin noted that since his memorandum had been written 7 further dive bombers had been delivered, 3 in March and 4 in April.
20 Bob Ruegg and Arnold Hague, *Convoys to Russia 1941-1945*, Kendal, World Ship Society, 1992, p. 81.
21 Naval War Diary, 6 May 1943, cited in Dr Hans-Adolf Jacobsen and Dr Jurgen Rohwer, *Decisive Battles of World War II*, London, Andre Deutsch, 1965, p. 302.
22 G.H. and R. Bennett, *Hitler's Admirals*, Annapolis, Naval Institute Press, 2004, p. 182.
23 Report by United States Navy, 1943, Harry Hopkins Papers 24/155.
24 D. Wragg, *Second World War Carrier Campaigns*, Barnsley, Pen and Sword, 2004, p. 224.

SOURCES

The essential sources of information for the writing of this book have come from the large number of wartime veterans who, in the course of the last thirty years, have allowed us access to their experiences, whether directly – by interviews, telephone conversations, correspondence, diaries and papers – or indirectly through intermediaries. Their experiences aroused our admiration: their kind co-operation and generosity deserve our grateful acknowledgement.

Squadron Leader Leon Armstrong, Founder and Chairman of the British Pensacola Veterans – the oldest organization for British aircrew trained in the United States 1941-5 – has supported this project from the beginning. Flight Lieutenant Frank Robinson, compiler and illustrator of *The British Flight Battalion at Pensacola and Afterwards*, very generously granted us the use of his personal research materials, drawings and correspondence, without which this book might not have been published. Fleet Air Arm volunteers from New Zealand – indicated below by [NZ] before their names – were also kind enough to share their training and operational experiences.

Where ranks are listed, they will generally be the rank attained before leaving the service at the end of World War II, but, for those who are known to have pursued postwar careers in the services or civil aviation, the ranks listed may be those held at the time we were able to gather information about them.

Post-war involvement in aviation, when known, is italicised within square brackets. To give even the briefest indication of the splendid wartime services rendered by the airmen trained under the Towers scheme, much information has had to be compressed by use of abbreviations. Most of the abbreviations are easy to interpret, but a glossary of abbreviations appears on pages 197-201.

(i) Former British training staff involved with the Towers scheme

Gibson, V/Adml Sir D., KCB, DSC, JP   SBNO, Miami
Hogan, AVM H.A.V., CB, DFC   Director, UK Training in USA, 1942-3
Jackson, Lt/Cdr P.B.   SBNO, St Louis & Bunker Hill
Lawrie, J., DSC   Ground School instructor, Bunker Hill
Rossiter, Lt(A) W.T.F.   Navigation instr., Pensacola & Corpus Christi
Suthers, Cdr S.H., DSC, DFC   SBNO, St Louis & Bunker Hill
Whatley, Lt/Cdr D.   SBNO, Pensacola & Corpus Christi

(ii) Royal Air Force:
Trained in the USA under the Towers scheme as Flying Boat pilots

Name/Rank/Decorations   Wartime Aircraft Squadrons/*Ships* *[Postwar Theatres etc aviation]*

Allen, F/Lt L.T.   PBY (S. Africa)   262/35SAAF/*Fencer*
Archibald, F/Lt W.W.   PBY/Hali/York   295/298/644
Armstrong, S/Ldr L.V.   Whitley/Welli   612/458
                         Founder & chairman, British Pensacola Veterans
Ashley, F/Lt J.H.   PBY/B'ftr/B'frt   62 TC/SEAC
Baker, F/Lt P.A.   PBY/Gliders   117/436 SEAC
Banton, Capt D.H.F.   PBY/Sunderland   212/240/230 SEAC *[CA]*
Barr, F/Lt J.J.   PBY/Hud/Lib   Atlantic anti-sub ops
Barrett, Capt J.S.P.   PBY/Lib/Sund   Ferrying   *[CA]*
Bassett, Capt D.S.   PBY/Lib/Lanc   224 Atl anti-sub ops *[CA]*
Bates, F/Sgt G.A.D.   PBY   Last Pensacola course as war ended
Batt, F/Lt L.N.   PBY/Wellington   38/221 Middle East
Bazalgette, A/Cdre J.E. PBY/Beaufighter   272/206   *[RAF]*
Beaumont, F/Lt M.   PBY   202/240 SEAC
Belton, F/Lt R.O.   Welli/Dak/York   223/512   *[A-1 Inst CA]*
Bennett, W/O H.   PBY/Beaufighter   236 Channel/N. Sea
Bleach, W/Cdr D.G.   PBY/Sunderland   209 Indian Ocean *[RAF]*
Blevins, Capt K.R.   PBY/B'ftr/Mos   39 Ferrying   *[CA]*
Borrowdale, F/O H.V., DFM PBY/B'ftr   47   *[ATC]*
Brew, F/Lt R.E.   PBY/Welli/Lanc   Also Flt Engineer   *[ATC]*
Brown, Sgt J.   PBY   Last Pensacola course as war ended
Brown, F/Lt P.J.   PBY/Sunderland   202/270 Gib/Atlantic
Bunting, F/Lt G., DFC   PBY/Sunderland   228 Atlantic anti-sub ops
Burdekin, F/Lt J.   PBY/Whit/Welli   612 Ferrying

SOURCES

Carter, F/Lt B.K.	PBY/Welli/Lanc	101	Ferrying
Castle, F/Lt D.E.	PBY/Sunderland	202/209	MidE/SEAC
Chapman, F/O K.F.	PBY/Beaufighter	254	sixty sorties
Clark, LAC M.	Injured and invalided out of RAF		
Cole, W/O R.J.	PBY	191/240	SEAC
Collier, W/O H.A.	PBY	240	SEAC
Colman, Capt R.F.	PBY/Gliders	SEAC,	[CA]
Cooper, F/Lt L.	PBY/Wck/Sund	282/204/278	Atl ASR
Cowper, The Rev'd M.C.	PBY	Psych Research, Cambs	
Cruickshank, F/Lt J.A.,VC	PBY	210 UK/anti-sub ops Sank *U-347*	
Cundy, F/Lt D.H.	PBY	Staff pilot	
Daniel, G/Capt J.M., DFC	PBY/Lancaster	106 Assistant Air Attaché	[RAF]
Davis, F/O P.R.	PBY/Sunderland	212/209	SEAC
Dow, W/O J.M., MBE	PBY/Wellington	179	
Dowson, S/Ldr G.R.	PBY	210/190 India/MidE Pensacola instructor	
Dugdale, F/Lt A.T., DFC	PBY/Welli/Lanc	115/195/232	SEAC
Edwards, F/Lt B.N.	PBY	End of war	[CA]
Emmott, Capt K.	PBY/Liberator	191/357	[CA]
Evans, Capt A.C.T., MiD	PBY	270/210	[CA]
Ewart, F/Sgt G.	PBY/Sea Otter/Dak	48 ATC	
Fenton, W/O J.N., MiD	PBY/Beaufighter	236 Anti-shipping ops	
Finke, Capt R.K.	PBY	Instructor	[CA, helicopters.]
Ford, W/O T.J.	PBY/Welli/Hali	36/644	MidE/UK
Fox, F/Lt D.C.	PBY/Wellington	172/22	N Atl/Med
Froom, Capt D.R.	PBY	259/262	[CA]
Fry, F/O D.J.	PBY/Whit/Hali	640 Europe PoW	
Fry, W/Cdr H.B.	PBY/Mosquito		[RAF]
Fry, Capt P.J., DFC, CdeG	PBY/Beaufighter	236	[CA]
Gammon, F/Lt A.	PBY/Liberator	358 SEAC	
Gamper, F/Lt H.R.	PBY/Welli/Wck	276/277 ASR	
Garside, Capt E.A., DFC	PBY/Sunderland	246/230 SEAC/Pac	[CA]
Garvey, P.	Transferred to Canadian EFTS		
Gazzard, F/Lt K.W.	PBY/Wellington	612/283 Atl/anti-sub ops	
Glazebrook, F/Lt J.J.V., DFC	PBY/Lib	206 Anti-sub ops	[MAF]
Glover, Capt W.N.	PBY/Welli/B-26	172/36/39	[CA]
Goodall, F/Lt D.W.	PBY/Lib/Dak	FC/TC	
Gooding, F/Lt D.W.	PBY/Dakota	202 N. Atlantic	

Gordon, F/Sgt M.L.	PBY/Gliders	Rhine crossing
Gough, W/O R.E.	PBY/Dakota	SEAC/Pacific
Griggs, F/Lt C.A.	PBY	270/212/202 West Africa/SEAC
Gwyther, S/Ldr H.V.	PBY/Liberator	240/210 Gibraltar/SEAC
Harding, K.J.I.	PBY	
Hartley, F/Lt R.C.	PBY/Welli/Wck	179 Gibraltar/Atlantic
Heady, F/Lt R.	PBY	
Herbert, S/Ldr E.D., AFC	PBY/Welli/Dak	458/38 Med/MidE
Higgs, W/O R.	PBY/Sunderland	Pre-AFU when war ended
Hine, S/Ldr I.F.M.	PBY	212 SEAC
Hirons, W/O R.W.	PBY/Welli/Hali	517 [CA Air Traffic Cont]
Hufton, R.E., MBE	PBY/Welli/Dak	SEAC/Pacific
Ingold, Sgt G.A.	PBY/Avenger	
Jay, W/Cdr J.B.	PBY/Mos/Sund	209/230 SEAC [RAF]
Kerr, J.M.	PBY/Gliders	671 as war ended
Landers, F/Lt B.W.	PBY/Sunderland	204/201 W.Africa/Atl
Landreth, F/Lt P.J.,	PBY/Wellington	194
Lane, Capt S.M.B.	PBY/Sunderland	201/230 Atl/SEAC [CA]
Lees, F/Lt E.J.	PBY/Wellington	FC/CC SEAC
LeFebure, P/O J.V.	Wellington	294 Middle East/ASR (Trained in Canada)
Ludgate, F/Lt P.F.H.	PBY	358 SEAC/Pacific
McAlpine, F/O J.M.	PBY	Weather flights/E. Africa
Machon, W/O D.E.	PBY	AFU/crash/invalided out
McKendrick, F/Lt G.G., DFC	PBY/Sund	265/209 SEAC/Pacific
McLoughlin, Father J.	PBY	Compass work/disabled
Mahoney, W/O D.J.	PBY/Liberator	628/212/210 SEAC/UK
Marsh, Dr H.	PBY/Sunderland	Convoy/Anti-sub ops
Meyer, W/O M.L.	PBY	210/191 UK/SEAC
Miles, F/Lt A.E.	PBY/B-25	45 Gp/FC Elizabeth Cty
Miles, Capt D.J.	PBY/Sunderland	205/250 SEAC/UK [CA]
Moore, W/O P.H.	PBY/Dakota	SEAC ATC
Morley, Capt R.H., MBE	PBY/Liberator	210/86 [CA]
Mort, W. A.	PBY	Further training in Canada
Morton, W/O A.S.	PBY	Staff pilot
Munro, F/Lt Sir H., JP, DL, MP	PBY/Sund	Ferrying/240/209 SEAC
Myers, Capt G., DFC	PBY	212/292 SEAC [CA]
Page, F/Lt C.S.V.	PBY/Liberator	212/202/220 SEAC
Palmer, W/O S.R.	PBY	Staff pilot [ATC]

SOURCES 181

Parsons, F/Lt D.I.	PBY	AFU when war ended
Pearson, W/O A.	PBY/Wellington	8/294 N. Africa/SEAC
Peck, S/Ldr E.C., AFC	PBY/Halifax	*[RAF]*
Phillips, Capt R.H.	PBY/Liberator	206 ATC *[CA]*
Pleasance, Capt C.R.	PBY/Sund/Lanc	191/212/38/37 *[CA]*
Plunkett, Capt G.P.	PBY	621 Middle East *[CA]*
Pope, A/Cdre W.H., OBE	PBY/Welli/Dak	458/36/96 Med/SEAC Air Traffic Control *[RAF]*
Potter, F/Lt E.	PBY/Hali/Lanc/Dak	FC/TC
Revill, Capt J.R.	PBY/Lib/Dak	Ferrying *[CA]*
Robinson, F/Lt F., DFM	PBY	270/210
Russell, W/O R.B.	PBY	205 SEAC
Russell-Vick, F/Lt C.	PBY	210/240/628
Satchwell, F/Sgt R.H.	PBY	Pre-AFU as war ended
Scargill, F/Lt M., DFC	PBY/B'ftr/Mos	236/618
Sharples, W/O R.E.V.	PBY	502/206
Sheppard, E.C.	PBY/Hud/Sund	AFU/OTU/as war ended
Smith, W/O R.W.	PBY/Wellington	Middle East Injured hand
Smyth, W/O R.P.	PBY/Beaufighter	Ferry/SEAC/war ended
Sparks, W/O D.	PBY/Gliders/Dak	194 SEAC/TC
Stevens, F/Lt G.	PBY/Sunderland	270/230 Ferry/ATC
Tebbit, Capt P.L.	PBY/Sunderland	270/259/209 *[CA]*
Tipple, F/Lt P.C., DFC	PBY/Beaufighter	272 Malta/Mediterranean
Todd, F/Sgt L.	Canada trained	Staff pilot as war ended
Trotman, E.J.	PBY/Wellington	517
Vincent, F/O A.P.	PBY	War ended
Wakeford, A/M Sir R., KCB, OBE, MVO, AFC, MiD		202/212/210 PBY/Sund/Lib Gib/SEAC/UK *[RAF]*
Warner, S/Ldr W.C., MiD	PBY	Air Intelligence SHAEF Awarded US decoration
Whitehead, F/O G.	PBY	Ground duties/SEAC
Willard, F/Sgt C.	Canada trained after Pensacola/war ended	
Windmill, F/Lt K.H.	PBY/Welli/Dak	38/201 Gp Middle East
Winters, P/O P.A.	PBY/Gliders/Dak	War ends
Woodland, W/O R.	PBY/Sunderland	240/207 SEAC

(iii) Royal Air Force:
Trained in the USA under the Towers scheme as Navigators (Nav), Wireless Operator/Air Gunners (WOp/AG) or for other roles

Name/Rank/Decorations	Wartime Aircraft	Role/Squadrons Theatre etc	[Postwar aviation]
Austin, W/O C.	Sunderland	WOp/AG 228 19 ops Wounded	
Barrett, F/Sgt A.G.	PBY/Halifax	WOp/AG Ferrying/148	
Bartlett, Sgt R.S.		Navigator 276/613 Compass adjuster	
Bates, W/O A.S	PBY/Welli/Lanc	WOp/AG 619/617 Europe/India 41 ops	
Bell, A.R.		Air Bomber/Canada-trained	
Brantingham, S/Ldr G.F., DFC & Bar	Lancaster/Liberator	Navigator 97/150 SEAC	
Brown, Sgt H.V.	Lancaster	Navigator 9 PoW	
Burgoyne, F/Lt D.G.	PBY/Blen/B-25	Navigator 98	
Cecil, W/O B.		WOp/AG 15 thirty ops	
Clawson, P/O S.		WOp/AG 612	[RAF]
Clayton F/Lt T.H., MiD	Dakota	Navigator 216 MidE Trained in S. Africa	
Farrow, W/O R.R.	Halifax/Dakota	WOp/AG 58 fifty ops	
Fish, Sgt F.	PBY/Wellington	WOp/AG 283	
Foley, F/O J.E., DFC	Welli/Lanc/Mos	Nav 156/608 82 ops	
Hanson, F/Lt S.B.	PBY/Sund	WOp/AG 202/270 60 operations	
Hewlett, F/Lt C.A., DFC		Navigator PoW	
Hunt, Sgt D.W.	PBY/Sund	WOp/AG 262/270/ 35 SAAF Indian Ocean	
Jarvis, Dr H.C.M., MD, MBE	PBY	Nav/Bomber OTU PoW	
Johnson, Sgt J.R.	PBY	WOp/AG	
Kirkpatrick, W/O R.	PBY/Welli/Lib	WOp/AG 203 SEAC	
Nye, A.E.		Nav/trained in Canada	
Oliver, W/Cdr S.F., MBE	PBY/Welli/Hali	Nav 148/171 MidE/Eur 2 tours of operations	
Scott, Sgt C.C.	PBY/Wellington	WOp/AG Middle East RAF HQ, Cairo	
Spencer, F/Lt A.H.G., DFC	PBY/Lanc	Navigator 97 PFF	

SOURCES 183

Venn, P/Off P.O.   Nav/Bomb aimer 109
                        Canada/UK
Warner, F/Lt D.M.   PBY/Wellington Navigator   Med/SOE
Windett, F/O R.V.   Welli/Sund   WOp/AG/Radar 458/
                                     46 Gp MidE/Med ASR

(iv) Royal Navy: Trained in the USA under the Towers scheme as Fleet Air Arm Pilots

Name/Rank/Decorations   Wartime Aircraft   Squadrons/*Ships*   *[Postwar Theatres etc   aviation]*

Allen, S/Lt(A) R.A.F.   Buffalo
Bailey, S/Lt K.S.   Buffalo/Wildcat   Transf to RN, flying ends
Barnfield, S/Lt(A) J.H.   Corsair
Beechinor, Lt(A) E.A.   Corsair   1846/790/801/*Implacable*/
                                                Air Traffic Control
Bird, Lt(A) G.R.   Avenger/Barracuda Trained in Canada
                                                813/821/828/*Formidable* Med/Home Fleet
Blaikie, S/Lt(A) J.W., DSC   Corsair   1841/*Formidable* BPF
Borthwick, Lt/Cdr(A) S.H.   Corsair   *Reaper*   *[RN]*
Brewer, S/Lt(A) W.I.   Avenger   853/*Arbiter*/*Tracker*
                                                Convoy escort
Brown, Lt(A) J.F.   Avenger   849/*Victorious* BPF
Burstall, Capt J.F.   Corsair   1831/*Glory*   *[CA]*
[NZ] Canter, Lt/Cdr(A) P.J.M., MBE, DSC   894/882/*Searcher*/*Illustrious*
                             Cors/W'cat/Seafire UK/Mediterranean
Carmichael, Lt/Cdr P., MBE, DSC   Cors/Seafire 889/1834/*Victorious*
                                                Served also in Korean War: 1 Mig destroyed
Carter, Lt(A) C.M.   Seafire/Hellcat   879/779 Norway/Gib
Chute, Lt/Cdr(A) D.T., DSC, MiD   1836/1837/*Illustrious*/
                             Buffalo/Corsair   *Victorious* BPF
Cole, S/Lt(A) C.S.   Buffalo
Coupe, S/Lt(A) D.R.   Avenger   Training as war ended
Crosland, Lt(A) J.K., DSC   Corsair   *Formidable* BPF
Dallosso, Lt/Cdr(A) P.R.   Corsair   1851/*Venerable*   *[RN]*
Dunn CPO D.P.   PBY   Tr'sfer to RN/flying ends
Duxbury, S/Lt(A) S.   Avenger   763/744/*Tracker*/*Queen*
                                                Convoy escort
Earp, S/Lt(A) D.E.   Corsair   748/TC   *[CA]*

Emberton, Lt(AE) F.C.	Buff/Skua/W'cat	882/*Victorious* BPF
		Also test pilot *[MRAeS]*
Evans, Cdr(A) T.C.	Avenger	BPF as war ended *[RN]*
Fleischmann-Allen, Lt(A) R.A., DSC & Bar	Fencer/*Campania*	
	Wildcat	Destroyed Condor & Ju88
[NZ] Ferguson, L	Pilot under training when Lease-Lend ended	
Frampton, Lt(A) D.G., MiD	Avenger	849/*Battler*/*Victorious*
George, S/Lt(A) E.P.	Corsair	1850/*Vengeance*/*Venerable* BPF
Gibbs, Mid(A) H.J.M.	Pilot/trained Canada	OTU as war ended
[NZ] Glading, Lt(A) R.H., DSC, MiD	1841/*Formidable* BPF	
	Buffalo/Corsair	
Goss, S/Lt(A) J.	PBY/B'ftr/Dak	603/22 Med/SEAC
Gough, S/Lt(A) R.G.	Avenger/Barracuda	
Grinstead, S/Lt(A) S.G.		1851/*Venerable*
Guest, S/Lt(A) P.	PBY	Medically unfit/grounded
Hart, The Rev. Canon D.D.	PBY/Barracuda	*Smiter* Transfer to RN
Hiller, S/Lt(A) R.	Cors/Barracuda	814/*Venerable* Med/SEAC/BPF
Hutchison, Lt(A) W.C.	Corsair	1843/*Trouncer* BPF
Hyde, S/Lt(A) C.G.	W'cat/Cors/Seafire	Crash on *Charger*
Johnson, S/Lt(A) R.K.H.	Avenger	855/UK PoW
Jones, Cdr(A) J.M., MBE	Corsair	*Vengeance* SEAC/BPF
Laidlaw, S/Lt(A) W.M.	Buff/Cors/W'cat	772 Middle East
Large, Lt(A) D.C.	Avenger	848
Lawler, Lt(A) E.	Buff/W'cat/Seamew	Ferrying
	Crashed, legs amputated, invalided out	
Lees-Jones, Lt(A) J.R.	Avenger	855/846/*Trumpeter*
Mann, Capt M.G.	Training when war ended	*[RAF/CA]*
Michie, Lt(A) A.R.	Avenger	1837/*Victorious* SEAC/BPF
Neale, S/Lt(A) V.H.J.		
Nuttall, Lt/Cdr(A) R.W.	Avenger	780/745/752 Canada
Parr, Lt(A) N.H.	Corsair	1844/*Colossus* BPF
Peffers, Lt/Cdr A.S.R., MD	Flight Surgeon	*[Med. director CA]*
[NZ] Perret, Lt/Cdr(A) N.P., MBE, MiD	882/896/*Victorious*	
	Buffalo/Wildcat/Hellcat	
[NZ] Price, Capt M.A.	Avenger	854/*Illustrious* *[CA]*
Purdon, S/Lt(A) W.T.	Avenger	SEAC
[NZ] Reynolds, Lt(A) A.H.	Avenger	854/*Indomitable*/*Illustrious*

[NZ] Rhodes, Lt/Cdr(A) H.A., DSC & Bar	Corsair/Avenger	849/*Victorious*
[NZ] Richards, Lt(A) J.H., DSC	Buffalo/Corsair	*Victorious* BPF
Roberts, Lt(A)K.	Buffalo/Wildcat	*Formidable*
Seymour, Lt(A) B.	Postwar Avenger pilot, trained at Pensacola	
Sheppard, Lt/Cdr(A) W.J.	Buff/Fulmar/W'cat	898/*Victorious/Searcher* BPF/UK
Shippey, Lt/Cdr(A) M.R.H.	Corsair	851/*Thane/Venerable*
Singleton,Lt(A) C.H., OBE, MiD	Corsair/Hurricane/Seafire	1836/*Victorious* MidE/BPF
Singleton, Lt(A) Sir E.	Hurricane/Seafire	804/889/880/*Implacable* Mediterranean/BPF
[NZ] Sisley, Lt(A) J.G.	Swordfish/Albacore/Roc/Barracuda	BPF 754/798/755/758/*Glory*
Smith, S/Lt(A) W.H.A.	Corsair	1851/*Venerable* Med/SEAC/BPF
Southern, S/Lt(A) H.E.	Avenger	Ferrying
Spencer, Lt(A) H.J.C., MiD	Avenger Goldfish Club	738/853/768/*Arbiter/ Tracker/Queen* BPF
Staniforth, S/Lt(A) T.H.	Avenger	738/857/*Indomitable* BPF
Stovin-Bradford, S/Lt(A) F.R., MiD	Avenger Goldfish Club	738/857/*Rajah/Indomitable* BPF
Styles, Rev Canon L.E.	Albacore/Barr	820/*Formidable/Indefatigable*
Thurstans, Lt(A) S.H.	Avenger	846/*Ravager/Tracker/Trumpeter* Convoy escort
Toseland, S/Lt R.N.	Corsair	1851/*Glory*
[NZ] Waite, Lt(A) G.	Buff/Martlet	892/898/*Victorious/Searcher*
Webb, Mid(A) J.T.	Avenger	War ended while training
Wheeler, Lt(A) M.F.	Avenger	846/*Tracker/Trumpeter/* Convoy escort
White, Cdr(A) D.C.B., OBE	W'cat/Fulmar	UK/BPF [MRAeS] DLCO on aircraft carrier
Winandy, S/Lt(A) J.C.	Wildcat	761 [RAF]
Wood, Lt(A) D.	Buff/W'cat/Cors	1841/*Formidable* BPF
Woodwards, Lt(A) B.A.G.	Wildcat	825/853/815/761/*Fencer* Convoy escort
Wort, Lt/Cdr(A) L.C., DSC	W'cat/Hurricane	842/1772/*Fencer/Indefatigable* BPF
Wreford, Lt/Cdr(A) P.J.	PBY/Barr/Firefly/Walrus	814 BPF [RN]

Wright, S/Lt(A) G.E.	Avenger	853/957/*Indomitable*	BPF
Yeo, Lt(A) R.K.L., MiD	Wildcat	895/892/819/833/856	
	Shot down JU88 & Bv138		Convoy escort

(v) Assistance with research

Acott, A/Cdre W., Air Historical Branch, Ministry of Defence, London.
Allam, A.J., British Flying Training School No 1.
Allard, Dr D.C., Head, Operational Archives Branch, US Navy Historical Center, Washington Navy Yard DC.
Ashenden, G., RAF Ferry Command Radio Officer, Elizabeth City and Takoradi.
Bains, L., USN instructor, first Royal Navy Class, Corpus Christi.
Bate, N., Arnold Scheme Registrar.
Brown, J.D., Naval Historical Branch, Ministry of Defence, London.
Brown, R.R., Registrar, Falcon Field Association.
Cardwell, Mrs R.L., Howard County Public Library.
Cavalcante, B.F., Assistant Head, Operational Archives Branch, US Navy Historical Center.
Chalmers, E., Librarian, Indian River County Library Association, Vero Beach, Florida.
Davies, G/Capt H.G., British Flying Training School No 4 and instructor, Greenville, Texas.
Duxbury, T. & E., Wife and daughter of S/Lt(A) S. Duxbury.
Elliott, Cdr E.W., US Navy instructor, Bunker Hill.
Francis, A.J., Naval Historical Library, Ministry of Defence, London.
Harding, J.M., Wife of the late K.J.I. Harding.
Hare, Professor A.T., Director, and staff, Larry A. Jackson Library, Lander University, Greenwood, South Carolina.
Higham, Dr. R., Historian, professor and editor, Kansas State University; publisher of the British Pensacola Veterans volume.
Hills, N., Wife of RAF pilot.
Hodges, M.J., Reference Librarian, Brunswick-Glyn Cty Regional Lib., Ga.
Hughes, Capt. W., USN (retd), Director, United States Naval Aviation Museum, Pensacola, Florida.
Jarvis, G/Capt J.F., OBE, Director, RAF Personnel Management.
King, Mrs L.O., Assistant Curator, Coastal Georgia Historical Society, St Simons, Georgia.
Lee, D., Librarian, Larry A. Jackson Library, Lander University, Greenwood, South Carolina.
McCash, W., Chairman, Falcon Field Association.

McMichael, T.
Malayney, N., Assistance re W.C. Warner.
Neal, S.F., MBE, Secretary General, RAF Association.
O'Brien, J., Reference Librarian, Thomas Crane Public Library, Quincy, Massachussetts.
Oulton, AVM W.E., CB, CBE, DSO, DFC, Navigation expert, RAFDEL.
Penaluna, A.J., Student.
Probert, A/Cdre H., Director, Air Historical Branch & RAFHS.
Pyle, F/Lt G.F., RAF fighter pilot, trained under the Arnold scheme.
Rich, G.J., Archivist, US Naval Aviation History Center, Washington Navy Yard.
Robson, R., Tippecanoe County Public Library.
Rush, Capt. T.F., USN (retd), US Navy aviator.
Sharples, E., Wife of a Pensacola pilot.
Snyder, K., Research, Emil Buehler Naval Aviation Library, Pensacola, Florida.
Staff, John C. Pace Library, University of West Florida, Pensacola, Florida.
Staff, United States Air Force Simpson Historical Research Center, Maxwell Air Force Base, Alabama.
Stern, E.J. Jr.
Strauss, L., Librarian, Larry A. Jackson Library, Lander University, Greenwood, South Carolina.
Walker, Capt. G., USN (retd), Director, United States Naval Aviation Museum, Pensacola, Florida.
Ward, Ms O., WAAF, RAF Transport Command, Elizabeth City, NC.
West, B. K., FAA aircrew, Canadian Register.
Williams, B., Librarian, Larry A. Jackson Library, Lander University, Greenwood, South Carolina.
Wingham, S., Treasurer, RAFA, Branch 276, Bury St. Edmunds.
Wooldridge, P/Off L.P., DFC, RAF Air Gunner, 51/578 Squadrons.

(vi) Private Papers

Armstrong, S/Ldr L. V., The British Pensacola Veterans (nominal rolls), 1969 onward.
Duxbury, S/Lt(A) S.   Papers 1943-54.
Gough, S/Lt(A) R.G.   Papers 1942-5.
Guinn Aviation History Archive, Special Collections, Thomas Cooper Library, University of South Carolina.
Robinson, F/Lt F.C.   Papers 1939-46; 270 Squadron, Coastal Cmd.
Roosevelt, Franklin D.   Papers 1939-45.
Suthers, Cdr S.,   Papers 1944; SBNO, Bunker Hill, Indiana.

Warner, F/Lt D.M.   Papers of Pensacola-trained navigator.
Warner, S/Ldr W.C. Papers, and issues of the *Limey* 1941-5.

(vii) Official Records

The National Archives of the United Kingdom, Richmond, Surrey

ADM 1/11941
ADM 1/13328
ADM 1/15862
ADM 1/16408
ADM 1/16464
ADM 1/18120
ADM 1/18499
ADM 177/17286
ADM 199/166
ADM 199/167
ADM 199/1236
ADM 199/1468   File 9241
ADM 199/1469   9242
ADM 199/1470   9243
ADM 199/1471   9244
ADM 199/1479   9268
ADM 199/1480   9269
ADM 199/2383
ADM 199/8228
AIR 2/4981   File 31173

AIR 2/7513   Training of British Pilots by the US Navy (Towers Scheme)
AIR 19/297
AIR 19/298
AIR 20/10
AIR 20/309
AIR 20/1387
AIR 20/1388
E.690 File H.30. American Women Pilots in Britain, London, 25 May 1943
AIR 29/860
AIR 32/14
AIR 42/2
AIR 45/11
AVIA 38/580
AVIA 38/914
CAB 122/6
CAB 122/663

The National Archives, Washington DC
RECORDS GROUP 18, Box 537
RECORDS GROUP 72, BuAer, US Navy, Boxes 1137 & 1138

The United States Naval Archives, Washington Navy Yard, Washington DC
History of the US Naval Air Station Bunker Hill, Indiana.
History of the US Naval Air Station Corpus Christi, Texas.
History of the US Naval Air Station Fort Lauderdale, Florida.
History of the US Naval Air Station Grosse Ile, Michigan.
History of the US Naval Air Station Miami, Florida.
History of the US Naval Air Station Pensacola, Florida.

History of the US Naval Air Station St. Louis, Missouri.
History of the US Naval Air Station Vero Beach, Florida.
Office of the Chief of Naval Operations in U S Naval Administration in World War II.
Office of the Deputy Chief of Naval Operations (Air) and Air Divisions in US Naval Administration in World War II.
Royal Navy Activities in USA, 1941-3, November 1944.
Training Division Diaries, Bureau of Aeronautics, Washington, 1944.
Training, Towers Scheme, Naval Aviation History OP-05D2, 'Survey of RN Air Training'.

The United States Naval Aviation Museum, Pensacola, Florida
Flight Jacket, Aviation Cadet Yearbook, 1941.
Flight Jacket, Aviation Cadet Yearbook, 1942.
Flight Jacket, Aviation Cadet Yearbook, 1943.
Flight Jacket, Aviation Cadet Yearbook, 1944.
Release of Primary Air Stations, Pensacola, Naval Air Training Command, 13 July 1944.
The Gosport, 1941.
The Gosport, 1942.
The Gosport, 1943.
The Gosport, 1944.

(viii) Newspapers

Daily Advance, Elizabeth City, NC, 1941-4.
Daily Mirror, no. 11,688, London, 28 May 1941, 40th anniv. reprint, 1981.
Ibid., no. 11,710, London, 23 June 1941, 40th anniversary reprint, 1981.
Daily Telegraph, London.
Detroit Free Press, Detroit, Mich, 1 July to 31 Dec. 1941.
Florida Times-Union, Jacksonville, Fla, 1941-2.
Limey: British Flight Battalion Weekly, Pensacola, Fla, vol. I, Nov-Dec 1941; vol. II, nos. 1-15 & special summer edition, 1942.
Manchester Guardian, Manchester.
Montgomery Advertiser, Montgomery, Ala, 1941-3.
Patriot Ledger, cuttings re US Naval Air Base Squantum, Mass, courtesy Ms J. O'Brien of the Thomas Crane Public Library, Quincy, Mass.
Pensacola Journal, Pensacola, Fla, 1941-4.
Pensacola News Journal, Pensacola, Fla, 1941-3.

Pensacolian, vol. II, no. 5, May 1985.
Quincy Patriot, 17 Apr. 1943, 8 Dec. 1943, and 29 Aug. 1945, courtesy of Ms. J. O'Brien of the Thomas Crane Public Library, Quincy, Mass.
Tampa Morning Tribune, Tampa, Fla.
Vero Beach Press Journal, Vero Beach, Fla, 1943.

(ix) Books

Adams, Henry H., *Harry Hopkins: A Biography*, New York, G.P. Putnam's Sons, 1977
Air Ministry, *Flying Training*, I, London, Air Historical Branch, 1952.
Allward, Maurice, *An Illustrated History of Seaplanes and Flying Boats*, New York, Barnes & Noble, 1981.
Apps, Lt/Cdr M., *Send Her Victorious*, London, Purnell, 1971.
Ashworth, C., *RAF Coastal Command 1936-1969*, Sparkford, Patrick Stephens, 1992.
Balfour, Harold, *Wings Over Westminster*, London, Hutchinson, 1973.
Banks, A., *Wings of the Dawning: The Battle for the Indian Ocean 1939-1945*, Malvern Wells, HMR, 1997.
Barker, Ray, *Victorious the World Over*, Worcester, Square One, 1991.
Barnett, Correlli, *Engage the Enemy More Closely; The Royal Navy in the Second World War*, London, Hodder & Stoughton, 1991.
Beaton, C., *Winged Squadrons*, London, Hutchinson, nd.
Beaumont, Joan, *The Australian Centenary History of Defence: Volume IV, Australian Defence Force*, Melbourne, Australia, OUP, 2001.
Beaumont, Joan, *The Australian Centenary History of Defence: Volume V, Australian Defence Force*, Melbourne, Australia, OUP, 2001.
Beaumont, Joan, *The Australian Centenary History of Defence: Volume VI, Australian Defence: Sources and Statistics*, South Melbourne, Australia, OUP, 2001.
Bekker, C., *Hitler's Naval War*, New York, Doubleday, 1974.
Bennett, G.H., *British Foreign Policy During the Curzon Period 1919-1924*, Basingstoke, Macmillan, 1995.
Bennett, G.H., *Roosevelt's Peacetime Administrations 1933-41: A Documentary History*, Manchester University Press, Manchester, 2004.
Bennett, G.H., and R., *Hitler's Admirals*, Annapolis, Naval Institute Press, 2004.
Bishop, E., *The Daily Telegraph Book of Airmen's Obituaries*, London, Grubb Street, 2002.

Brief History of US Naval Air Station Bunker Hill, Indiana, 1942-1945.
Brock, Horace, *Flying the Oceans*, New York, Jason Aronson, 3rd edn, 1978.
Brown, David, ed., *The British Pacific and East Indies Fleets: The Forgotten Fleets*, Liverpool, Brodie Publishing, 1995.
Buchanan, A.R., *The Navy's Air War: A Mission Completed*, New York, Harper & Brothers, 1946.
Carlisle, Robert L., *P-Boat Pilot*, Santa Barbara, Fithian Press, 1993.
Charlton, Air Commodore L.E.O., *Britain at War: The Royal Air Force and USAAF*, London, Hutchinson, 1945.
Churchill, Winston S., *The Second World War*, London, Reprint Society, 6 vols, 1950-6.
Courtney, Frank T., *The Eighth Sea*, Garden City, New York, Doubleday, 1972.
Creswell, Commander John, *Naval Warfare: An Introductory Study*, London, Sampson Low, 2nd edn, 1942.
Cull, Brian and Newton, Dennis, *With The Yanks in Korea*, I, London, Grub Street, 2000.
Douglas, William A.B., *The Creation of a National Air Force: Vol. II of the Official History of the Royal Canadian Air Force*, Toronto, University of Toronto Press, 1986.
Dowling, John, *RAF Helicopters: The First Twenty Years*, London, HMSO, 1992.
Erickson, Captain Frank, USCG (retd), *Fishers of Men: The Story of the Development of Seagoing Helicopters*, Washington, Naval Historical Center, manuscript volume, nd
Joubert de la Ferté, Air Chief Marshal Sir P., *The Third Service: The Story Behind the Royal Air Force*, London, Thames and Hudson, 1955.
Fiske, Rear-Admiral Bradley A., *From Midshipman to Rear-Admiral*, New York, The Century Company, 1919.
Fopp, M., *High Flyers*, London, Greenhill Books, 1993.
Foster, D., *Wings over the Sea*, Canterbury, Harrop, 1990.
Fowler, Simon; Elliott, Peter; Nesbit, Roy Conyers; and Goulter, Christina, *RAF Records in the PRO*, London, Public Record Office, 1994.
Freeman, Roger A., *The British Airman*, London, Arms and Armour Press, 1989.
Friedman, Norman, *British Carrier Aviation*, London, Conway Maritime Press, 1988.
Goulter, C.J.M., *A Forgotten Offensive: Royal Air Force Coastal Command's Anti-Shipping Campaign 1940-1945*, London, Frank Cass, 1995.

Great Britain, Admiralty, *East of Malta; West of Suez*, London, HMSO, 1943.
Great Britain, Admiralty, *Fleet Air Arm*, London, HMSO, 1943.
Great Britain: Air Ministry, *Coastal Command*, London, HMSO, 1943.
Great Britain, Commonwealth War Graves Commission, *Cemeteries in the United States of America: The War Dead of the British Commonwealth and Empire 1939-1945*, Maidenhead, England, Commonwealth War Graves Commission, 1980.
Great Britain, HMSO, *Sectional List 60: Histories of the First and Second World Wars and Peacetime Series*, London, HMSO, 1976.
Greenhous, Brereton; Harris, Stephen J.; Johnston, William C.; and Rawling, William G.P., *The Crucible of War, 1939-1945, Volume III of the Official History of the Royal Canadian Air Force*, Toronto, University of Toronto Press, 1994.
Grey, C.G., *A History of the Air Ministry*, London, 1940.
Hadley, D.L., *Barracuda Pilot*, England, Airlife, 1992.
Halley, James J., *The Squadrons of the Royal Air Force and Commonwealth 1918-1988*, London, Air-Britain, 1988.
Hanson, Norman, *Carrier Pilot*, Cambridge, Patrick Stephens, 1979.
Hargis, R., *US Naval Aviator 1941-45*, Oxford, Osprey, 2002.
Harris, MRAF Sir Arthur, *Bomber Offensive*, Barnsley, Pen & Sword paperback, 2005.
Hastings, Max, *Bomber Command*, New York, The Dial Press, 1979.
Hayward, Roger, *The Fleet Air Arm in Camera 1912-1996*, Stroud, Gloucestershire, Sutton, 1998.
Hendrie, Andrew, *Flying Cats: The Catalina Aircraft in World War II*, Shrewsbury, Airlife, 1988.
Houston, R., *Changing Course: The Wartime Experience of a Member of the Women's Royal Naval Service 1939-1945*, London, Grub Street, 2005.
Jane's, *Jane's Fighting Ships of World War II*, London, Random House, 2001.
Jefford, C.G., *RAF Squadrons*, Shrewsbury, Airlife, 1988.
Jefford, C.G., *Observers and Navigators and other Non-Pilot Aircrew in the RFC, RNAS and RAF*, Shrewsbury, Airlife, 2001.
Lambert, John W., *Naval Aviation in the First World War: Its Impact and Influence*, London, Caxton Editions, 2002.
Lowry, Thomas P., and Wellham, John W.G., *The Attack on Taranto*, Mechanicsburg, Pa, Stackpole Books, 2000.
Lundstrom, J.B., *The First Team: Pacific Naval Air Combat from Pearl Harbour to Midway*, Annapolis, Naval Institute Press, 1990.
Mackenzie, H., *Observations*, Edinburgh, The Pentland Press, 1997.

Marolda, E., ed., *FDR and the U.S. Navy*, Basingstoke, Macmillan, 1998.
Middlebrook, Martin, and Everitt, Chris, *The Bomber Command War Diaries: An Operational Reference Book 1939-1945*, Leicester, Midland Publishing, 2000.
Miller, Lieutenant Harold B., *Navy Wings*, New York, Dodd, Mead & Co., 1937.
Mingos, Howard, ed., *The Aircraft Yearbook For 1946*, New York, Lanciar Publishers, 1946.
Nesbit, R.C., *The Strike Wings: Special Anti-Shipping Squadrons 1942-45*, London, William Kimber, 1984.
Pape, Richard B., *Boldness Be My Friend*, London, Elek Books, 1953.
Patillo, Donald M., *Pushing the Envelope: The American Aircraft Industry*, Ann Arbor, University of Michigan Press, 2000.
Pearcy, A., *Lend-Lease Aircraft in World War II*, Shrewsbury, Airlife, 1996.
Pelant, Reg., *St Clement Danes: Church of the Royal Air Force, Strand*, Leicester, Blackfriars Press, 1971.
Pickersgill, J.W., *The Mackenzie King Record*, Toronto, University of Toronto Press, vol. I, 1960.
Pickersgill, J.W. & Forster, D.F., *The Mackenzie King Record*, Toronto, University of Toronto Press, vol. II, 1968.
Popham, H., *Sea Flight: A Fleet Air Arm Pilot's Story*, Par, Old Ferry Press, 1994.
Raff and Armstrong, Anthony, *Nice Types*, London, Methuen, 1943.
Ranft, Bryan, ed., *Technical Change and British Naval Policy 1860-1939*, London, Hodder & Stoughton, 1977.
Renwick, Robin, *Fighting With Allies*, New York, Random House, 1996.
Reynolds, David, *The Creation of the Anglo-American Alliance 1937-1941: A Study in Competitive Co-operation*, Chapel Hill, University of North Carolina Press, 1982.
Richards, Denis, and Saunders, Hilary St. George, *Royal Air Force 1939-1945*, London, HMSO, 3 vols, 1993.
Robinson, Frank (compiler and illustrator), *The British Flight Battalion at Pensacola and afterwards*, Manhattan, Kansas, Sunflower University Press, 1984.
Roskill, Stephen, *The Navy at War 1939-1945*, Ware, Hertfordshire, Wordsworth Editions, 1998.
Roskill, Stephen, *The Strategy of Sea Power: Its Development and Application*, London, Collins, 1962.
Ruegg, Bob, and Hague, Arnold, *Convoys to Russia 1941-1945*, Kendal, World Ship Society, 1992.

Rutter, Owen, *The British Navy's Air Arm*, Washington, HMSO/Penguin Books, 1944.
Saward, D., *Bomber Harris*, Sphere, London, 1990.
Sayer, L., and Ball, V., *TAG on a Stringbag*, Dyfed, Aspen Publications, 1994.
Serling, Robert J., *When the Airlines Went to War*, New York, Kensington Publishing Corporation, 1997.
Sherwood, Robert E., *Roosevelt and Hopkins: An Intimate History*, New York, Harper & Brothers, 1948.
Shettle, M.L., *United States Naval Air Stations of World War II: Volume 1 – Eastern States*, Georgia, Schaertel Publishing, 1995.
Slessor, Sir John, *The Central Blue: Recollections and Reflections*, London, Cassell, 1956.
Smith, P.C., *Into the Assault: Famous Dive Bomber Aces of the Second World War*, London, John Murray, 1985.
Stephenson, William, ed., *The Secret History of British Intelligence in the Americas 1940-1945*, New York, Fromm International Publishing, 1999.
Sturtivant, Ray, *The Squadrons of the Fleet Air Arm*, Tonbridge, Kent, Air-Britain, 1984.
Sweetman, John, *Tirpitz: Hunting the Beast*, Stroud, Sutton, 2000.
Terraine, John, *A Time for Courage: The Royal Air Force in the European War 1939-1945*, New York, Macmillan, 1985.
Terraine, John, *The Right of the Line: The Royal Air Force in the European War 1939-1945*, London, Sceptre, 1988.
Turnbull, Captain Archibald D., and Lord, Lt/Cdr Clifford L., *History of United States Naval Aviation*, New Haven, Yale University Press, 1949.
Van Deurs, Rear-Admiral George, *Wings For the Fleet*, Annapolis, Naval Institute Press, 1966.
Winterbotham, F.W., *The Ultra Secret*, New York, Harper & Row, 1974.
Wise, Sydney F., *Canadian Airmen and the First World War: Volume I of the Official History of the Royal Canadian Air Force*, Toronto, University of Toronto Press, 1979.
Woodhouse, Henry, *Textbook of Naval Aeronautics*, New York, The Century Company, 1917.
Woods, G., *Wings at Sea: A Fleet Air Arm Observer's War 1940-45*, London, Conway, 1985.
Wragg, David, *Carrier Combat*, Stroud, Gloucestershire, Sutton, 1997.
Wragg, David, *The Fleet Air Arm Handbook 1939-1945*, Stroud, Gloucestershire, Sutton 2001.

Wragg, David, *Second World War Carrier Campaigns*, Barnsley, Pen and Sword, 2004.

(x) Articles and Periodicals

Aeroplane, London, 1943-9.
Aviation News Magazine, Berkamstead, Hertfordshire,, vol. XV, no. 25, 1-14 May 1987.
Campbell, Debra M., 'WWII Brits Return For Last Pensacola Reunion,' for the Pensacola Convention & Visitors Information Center.
Clark, M., 'Change Course for the Dentist,' *FlyPast*, Dec. 1985, pp. 34-5.
Collins, John J., 'The Brits who invaded Grosse Ile,' *Michigan History*, May-June 1990, pp. 40-5.
Deacon, Shirley M., ed., *From Pirates to Pilots: A Pictorial History of Pensacola Navy, 1528 to present*, Pensacola, Pensacola Engraving Co., 2nd edition, 1975.
Donaldson, W/Cdr Edward M., DSO, 'Notes on Gunnery' (copy provided by Mrs. Edward M. Morgan, Memphis, Tennessee).
Dowling, W/Cdr J.R., 'Wartime Developments,' excerpt from *RAF Helicopters: The First Twenty Years*, Air Historical Branch publication.
Flight, vol. II, no. 5, 'US Naval Air Station Grosse Ile, Michigan' (Copy provided by George A.D. Bates).
FlyPast, London, December 1985.
Guinn, G., 'British Aircrew Training in the United States 1941-45,' *Journal of Southwest Georgia History*, vol. VII, 1989-92, pp. 59-80.
Hearon, Olive H., ed., *Campus: The Navy Education and Training Monthly*, April 1975.
Limey, Pensacola, Royal Navy & Royal Air Force, November 1944.
Naval History, Annapolis, US Naval Institute, vol. III, no. 1, 1989.
Oliver, David, 'They Float, They Fly: Seaplanes on the Wing and Water,' *Mayfair*, vol. XXI, no. 9, 1987, pp. 106-11 (copy courtesy of Douglas Goodall).
Pinfeather, US Naval Air Station Bunker Hill, Indiana, September 1944.
Portz, Captain M., 'Aviation Training and Expansion,' in *Naval Aviation News*, July-August 1990.
Portz, Captain M., 'Aviation Training and Expansion, part 2,' *Naval Aviation News*, September-October 1990.

'Quonset Point Naval Air Station' and 'List of Early Helicopter Pilots' (appendix 31), http://www.nuwc.navy.mil/hq/, *The Navy and Rhode Island History Page*, 5 January 2001.

Rea, Robert C., *British Pensacola, 1763-1781* (excerpt from Professor Rea's *Colonial Pensacola*, 1974).

Read, Captain A.C., 'Training the Naval Aviator,' *Flying and Popular Aviation*, January 1942.

Rowe, Michael, 'We are learning to Fly in the USA,' *War Illustrated*, 30 January 1942, article reprinted from the *Surrey Comet* (copy supplied by A.J. Penaluna).

St. Louis Blues, US Naval Air Station Lambert Field, St. Louis, Missouri, August 1944.

Scheina, Robert L., 'A History of Coast Guard Aviation,' in *Commandant's Bulletin 21-86*, 10 October 1989.

Sea Classics, vol. XXVI, no. 9, September 1993.

Steward, Davenport, 'As the English See Us,' *Saturday Evening Post*, 11 Oct. 1941, pp. 24-5, 94, and 96.

Stovin-Bradford, F., 'Last Off, Last Back,' *Aeroplane*, Dec. 2002, p. 44.

The Turret, Official Magazine of the Air Gunners Association, (J.A.G. Skinner, DFC, President) New Series, nos 32 & 33, April & August 1985.

The WAG, Magazine of WOp/AG students at Jacksonville/Pensacola, Florida, 1941-2.

Thomas, A., 'Nigerian Sea Searchers,' *Aviation News*, vol. XV, no 25, 1-14 May 1987, pp. 1230-3.

Till, Geoffrey, 'The Fleet Air Arm Controversy and Its Implications for British Defence,' *Army Quarterly*, vol. CVII, no 4, Oct. 1977, pp. 406-7.

Vikkee, Publication of the Navy Relief Society, US Naval Air Station Jacksonville, Florida, (first anniversary edition).

(xi) Brochures

Tour Guide, Historic Pensacola.
US Naval Aviation Museum, *Foundation*, vol. XV, no 1, Spring 1994.
US Naval Aviation Museum, Pensacola, Florida.
US Naval Aviation Museum, *The NC-4: The First Transatlantic Flight*.

GLOSSARY OF ABBREVIATIONS

(A)	Royal Navy officer-aviator in Fleet Air Arm
AC2	Aircraftman 2nd Class
A/Cdre	Air Commodore
ACM	Air Chief Marshal
ACRW	Air Crew Receiving Wing
ADDL	Aerodrome Dummy Deck Landing
AFC	Air Force Cross
AFU	Advanced Flying Unit
AHB	Air Historical Branch
Ala	Alabama
A/M	Air Marshal
AMC	Armed Merchant Cruiser
AMT	Air Member for Training
ASR	Air Sea Rescue
ATC	Air Traffic Control
[ATC]	Air Training Corps postwar
Atl	Atlantic Ocean
ATTS	All Through Training Scheme
AVM	Air Vice-Marshal
AWOL	Absent without leave
B-17	Boeing Flying Fortress aircraft
B-25	North American Mitchell aircraft
B-26	Martin Marauder aircraft
BAD	British Admiralty Delegation in Washington
Barr	Fairey Barracuda aircraft
BBC	British Broadcasting Corporation
BC	RAF Bomber Command
B'frt	Bristol Beaufort aircraft

B'ftr	Bristol Beaufighter aircraft
BFTS	British Flying Training Schools
Blen	Bristol Blenheim aircraft
BOQ	Bachelor Only Quarters
BPF	British Pacific Fleet
Buff	Brewster Buffalo aircraft
[CA]	Civil Aviation postwar career
CAA	Civil Aeronautics Authority
CAM	Civilian Air Mechanic
Capt	Captain
CB	Companion of the Order of the Bath
CBE	Companion of the Order of the British Empire
CC	RAF Coastal Command
CdeG	Croix de Guerre
Cdr	Commander
Cdre	Commodore
Cmd	Command
CNR	Canadian National Railways
CO	Commanding Officer
Cors	Chance Vought Corsair aircraft
CPO	Chief Petty Officer
CPTP	Civilian Pilot Training Program
CTD	College Training Detachment
Dak	Douglas Dakota aircraft
DC	District of Columbia
DFC	Distinguished Flying Cross
DFM	Distinguished Flying Medal
DFT	Director of Flying Training
DL	Deputy Lord Lieutenant
DLCO	Deck Landing Control Officer
DSC	Distinguished Service Cross
DSO	Distinguished Service Order
EFTS	Elementary Flying Training School
FAA	Fleet Air Arm
FB	Fighter bomber
FC	RAF Ferry Command
Fla	Florida
F/Lt	Flight Lieutenant
F/O	Flying Officer
F/Sgt	Flight Sergeant

GLOSSARY OF ABBREVIATIONS

Ga	Georgia
G/Capt	Group Captain
Gib	Gibraltar
GR	General Reconnaissance
Grp	Group
Hali	Handley Page Halifax aircraft
H'cat	Grumman Hellcat aircraft
HMS	His Majesty's Ship
Hud	Lockheed Hudson aircraft
Ind.	Indiana
ITW	Initial Training Wing
JP	Justice of the Peace
KCB	Knight Commander of the Order of the Bath
LAC	Leading Aircraftman
Lanc	Avro Lancaster aircraft
Lib	Consolidated Liberator (B-24) aircraft
Lt	Lieutenant
Lt/Cdr	Lieutenant-Commander
Lt (jg)	Lieutenant (Junior Grade) in USN
[MAF]	Missionary Aviation Fellowship
Mass	Massachusetts
MBE	Member of the Order of the British Empire
MC	Military Cross
MD	Doctor of Medicine
Med	Mediterranean Sea
Mich	Michigan
MiD	Mentioned in Dispatches
Mid	Midshipman
MidE	Middle East
Mos	De Havilland Mosquito aircraft
MP	Member of Parliament
MRAeS	Member of the Royal Aeronautical Society
MRAF	Marshal of the Royal Air Force
MVO	Member of the Royal Victorian Order
Nav	Navigator
NC	North Carolina
NCO	Non-Commissioned Officer
NJ	New Jersey
[NZ]	New Zealand volunteer in Fleet Air Arm
OBE	Officer of the Order of the British Empire

ops	operations
ORTU	Operational Refresher Training Unit
OTU	Operational Training Unit
Pac	Pacific Ocean
PBY	Consolidated Catalina flying boat
PFF	Pathfinder Force
PLM	Production Line Maintenance
P/O	Pilot Officer
PoW	Prisoner-of-war
PRC	Pilots' Reception Centre
PRO	Public Record Office
R/Adml	Rear-Admiral
RAF	Royal Air Force
[RAF]	Royal Air Force postwar career
RAFA	Royal Air Forces Association
RAFDEL	Royal Air Force Delegation, Washington
RAFHS	Royal Air Force Historical Society
RAFVR	Royal Air Force Volunteer Reserve
RCAF	Royal Canadian Air Force
Retd	Retired
RN	Royal Navy
[RN]	*Royal Navy* postwar career
RNVR	Royal Naval Volunteer Reserve
RNZAF	Royal New Zealand Air Force
RT	Radio telephony
SAAF	South African Air Force
SBNO	Senior British Naval Officer
SC	South Carolina
SEAC	South East Asia Command
SHAEF	Supreme Headquarters, Allied Expeditionary Force
S/Ldr	Squadron Leader
S/Lt	Sub-Lieutenant
Sgt	Sergeant
Sq	Squadron
Sund	Short Sunderland flying boat
TAG	Telegraphist/Air Gunner
TBR	Torpedo/bomber/reconnaissance aircraft
TC	RAF Transport Command
Tex	Texas
TNA	The National Archives (UK)

GLOSSARY OF ABBREVIATIONS

UK	United Kingdom
USA	United States of America
USAAF	United States Army Air Force
USMC	United States Marine Corps
USN	United States Navy
USNAS	United States Naval Air Station
USO	United Services Organization
USS	United States Ship
V/Adml	Vice-Admiral
VC	Victoria Cross
VE	Victory in Europe
WAAF	Women's Auxiliary Air Force
W'cat	Grumman Wildcat aircraft
W/Cdr	Wing Commander
Wck	Vickers Warwick aircraft
Welli	Vickers Wellington aircraft
Whi	Armstrong Whitworth Whitley aircraft
W/O	Warrant Officer
WOp/AG	Wireless Operator/Air Gunner

INDEX

Names of ships are printed in italics; nationality is British, unless otherwise indicated.

Abyssinia, 4
Admiralty, 5, 11, 21, 23, 92, 120-1, 126, 148, 150, 155, 161
advanced fighter training, 106-9
advanced flying training, 20, 24, 79, 104-14
aerodrome dummy deck landing (ADDL), 78, 124-5, 128
aerology, 24-6, 85-6, 107, 110
Air Council (RAF), 122
air gunners,
   see gunnery, telegraphist/air gunner, wireless operator/air gunner
Air Ministry, 5-6, 7, 11, 14-15, 18, 19, 23, 28, 29, 113, 116-18, 121-2, 151, 153, 162
Air Operational Training Command (US), *see* Operational Training Command
air-sea rescue, 114, 119, 123, 140
air traffic control, 146
Air Training Conference (1942), 105

Air Training Corps, 33, 146
Air Transport Command, 147
aircraft carriers, vii, x, 2, 3, 7, 10, 20, 21, 106, 108, 109, 111, 125, 141-6, 150-1, 155, 156-7, 159, 160-1, 163, *see also* escort aircraft carriers, *and names of individual ships*
aircraft maintenance (PLM), 28-30, 112, 122
aircraft recognition, 26-7, 37
aircrew, demand for, x, 4, 7-8, 16, 21, 28-30, 118, 123, 126, 138, 156, 164
aircrew receiving wing (ACRW), 11, 33, 36, 39, 90
   No. 2 Receiving Wing, 33
aircrew training, x-xii, 1, 4-9, 11-13, 17, 21, 24-9, 152-3, 156-7, 164 *see also* Arnold scheme, Towers scheme, *and specific aspects of training*
Albacore (Fairey) aircraft, 132
All Through Training Scheme (ATTS), 17-18
Allen, Richard, 55, 58, 64-6, 67, 75
Ameer, HMS, 165

American Legion, 131
Andes, 98
Andaman Is, 143, 145
Anglo-American:
   cultural contrasts, xi, 28, 29, 46, 49-58, 70, 72, 75-6, 131-3, 164,
   food, 45-6, 53, 57, 62, 72-3, 78, 82-3, 100, 164
   language differences, 50, 53-4, 56, 67-8
   marriages, 147, 164
   relations, xi, 2, 13, 49, 51-2, 159, 164-5
   understanding, campaigns to improve, 49-52, 61-3
Anson (Avro) aircraft, 134-5, 151
anti-British prejudice in USA, 53-54, 60, 63, 64, 72, 81-2, 132
Arctic Ocean, 133
Argentia, 137
Argus, HMS, 150, 163
Ark Royal, HMS, 151, 156, 160
Armstrong, Leon, 59, 65
Armstrong, Lt (jg), 79-80
Arnold, Major-Gen, H.H., 18, 19
Arnold-Portal Accord (1942), 22, 119
Arnold scheme, 18, 30, 91, 98, 104
Asbury, HMS, 23
Asbury Park, NJ, 23
Ashley, J.H., 37, 77-8, 86, 114-15, 134-5
assessment of aircrew trainees, xi, 18, 20, 28-29, 40-1, 49, 57, 62, 63, 76, 78-82, 86-9, 95-6, 100, 104-5, 111, 115, 130, 157
Assistant Chief of Naval Staff (RN), 112
Assistant Naval Attaché (Air), 23
Athlone Castle, 134
Atlantic City, 130
Atlantic Ocean, vii-ix, 9, 12, 13, 19, 21, 39, 42, 43, 92, 114, 122, 126, 133, 135, 140, 152, 156, 160, *see also* Battle of the Atlantic, convoys
atomic bomb, 140, 146
Australia, 44, 143
autogiros, 119-20
Avenger (Grumman) aircraft, 22, 80, 109, 110, 111, 123, 124, 125, 126, 128-130, 144-5, 146, 157, 165
Aviation Radio School (USN), 93-5

Bader, G/Capt Douglas, 97
Bahamas, 109, 115, 135
Baldwin, Stanley, 3
Baltic Sea, 155
Banton, David H.B., 34, 134
Bar Harbor, Me, 125
Barham, HMS, 156
Barracuda (Fairey) aircraft, 106, 113, 142-3, 157
Bartlett, Richard, 100-1, 115
Bathurst, Gambia, 136
'batsman', *see* deck landing control officer (DLCO)
Battle of Arnhem, 138
Battle of Britain, viii, x, 8, 36, 40, 51-2, 95, 97, 152
Battle of Matapan, 155-6

INDEX

Battle of Midway, 113, 163
Battle of the Atlantic, 16, 45, 119, 161
Battle of the Coral Sea, 163
battleships, 3, 143, 149-51, 154-6, 162-3, *see also names of individual ships*
Bay of Biscay, 138, 160
Bazalgette, John, 70
Béarn (Fr), 150
Beaton, Cecil, 141
Beaufighter (Bristol) aircraft, 86, 113, 134
Beaverbrook, Lord, 8
Begum, HMS, 126
Bell, Alan R., 43, 73, 79-80
Belem, Brazil, 136
Bergen, 155
Bermuda, 20, 135, 136
Bird, Geoffrey, 46, 64
Bismarck (Ger), 3, 71, 156
Blackpool, 115
Blenheim (Bristol) aircraft, 6, 134
Blevins, Kenneth R., 33, 77, 135-136
blitzkrieg, 7
Bomber Command (RAF), 5-6, 8, 15, 16, 103, 117, 118-19, 147, 151, 153-4
bombing, 2-3, 4, 6, 8, 10, 52, 79, 102, 106, 109, 112, 113, 115, 125, 130, 142, 151, 153-5
Boston (Douglas) DB-7 aircraft, 22
Boston, Mass, 44
Botha (Blackburn) aircraft, 138
Brest, 155
Brie, W/Cdr Reginald, 120
Briggs, S/Ldr, 71

British Admiralty Delegation (BAD), 22, 82, 122
British Air Commission, 22, 120
British Air Delegation, 23, 29
British Broadcasting Corporation (BBC), 50, 59, 60
British Commonwealth Air Training Plan, 10, 12, 13, 49, 156
British Flying Training Schools (BFTS), 17-18, 30, 91, 98, 104, 159
British Naval Staff, Washington, DC, 165
British Pacific Fleet, 143-4, 145-6, 163
British Pensacola Veterans, 164-5
British Purchasing Commission, 15, 114
Brize Norton, 9
Brogan, G.F., 113
Brown, J.F., 53
Brunswick, Maine, 112, 124, 126-7, 129
Buffalo (Brewster) aircraft, 107, 108
Bunker Hill, Indiana, 20, 22, 59, 80-3, 88-9, 147
Bureau of Aeronautics (USN), 19, 118, 120, 159
Burgoyne, Dennis, 99-100
Burma, 138, 145
Byrd, Adml Richard E., 122

Canada, 12, 15, 19, 27, 29, 43, 46-7, 74, 89-91
Caribbean, viii
Carnegie, G/Capt D.V., 17, 92-3, 95, 117-19

carrier landings, 78, 106, 124, 126, 128, 129-30
'cash and carry', viii, 15-16
casualties, 4, 6-8, 55, 56, 62, 70, 86-7, 111, 115, 124, 127-9, 136, 145-7
Catalina (Consolidated) PBY flying boat, 22, 71, 93, 97, 98, 100, 101, 114, 115, 117-19 135-7, 140, 152, 156, 159, 161
catapult launching, 160-1
Cecil, Ben, 95-8
censorship, 60, 62, 89
Central Flying School (RAF), 116
Cessna aircraft, 38
Ceylon, 144, 165
Chamberlain, Neville, 3, 35
Charger, USS, 126, 128, 130
Charlottetown, 118, 134
Cheduba Is, 145
Chesapeake Bay, 129, 131
Chicago, 30, 59
Chief of Naval Air Services (RN), 153-4
Chief of Naval Operations (US), 122
China, 2, 4, 10, 145
Churchill, Winston, vii-ix, 2-4, 7, 17, 18, 154
Cierva Autogiro Company, 120
Civil Aeronautics Authority (US), 38
Civilian Pilot Training Program (CPTP), 38
Clayton, Thomas H., 35
climate (US), 14, 55-8, 74, 78, 80, 84, 86, 110, 111, 114, 130, 152

Coastal Command (RAF), xi, 8, 10, 15, 17, 21, 94, 103, 114, 115, 118-19, 133, 135, 138, 139-140, 147, 151-2, 153, 154, 156, 161, 162
Cobb, USCG, 120
Cold War, 133, 165
College Training Detachments (CTD), 38
Collishaw, F/O Dick, 138
Colossus, HMS, 161
Committee of Imperial Defence, 148
Conte Rosso (It), 150
convoys, vii, 9, 45, 114, 120, 129, 141, 151, 152, 154, 155, 160-2, see also Battle of the Atlantic
Coral Gables, Florida, 17
Corpus Christi, Texas, 20, 22, 83, 104, 108, 158
Corsair, (Chance-Vought) F4 aircraft, 21, 22, 80, 108, 123-5, 127, 128, 141-2, 144, 157, 159
Courageous, HMS, 7, 150, 160
Cowan, R/Adml Sir Walter, 148
Cranwell, 137
Cresswell, Cdr John, 149
Crete, 155, 163
Critchley, A/Cdre A.C., 89-91
Cullum, F/Lt, 78

D-Day, 44, 162
Daghestan, 120
Dakota (Douglas) DC-3/C-47 aircraft, 22, 136
Dardanelles, 163
Darr Aero Tech Inc, 98-9

INDEX

Dauntless (Douglas) aircraft, 80, 110, 113
Davies, Lt/Cdr R.B., 148
deck landing control officer (DLCO), 125, 128, 129
Defence Requirements Committee, 3
demerit punishment system, 65-6, 72, 75, 85, 96
Deputy Director, Naval Air Warfare (RN), 165
'destroyers for bases' deal, viii, 13, 63
Detroit, 30, 53, 58, 72-4, 78
Detroit Free Press, 62
Dilbert Dunker, 110-11
Dinner Key, Florida, 17
Director, Air Warfare and Flying Training (RN), 22, 121
Director, Flight Training (RAF), 92, 117
Director, Naval Air Division (RN), 121
Director, Naval Intelligence (RN), 165
Director, Personnel Services (RN), 121
Director, Pre-Entry Training (RN), 121
Director, Training (RAF), 15
Director, UK Training in the USA, 17
disarmament, 1-2
discipline while training, 65-6, 72, 75, 85-6, 89, 91, 96, 107-8
'ditching', 108, 110-11, 129, 145, 160
dive-bombing, 21, 112-14, 126, 160, *see also names of particular aircraft types*

Dominion Monarch, 136
Dönitz, G/Adml Karl, 9, 162
Dorval Airport, 135-6
Douglas Aircraft Company, 115
Dreyer, Adml Sir Frederic, 153-4
'dropouts', *see* 'washouts'
Dunkirk evacuation, 9, 52, 95, 163
Duxbury, Stanley, 72-3

Eagle, HMS, 150, 160
East Indies, 143-5
Eastern Fleet (RN), 143
Edwards, Bryn Noel, 70
elementary flying training schools (EFTS), 38-9, 43, 92
No. 9 EFTS, 38
No. 28 EFTS, 39
No. 29 EFTS, 43
elementary training, *see* primary training
Elizabeth City, NC, 20, 115, 135-7
emergency landings, 69, 78
Empire Air Training Scheme, *see* British Commonwealth Air Training Plan
Empire Mersey, 120
Empress of Asia, 44, 47
Empress of Scotland, 42
English Channel, vii-viii, x, 9
escort aircraft carriers, 21, 112, 126, 129, 145, 160-3
21st Aircraft Carrier Squadron (RN), 145
Everglades, Florida, 55, 107, 109

failures, *see* 'washouts'

Farrow, Robert, 46, 97, 138
Ferguson, Leo, 41, 45
Ferry Command (RAF), 20, 21, 116, 118, 122, 135-6, 147
Fighter Command (RAF), 151
films in training, 27, 159
Firefly (Fairey) aircraft, 144, 157
Fiume (It), 156
Fleet Air Arm (RN), x-xi, 3, 5, 7-10, 12, 19-21, 23-4, 28-9, 31-3, 40-1, 83, 92-4, 101-2, 105, 133, 140, 141-5, 146-7, 151, 155, 156-7, 162-3, *se also under* Squadrons
FAA Dive-Bomber Training Unit, 113
Fleischmann-Allen, Richard, *see* Allen
flight grading, 28, 36, 38-40, 42-3, 91-3
Floyd Bennett Field, NY, 122
flying boats, 10, 19, 20, 55, 83, 100, 104, 114-19, 139, 151, 153, *see also names of particular aircraft types*
Flying Training Command (RAF), 12
Ford, Trevor, 134
formation flying, 69-70, 78, 86-7, 106-7, 113, 125, 127-8, 132
Formidable, HMS, 131, 143, 146, 155
Formosa, 146, 165
Fort Lauderdale, Florida, 21, 22, 109, 111
Foster, David, 129-30
France, viii, 8, 15, 51, 63, 150, 151, 152
Fry, Denis James, 36, 46, 54
Fulmar (Fairey) aircraft, 132

Furious, HMS, 150, 163

Gander, Newfoundland, 136
Garrod, A/M A.G.R., 38, 91
general reconnaissance schools, (GRS) 115, 116, 118, 134-5
Germany, vii-x, 2-4, 13, 16, 18-19, 34, 51, 53, 63, 72, 119, 150, 151, 152, 154, 155, 160, 163
  air force (Luftwaffe), vii, x, 3, 5, 9, 112
  army, vii
  navy (Kriegsmarine), vii, 3, 6, 9, 154, *see also* U-boats, *and names of individual ships*
  High Command, 161
Gibraltar, 160
Gibson Commander, 108
Glazebrook, Jim, 35
Glider Pilot Regiment, 138-9
Glorious, HMS, 7, 150, 160
Gneisenau (Ger), 155
Goldsmith, F/Lt Paul, 48
Gordon, Mark, 138
Gosshawk, HMS, 102
Gough, Ray, 40, 45, 80, 82, 105-6
Grant-Sturgess, Robin, 113-14
Great Britain:
  financial problems, viii, 13, 15-16, 18, 27, 150
  war economy, vii-ix
Great Lakes, 74
Green, Hughie, 137
Greenock, 135
Grosse Ile, Michigan, 20, 22, 53, 62, 65, 71-8
ground school, 24-7, 69-70, 75-6, 78, 85-6, 106-7, 109

INDEX

Guest, Philip, 42, 65, 110-11
Guinn Aviation History Archive, xii
Gulf of Mexico, 100-1
gunnery, 6, 24-6, 54, 93-5, 97-8, 102, 106-7, 109, 113, 115, 137

Hadrian glider, 139
Halifax (Handley Page) aircraft, 22, 138
Halifax, Lord, 129, 160
Halifax, Nova Scotia, 19, 44-6, 134
Halliday, V/Adml Sir Roy 'Gus', 165
Hampden (Handley Page) aircraft, 6
Hampton, Fla, 55
Hanson, Norman, 58, 79, 88, 107, 128
Hanson, S.B., 55,
Harris, 128-9
Harris, A/Cdre (later MRAF Sir) Arthur T., 15, 119 154-5
Harrogate Reception Centre, 135
Harvard (North American) aircraft, 15, 65, 87
Heaton Park, 41-3
Heffer, Ben, 108
helicopters, 119-23
Heligoland, 6, 163
Hellcat (Grumman) F6 aircraft, 127, 142, 144, 145
Helldiver (Grumman) aircraft, 80, 126, 157
Hepburn Board (1938), 158
Hermes, HMS, 150, 160
Hiroshima, 140, 146

Hitler, Adolf, vii, 2, 4, 9, 51
Hill, A/M Sir Roderic, 120
Hollywood, 50
Home Fleet (RN), 141-3
homesickness, 60, 81
Honshu, 146
Hopkins, Harry, ix, 159-60
Hopkins, Lt R.D.B., 128
Horsa glider, 139
hospitality (US), 51, 53-4, 61-3, 74, 77-9, 82, 85, 97, 130-2, 164
Houchin, S/Ldr, J.F., 47-8
Hudson (Lockheed) aircraft, 15, 22
Hunt, Capt, 135
Hunt, Reg, 96
Hurricane (Hawker) aircraft, 22, 36, 152

Iceland, 13, 136
Illustrious, HMS, 143-4, 151, 160, 165
Implacable, HMS, 151
India, 137
Indian Ocean, 118, 143, 145, 157, 163, 165
Indiana, 80-1
Indefatigable, HMS, 144, 146, 151
Indomitable, HMS, 130-3, 143-4, 146
initial training wings (ITW), 11, 34-9, 89, 90, 93, 96
  No. 4 ITW, 36
initial training wings, continued,
  No. 5 ITW, 34
  No. 13 ITW, 34
instructors, xi, 4, 8, 9, 12, 17, 18, 27-8, 38-9, 52, 57, 63-5, 67, 74-82, 86, 88, 91, 95, 97, 100,

instructors, continued, 102, 104-6, 109-10, 113, 115-18, 125, 136, 157-9, 163
intermediate training, 20, 22, 24, 29, 71, 79, 83-7, 104, 158
invasion threat, vii, 8-10, 16
Italy, viii, 2, 4, 19, 63, 150, 155-6, 163
   navy, 155-6

Jackson, Lt/Cdr P.B., 71-2
Jacksonville, Florida, 21, 22, 64, 93-8, 107, 158
Japan, viii, 2, 4, 19, 20, 53, 63, 112, 140, 143-6, 151, 160, 164
Jarvis, Hilary, 100
'Jeep carriers', *see* escort carriers
Johnson, Joseph R., 98-9
Johnson, Cpl Leonard, 52
Jones, John, 76

Kaa Fjord, 141
kamikaze attacks, 146
Keflavik, Iceland, 136
Kennedy, Joseph P., viii,
Kennedy, Peter, 95
Kerr, James, 138
Keyes, Admiral of the Fleet Sir Roger, 148-9
King George V, HMS, 151, 156
Kirkpatrick, Robert, 137-8
Kitty Hawk, 136
Königsberg (Ger), 113, 155
Kra Isthmus, 145

Lambert Field, *see* St Louis
Lancaster (Avro) aircraft, 22, 95, 142, 157

Large, David, 55, 107
Largs Bay, Prestwick, 136
League of Nations, 1, 150
Lend-Lease Act (1941), ix-x, 13, 16-17, 19, 22, 27, 126, 129, 131, 141, 152, 156, 159, 161, 164
Lewiston, Maine, 112, 123, 124
Liberator (Consolidated) B-24 aircraft, 22, 136, 152
Limey, 57, 67, 84-5
Link Trainer, 14, 79, 87
Liverpool, 41-4, 134, 137
Lloyd, Capt R.M., 135
London, 35-6
London (Saro) flying boat, 151
Lofoten Islands, 95
Long Island, NY, 122
Lothian, Lord, 16
Lough Erne, NI, 136
Lubin, Isador, 159-60
Ludlow-Hewitt, ACM Sir Edgar, 5-6
Luton, 9

Macdonald, James Ramsay, 2
Mackenzie, Hector, 102-3, 131
'Mae West' lifejacket, 111
Magill, G/Capt Frank S., 47
Magister (Miles) aircraft, 9
Maine, 20-1
Malacca Str, 145
Malaya, 145
Malta, 155, 163
Manchuria, 2
Manus Is, 145
Martlet (Grumman) aircraft, 19, 21
Massachussetts, 20-1

INDEX 211

Mauretania, 43
Mediterranean Sea, ix, 86, 122, 131, 133, 155, 160
Merchant Navy, 154
merchant ships, losses, vii-viii, 9
Mexico, Gulf of, 100-1
Miami, Fla, 20-1, 62, 106-9, 113, 135
Michie, Alistair, 126
Milton, Ala, 85
Missouri, USS, 146
Mitchell, Gen William, 2
Mitchell (North American) B-25 aircraft, 22
Moncton, New Bruswick, 48, 93, 94, 97-8, 100, 135, 157
Monroe Doctrine, viii
Montreal, 47, 135, 136
More, HMS, 123
Murmansk, 136
Mustang (North American) P-51 aircraft, 22

N2S (Stearman) aircraft, 70, 74, 77, 79, 81, 83
N3N aircraft, 69, 77
NP-1 aircraft, 70, 77
Nagasaki, 140, 146
Nashville, Tennessee, 160
Naval Aviation Cadet Act (1935), 158
Naval Aviation Cadet Act (1938), 158
navigation, 11, 15, 17, 22, 24-6, 37, 40, 85-6, 100-2, 106-7, 116-17, 125, 130, 134-5, 149
navigators, 10, 12, 17, 19, 21, 29, 30, 35, 93, 98-102, 105, 115, 116, 137, 147

neutrality (US), viii, x, 8, 12, 51-52, 71, 74, 77
New Deal, ix, 158
New Orleans, 8, 135
New York, 23, 44, 45, 50, 80, 97-8, 122, 135
New Zealand, xii
NZ aircrew, 28, 40-1, 44-5, 77, 84, 108, 136, 164
NZ High Commissioner, 41
Newell, Professor Arthur, 50
Newfoundland, viii, 45, 136-7
Nicobar Is, 143, 145
night flying, 6, 37, 70, 78, 87, 101, 106-7, 115-17, 139, 141, 152, 157
Norfolk, Virginia, 123, 125, 130-2
Normandie (Fr), 97
North Sea, 7, 151
Northumberland, AMC, 39
Norway, 7, 9, 113, 160, 163

observer (RN), 8, 10, 11, 24, 33, 44, 94, 101-102, 120, 125, 130-1
Okinawa, 146
Oklahoma, University of, 30
Opa Locka, Florida, 20, 21, 106
Operation Lentil, 144
Operation Meridian I, 144-5
Operation Meridian II, 144-5
Operation Tungsten, 141-3, 157
Operation Varsity, 139
operational conversion course, 134
Operational Refresher Training Unit, 139
Operational Training Command (USN), 20, 158

operational training squadrons (FAA),
738 Sq, 123-5
732 Sq, 124
operational training units (OTU), 20-1, 34, 97, 115, 116, 134, 136, 140
No 14 OTU, 34
No 79 OTU, 134
operational training, 20-1, 104, 123-5
Oxford (Airspeed) aircraft, 138

Pacific Ocean, 21, 133, 142, 143, 145-6, 157, 163, 164
Padgate, 33, 34
Palembang, 165
Palm Beach, 54,
Palmer, Ensign, 74
Palmer, R., 72
Palmer, S.R., 42-3, 44
Pan-American Airways Navigation School, 17-18, 99
Panama Canal, viii,
Pankalan Brandan, 144
parachute, 9, 86-7, 110, 161
Pasteur (Fr), 135
Pearl Harbour, 20, 27, 53, 74, 77, 102, 115, 158, 163
PBY flying boats, *see* Catalina
Penang, 145
Pensacola, Florida, 19-20, 22, 29, 58, 61-2, 65, 67, 71, 83-5, 99, 101, 104, 110, 114, 116-18, 146, 152, 158, 165
Pensacola News Journal, 52, 61-2,
Pepsicola, 45
Perry, Missouri, 54
personnel embarkation centres, 41-2

physical fitness/training, 11, 25-6, 37, 40, 76-7, 84, 107
Pilots Reception Centre, 118
Pin Feather, 59
Piper Cub aircraft, 38
Pirie, G/Capt G.C., 17
Pladjoe, 144
Plan Z, 3, 9
Plymouth, 133
Pola (It), 155-6
Popham, Hugh, 8-9
Port Lyautey, 136
Portsmouth, Hants, 40, 133
Portsmouth, Virginia, 112, 119
post-war careers. 146-7, 165
Prentice, Lt/Cdr St John, 112-13
Price, Michael, 40, 66
Pridham-Whipple, Lt/Cdr R., 128
primary training, 20-2, 24, 29, 38, 69-83, 99, 104, 107, 123, 152, 158
Prince Edward, Island, 20, 115, 134-5
Prince Philip, (later HRH Duke of Edinburgh), 165
Prince of Wales, HMS, 130, 163
promotion on qualifying, 20, 29, 79, 97-8, 104-5, 136, 165
Puerto Rico, 136
Purdon, William, 72

quality of aircrew training in USA, xi, 24, 27-28, 52, 63-5, 75-8, 80-1, 94, 95, 97-8, 109
quality of training, continued, 11, 113, 115-17, 134, 140, 152-3, 156-9
Queen Elizabeth, 44, 97

Queen Mary, 44
Quimby, CPO, 96
Quonset Point, Rhode Island, 112, 123-5, 129

racial discrimination (US), xi, 55, 58-9, 131-2
radar, 93-4, 107, 137, 138, 162
Radford, Headley, 108
radio, 4, 11, 71, 79, 86, 93-100, 102, 115, 125, 132-3, 137-8
Rajah, HMS, 144
Ramree Is, 145
Rangoon, 145
Ravager, HMS, 129
rearmament, 3-4, 151
Renshaw, Dr Samuel, 26
Repulse, HMS, 130, 163
Revill, John R., 136
Rhine crossing, 139
Rhode Island, 20-1
Robinson, Frank, xii, 33, 39, 56, 60, 85, 135, 140, 146-7
Roc (Blackburn) aircraft, 157
rockets, 102, 106, 144
Rodney, HMS, 156
Roosevelt, President Franklin Delano, viii-ix, 13, 16, 18, 19, 84, 153, 159-60
Roosevelt, President Theodore, viii,
Roskill, Capt Stephen, 149
Royal Air Force (RAF), viii, x, 1, 2-4, 10-12, 14, 20, 28, 31, 33-8, 92, 118-19, 148, 151-4, *see also* Air Ministry, *names of RAF Commands and specific topics*
RAF Delegation in USA (RAFDEL), 22, 27, 116, 117, 119, 123, 152-3
RAF No 2 Receiving Wing, 33
RAF No. 11 Radio School, 138
RAF No 31 Personnel Depot, 48
RAF Transit Section, 48
RAF Volunteer Reserve (RAFVR), 8, 140
Royal Arthur, HMS, 40
Royal Canadian Air Force, 19, 43, 44
RCAF No 1 Manning Depot, 19, 47, 89-90, 134
RCAF No 1 Movements Group, 46-7
RCAF No.1 Port Transit Group, 47
RCAF No 2 Movements Group, 47
Royal Flying Corps, 1, 36, 112, 120
Royal Naval Air Service, 1, 162
Royal Navy (RN), vii-x, 1, 2-3, 16, 148-9, 151, 162, *see also* Admiralty, Fleet Air Arm *and specific topics*
RN Helicopter School, 123
RN 'Y' scheme, 33
Royal New Zealand Navy, 40-1
Russia (USSR), vii, 9, 115, 135-7, 141, 161

SNJ-3 aircraft, *see* Harvard
Sabang, 143
St Johns, Newfoundland, 45
St Louis, Missouri, 20, 79-83
St Vincent, HMS, 40-1, 92
Sakishima Gunto Is, 146, 165

Saker, HMS, 23
Saratoga, USS, 143
Scapa Flow, ix
Scharnhorst (Ger), 155
Schillig Roads, 6
schnorkel, 162
sea power, ix, 2, 9, 148-9, 151, 155, 156, 162
Seafire (Supermarine) aircraft, 142, 145, 146
selection of aircrew, 5, 10, 28-9, 31-40, 42, 81-2, 92-3, 121-2
Sewell, Jackie, 127-8
Shearer, Jock, 56
Sheppard, E.C., 70, 83
Shippey, Maurice, 107
Sierra Leone, 140
Sikorsky helicopters, 120-1
Sikorsky, Igor, 120
Sims, Lt(jg) John, 109
Singapore, 130, 145
Singleton, Clifford, 124, 126-9
Sinclair, Sir Archibald, 7
Sisley, John (Jack), 84
Skua (Blackburn) aircraft, 113, 157
Slight, Ldg/Airman Peter, 130
Smiter, HMS, 130
Smith, Harry, 95
social class (in UK), 10-11, 36, 39, 41, 53-4
Soengi Gerong, 144
Soerabaya, 143
solo flying, xi, 38-9, 65, 69-70, 74-8, 95-6, 113
sonar, 94, 138
Souray, D.A., 84-5
South-East Asia Command (SEAC), 145
Soviet Union, *see* Russia

Spanish Civil War, 4
Spitfire (Supermarine) aircraft, 22, 36, 152
squadron formation (FAA), 105, 112, 123, 125-6, 130
Squadrons (FAA)
 800 Sq, 142
 801 Sq, 142
 804 Sq, 142
 813 Sq, 165
 820 Sq, 144
 827 Sq, 131, 142
 828 Sq, 157
 829 Sq, 142
 830 Sq, 142
 831 Sq 142
 842 Sq, 142
 845 Sq, 165
 846 Sq, 129
 849 Sq, 144, 165
 854 Sq., 144
 856 Sq, 129-130
 857 Sq, 125, 130, 144
 880 Sq, 132-3, 142
 882 Sq, 142
 888 Sq, 145
 898 Sq, 142
 1770 Sq, 144
 1826 Sq, 144
 1830 Sq, 127-9, 144
 1833 Sq, 108, 144
 1834 Sq, 128, 141-2, 144
 1836 Sq, 141-2
 1837 Sq, 126-8
 1839 Sq, 144
 1844 Sq, 144
Squadrons (RAF)
 9 Sq, 142
 58 Sq, 138
 100 Sq, 157

INDEX 215

Squadrons (RAF) continued
  203 Sq, 137
  209 Sq, 118
  240 Sq, 118
  266 Sq, 36
  272 Sq, 86
  617 Sq, 142
Squantum, Mass, 112, 124-6, 129-30
Stirling (Short) aircraft, 95
Stopford, Capt the Hon. A., 148
Stovin-Bradford, S/Lt Frank, 125, 130, 144-5
Straits of Dover, 163
Stranraer (Short) flying boat, 151
Stratheden, 43
Stuart, Lt/Cdr W. 'Doc', 130
SU-2 Scout aircraft, 86
submarines, *see* U-boats
Sumatra, 143-5, 165
Sunderland (Short) flying boat, 118, 152
Superintendent of Aviation Training, 95
Suthers, Cdr S.H., 81-2, 147
Swinton, Lord, 14
Swordfish (Fairey) aircraft, 71, 125, 142, 156, 157
syllabuses, 11, 17, 24-7, 37, 70, 78, 86, 106-7, 109-10, 112, 114

Taranto, 155
Taylor, Lt/Cdr, 109
Technical Training Command (RAF), 12
Tedder, A/Cdre A.W.J. (later MRAF Lord), 15

telegraphist/air gunner (TAG), 10, 29, 33, 102, 124-5, 130
The Wag, 60-1, 64, 67-8, 99
Tiger Moth (De Havilland) aircraft, 38, 39, 43
Till, Geoffrey, 5
Tipple, Peter, 86
Tirpitz (Ger), 3, 141-3, 157
Todd, Lindsay, 74-5
Tokyo, 146, 163
Tomahawk (Curtis) P-40C aircraft, 22
Toronto, 19, 46-8, 89-91, 100, 135
Toronto Star, 90
torpedo/bomber (TBR), 5, 21-2, 71, 105-7, 109-13, 123, 132, 146, 151, 154, 156
Towers, V/Adml J., 19, 118
Towers scheme, xi, 19-21 ff, 28-30, 34, 43, 63, 91, 99, 102-3, 115, 117, 126, 133, 134, 137, 138, 141, 144, 146, 152-4, 156-8, 162-5
Training Command (RAF), 5, 12
Treasury (UK), 23
Trenton, 78, 89-90, 93, 95-6, 99, 100
Trevallion, Leonard, 54
Trincomalee, 144
Trinidad, 102
Trinity House, 146
Truk, 146
Turnhouse, 37-8
Typhoon (Hawker) aircraft, 22

U-29 (Ger), 7
U-boats, x, 2, 3, 9, 13, 42, 45, 90, 109, 114, 115, 119, 120,

U-boats, continued, 122, 124, 125, 138, 140, 152, 155, 161-2, 165
Unicorn, HMS, 163

United Services Organization (US), 73-4, 101
United States of America (USA), viii, 12-14 *and passim*
US Army Air Corps/ Force, 15, 17, 18, 38, 99, 105, 115, 122-3, 153, 159
US Coast Guard, 119-20, 122
US economy and industry, viii-x, 14, 16-17, 22, 126, 152, 159-62
US Marine Corps, 38, 94, 104, 119
US Navy, 17-19, 24, 46, 58, 63, 65, 72, 77, 78, 94, 97, 104, 110, 112-13, 116-20, 122, 126, 132, 142-3, 151, 152, 153, 156-9, 162, 165
US Naval Academy, 158
US Naval Aviation Radio School, 93-5
US Navy, Historical Unit, 158
US presidential election (1940), viii, 16
US public opinion, viii, 16, 51-2, 72, 142
Uxbridge, 10, 33-4, 36

Valiant, HMS, 156
Van Bruggen, Lt John, 77
Vengeance (Vultee) aircraft, 160
Vero Beach, Florida, 22, 113-14
Vian, R/Adml Sir Philip, 143-4
Victorious, HMS, 141-3, 144, 165

Victory, HMS, 40
Victory in Europe (VE), 106
Vildebeest (Vickers) aircraft, 151
Vincent, Anthony P., 36
Vincent, AVM Stanley, 36
Virginia, 20, 131-2
Vittorio Veneto (It), 155
Vought aircraft-makers, 127
Vought-Sikorsky helicopter-makers, 123

Waite, Gavin, 40
Wakeford, AM Sir Richard, 85, 165
War Illustrated, 19,
War Training Service (WTS), 38
Warner, William, xii, 42, 43, 45-7, 49, 53, 55, 57-60, 73-4, 76-7, 84-5, 114
Warspite, HMS, 156
'washouts', 20, 28-9, 38, 49, 63, 70, 72, 74, 75, 78-82, 88-92, 102, 111, 157
Washington, DC, 22
Washington, President George, 16
Washington Naval Conference (1921-2), 2, 63
Wellington (Vickers) aircraft, 6, 34, 137
Wells, James T., 108
Wessex, HMS, 144
West Indies, 102, 131
Wheeler, Morley, 109, 129
Whimbrel, HMS, 165
White, Dennis, 66
Wildcat (Grumman) aircraft, 80, 125, 127, 132, 142
Wilhelmshaven, 6
Williams, Douglas, 157

Wilmot, CPO, 41
Winandy, Joe, 72, 76, 85, 140
wireless operator/air gunner (WOp/AG), 8, 10, 19, 29-30, 55, 57, 64, 93-9, 116, 137, 138
Wong, Jimmy, 108
Woffindin, S/Ldr, 95
'Woolworth' carriers, *see* escort aircraft carriers

world economic crisis, 150, 159
World War I, 1, 2, 7, 36, 48, 63, 112, 119, 148, 150, 153, 162, 163
Wright, Geoffrey, 67

Young, Lt/Cdr R.C., 71

Zara (It), 156